MY FIGHT AGAINST APARTHEID

MY FIGHT AGAINST APARTHEID

MICHAEL DINGAKE

KLIPTOWN BOOKS

LONDON

First published in 1987 by Kliptown Books Ltd,
Canon Collins House, 64 Essex Road, London N1 8LR.

ISBN No. 0 904759 82 2 (Paperback), 0 904759 83 0 (Hardback)

Phototypeset in 9½pt Melior and
printed in England by A.G. Bishop & Sons Ltd, Orpington, Kent.

Contents

CHAPTER I

Formative years

EARLY ENVIRONMENT

'Ee-ee-ee-ee!' a piercing cry rent the air, 'All men, assemble at the Kgotla! (village meeting place).' The village crier was summoning the villagers, men specifically, to the Kgotla. Stocky, dark, red-eyed and unshaven, he had a powerful voice. His summons reverberated across the village. He moved from one part of the village to another, repeating his shrill summons. It was his devout duty to ensure that villagers to the last man heard the call. Men popped out of their huts to check whether their neighbours had heard what they were hearing. Those who were still shaking or caressing the calabash sensed the impending interruption to their carousal and cursed the crier's illbreeding! They took a few more swigs to provide for the thirsty and uncertain hours ahead. One by one they emerged from the beer-hut. They wiped their beards, belched from the hastily-downed drink and blinked from the hot sun outside. Everywhere men abandoned their chores, picked up their thong chairs and dipora (wooden stools), and shouted reminders across to their dallying neighbours: 'Did you hear the cry?'

From all directions the villagers converged on the Kgotla – wide-brimmed hats on their heads and stools and chairs under their armpits.

It was 1941. In Europe the war had been going on for two years. It was spreading and intensifying as one victim of Hitler's aggression followed another. Life in Bobonong was beginning to display a new dimension. War talk. Rumour was rife about Hitler's objectives. According to the common talk in the village Hitler was the greatest tyrant ever heard of, worse than the most sadistic of the Boers across the Limpopo in the Union of South Africa. He was bent on enslaving all humanity, in particular the black masses. The Batswana were likely to be inspanned like draught animals by Hitler at the first opportunity. It was frightening.

'Ee-ee-ee-ee! All men assemble at the Kgotla!' The crier continued his dutiful cries as villagers poured into the Kgotla. Women, curious and full of anxiety, followed their men at a distance. As they trudged along the village's winding footpaths they circulated gossip about the imminent pow-wow and swore by their brothers that what they said about the objectives of the pow-wow was the gospel truth. At the Kgotla they settled on the ground along the fringes. We children, not to be outdone, arrived wide-eyed and ready to dart away if the elders judged our presence an unwelcome intrusion in adult affairs. We perched ourselves on the palisades surrounding the Kgotla. Some of us squatted on the ground alongside our mothers and watched the historic proceedings with childish vagueness.

Tshekedi Kgama, Ragonkgang to his people, was the star of the occasion. Many villagers had never seen Tshekedi before. He seldom visited villages like Bobonong unless grave matters were at stake. He was popular with the Babirwa regardless. They referred to him as Setlogolo (nephew). His mother was of Babirwa. Moreover he was a living legend. It is said when he was installed as regent after the death of his older brother, Sekgoma, the Ratshosa brothers were violently opposed. They tried to shoot him, but bullets just whizzed by without hurting him. The Ratshosa brothers paid dearly for that abortive regicide attempt. Another episode that made him a legendary figure was the whipping of a white youth. The Bangwato felt equal to anyone. Why not? Their chief could flog a white in the administration of justice. That made all equal before the law. No discrimination between a Mongwato and a white person. So here he was, TK (Tshekedi Kgama), come to honour Bobonong with his fabled eminence.

The District Commissioner and some of his senior staff were there, smiling affably and showing proper deference to TK in the presence of his people. All eyes were on TK. Pula (Rain)!, was the chant.

The events leading to the aggression against Poland and the war were briefly outlined to a tense Kgotla. The critical question of the moment was, what now? Could Batswana stand idly by and continue to enjoy their rustic peace when His Majesty's imperial government was locked in a life and death struggle? It was an open question and Babirwa went hammer and tongs into its merits and demerits – Chief, we can support the war effort through financial contributions. We have a lot of cattle. We'll sell them. They have never benefited us much except to keep the lions well fed and numerous. Chief, how do we come into this? England and Germany are at war. They know what their fight is all about. We don't know. It has nothing to do with us. Let them have it out. Ya gaetsho k e e e naka lehibidu (Mine (my bull) is the one with the red horn) – meaning, I'll back the victorious one. Chief, how can we fight the white man, with only our knobkerries, primitive spears and shields? The white man has powerful guns and flying machines. It's impossible – Chief, our forefathers resisted Mzilikazi and the Boers by force of arms when they tried to steal our land and cattle. We did not pay someone to fight for us. Hitler wants our land and our cattle. We must resist by force of arms. Chief, King George is our king in the same way you are our Kgosi. Can we desert you if you declare war on an enemy? Never! Voices were many and diverse. Affirmative and negative. Some asked simple and straightforward questions: Where is Germany? Where is England? Where is Poland? Who will look after our wives, our children, our cattle, goats and dogs while we are away in foreign lands fighting the war we did not provoke?

2

The sun was hot. Its rays impaled the earth and stirred cicadas to screeching sounds. Men wiped the perspiration that dripped from their foreheads with their forefingers and shook it off violently to the scorching ground. Others took out their snuff boxes with cool deliberation, tapped the box on the hard surface, sniffed the snuff and sneezed loudly. On the second day Ragonkgang summarized the pros and cons of the debate. The verdict was foregone: Babirwa, and every other tribe under the jurisdiction of TK, must to war! Men stood up. Some muttered misgiving and disagreement. Others applauded the sensible and irreversible verdict of the Chief. Women ululated and pranced around to mark the beginning of an era for the village. Bobonong limped into the international orbit under a dappled cloud of consensus.

Our dusty soccer field was soon transformed into a military ground. Left, right, left, right . . . Right about turn . . . 'Shun . . . By the right quick march . . . left, right, left, right . . ! Recruits in their sandals and barefeet stamped the ground and practised mock rifle drills with sticks. Maguge, lest it be said there were no conscientious objectors in Bobonong, skipped the border and sought sanctuary among his clan in Rhodesia. Children, perceptive saucy brats, immortalised his flight in song 'Maguge's shoe . . . He ran away from the drill . . . I said to you, is that why he remained behind?' And they danced to the rhythm of fleeing footfalls and the derisive tune. His cattle were placed under 'judicial management' for purposes of extorting an appropriate fine at a later stage. So it was rumoured.

My father missed the big Kgotla meeting. As usual he was away on the Reef, digging the yellow metal in one of the gold mines. The news of recruitment for active service up north had reached him while he was still on the mines. He returned to BP (Bechuanaland Protectorate) imbued with the spirit and philosophy of a gambler: Wafa wafa; wasala wasala ((if) you die, you die, (if) you survive, you survive). As a mineworker of many years standing he embraced this philosophy without reservations. Mine work was a risky and precarious business. Death, down there, came uninvited from rock fall. The miners could easily have changed the Lord's prayer to '. . . Give us this day our daily rock fall', without blasphemy. Every day as the mineworkers descended into the pit, they probably held their breath and wished for just one more day of survival. Life was worth a pittance.

The debate on Botswana's involvement in a war started in foreign lands and fought with foreign weapons was still raging among Babirwa in spite of the official decision. Dad expressed himself ready and willing to die in the quest of national and personal goals. The chief called for patriotism? Fine, as long as it earned his family a livelihood. That was it. Pragmatism of a responsible head of the family. Mom remonstrated tearfully. 'Father of Kitso, you can't do that. Who will look after the kids and me? You know your brothers are irresponsible. They cannot look after us when you are gone. They

3

can go. They are younger. In fact 'joining' for your age group is optional. Don't go!' Dad dismissed Mom's lacrimonious objections. 'Mother of Kitso, you puzzle me. You have never objected before to my going to the mines. The life of a mineworker hangs on a thread like that of a soldier. Luck is all that counts in both cases. War for a soldier is a job like any other job where one is paid or unpaid for his energies.' Pa was determined to volunteer in spite of mother's objections. He was like that. Uncompromising when his mind was made up.

I knew what was going on between my parents through eavesdropping – and sometimes their unguarded outbursts in front of us gave the secret away. I sympathised with Mom; the whole situation affected her badly. She suffered in spirit and her physical condition reflected it. 'Mom, don't worry, let him go. I'll look after you,' I tried to comfort her one day. 'You? look after me! You can hardly look after yourself . . .' she said in sarcastic rebuff to my chivalry. 'Moreover,' she continued, 'next year, you are going to school in Johannesburg.' The cat was out of the bag. School in Johannesburg! The city of gold! It was a dream.

Both my parents were very opinionated. Once they held extreme positions, no compromise was possible. They were similar in other respects. Kind, generous and sociable. To us children they were both loving and inclined to strict discipline. The difference probably came in their enforcement of their disciplinary codes.

Mom never hesitated to apply violence against our misconduct. It was not always a premeditated sort of punishment but more of an impulsive nature. You broke a cup or plate and, wham! 'Clumsy fool, these things cost money!' That sort of thing. So that if you did wrong and instinctively retreated out of harm's reach, the fury was spent in a moment and you could return to an atmosphere of restored peace. Of course in your nimble retreat you might be followed by a missile or two but those were usually wide of the target if your instincts, reflexes and past experiences worked in coordination. We were great chums, Mom and I. She could not read and write. I had to teach her. And very often it was the teacher who was on the receiving end instead of the other way round. For instance I would grab her resisting hand to show her how to write a letter of the alphabet and if she felt I was somewhat impatient in taking her hand, the same hand would break loose and come down on me, smack! 'I am your mother, don't try to be too smart!'

Dad laid down laws and interpreted them word by word. 'Children, I have no objection if you go to any part of the village to play with your friends. But, meal time be home. I don't want to go looking for you when it's time for food . . .' Should you happen to be late for meals, and it was not uncommon since neither the cooks nor ourselves had clocks to regulate punctuality, then you were in for it.

The timer would grill you. 'Why are you late, eh? What did I say to you? What are these for (he would be tugging your ears)? Are you deaf . . .?' But he seldom applied corporal punishment. On the rare occasions that he did, it would be slow and really painful before it was actually administered. The child itself would be asked to go and find the instrument to administer punishment after the interrogation. And while the blows rained on the poor child the lecture would be going on side by side. Wham! 'Don't do it again!' Wham! 'Next time I'll kill you!' Wham! 'I don't like delinquents!' Wham! 'You hear me?' All the same he was never unreasonable and always exercised a lot of patience with our little wayward ways.

My parents' kindness was manifested in the string of visitors who frequented our home and indigent relatives who stayed with us. We were not rich but in those days we had enough to sustain us and to share with a few others. Except for one year of drought, 1935, I do not recall a true pang of hunger from those years. The modest herd of cattle was always supplemented by crop raising and a nine months' stint in the mines by the head of the family. When it comes to hard work I have yet to see a man work harder than Pop. He was a true workaholic.

I was born of these two kind, loving and hardworking persons in 1928, 11 February. Unlike Topsie who just growed and growed, I was born. My mother expressed it in unprintable words whenever she was enraged by my mini-mischiefs. It made decent folks wince, but the expression conveyed to me in no uncertain terms that I was a waste product of her thankless system. Besides my Mom, other people have testified to the fact of my birth. Sarah, the Zimbabwean and cousin of my mother, says I was big and ugly, besides being a cry baby when I was born. She had the misfortune of serving as my nurse in my infancy. Yelling and heavy, she strapped me on her back and lulled me to sleep.

From my father I got the name Kitso (knowledge/skill). My mother named me Ditshale (ill will/envy). Granma simply named me Koketso (increase of the family). There were other less remarkable names. The family soon multiplied. Kabelo, a boy, came after me. He died at the young age of 14. We were big friends – except when Pop overpraised him and contrasted our IQ's on the basis of our school work in our respective classes. The village did not share my Dad's assessment. It was arbitrary and my little ego was hurt. Dad was unknowingly sewing seeds of jealousy. Khutsafalo our sister came third. She married in Zimbabwe. A boy and a girl followed, but they died in infancy. Mom died in 1944 and Dad married shortly after and increased the family by another eight, three girls and five boys . . .

I once asked my father how they could ever have chosen to settle on such a barren, drought-prone area like Bobonong. No, says Dad; drought in Bobonong is a relatively new phenomenon. Bobonong river after which the village is named was perennial when the Babirwa first settled there. Moreover, reminisces Dad, the site was chosen by Khama himself for the Babirwa. According to my paternal informant the settlement was to serve as a sort of a buffer zone against hostile intruders from the north and the east. In those days the threat of invasion from across the borders was ever present. In these conversations with my father I also came to hear about Malema, the hereditary chief of Babirwa. He was disgraced and deposed by Chief Khama because of alleged insubordination. Some outsiders believe Babirwa are a strongheaded and obstreperous group. And they are quick to cite Malema as an example. Some think the streak runs through all Babirwa – and wink an insinuating wink at the author.

Malema was at loggerheads with Khama for many years. Apparently he and some of his people had lived in the fertile area of Tuli Block after crossing from the Transvaal, long before the advent of British protection. He considered himself independent. He did not fall under Khama's political jurisdiction as far as he was concerned. Khama believed differently and acted to enforce his authority. Malema was forced out of Tuli Block to Molalatau in the vicinity of Bobonong. In the course of this some atrocities were apparently committed against Malema and his people. Thereupon Malema instituted claims against Khama. The judicial proceedings were long and unfruitful for Malema. The Commissioner, Sir Herbert Stoley, appointed to investigate Malema's claims against Khama however made a critical observation and a positive recommendation which was never implemented. 'The Commissioner suggested that the headman (Modisaotsile) at Bobonong be removed in order to bring happiness to the Babirwa. He could not understand why Khama regarded the Babirwa as a servile and subordinate people to be ruled by a Bangwato headman rather than by one of them . . .'*

Neither did the Babirwa understand. Least of all Malema. The discontent simmered below the surface for some time and eventually faded into the history of modern political developments. Time is the greatest healer.

As a child the political conflict was obscure yet it permeated my subconscious. I remember Chief Malema when I was a kid, erect and stately. A truly imposing figure. He looked every inch the chief. Towering in spite of his humiliation. I remember also how granny revered this man. Whenever he visited Bobonong from Molalata, granny would be beside herself, all a-flutter and in deep confusion about the day's priorities. Invariably we children would be shouted at, harassed and relegated to secondary position. Granny would be off to Moshate (Chief's place) to lotsha (pay homage) to the Chief and to

* Modisenyane Bobeng 'Babirwa-Bangwato conflict in the late nineteenth and early twentieth centuries', BA History dissertation, University of Botswana, 1976.

gaze upon and admire her idol. It is difficult to say how representative granny's allegiance was.

In late 1982 I was travelling from Bobonong to Phikwe in a bus full to capacity. It was one of the popular buses installed with an intercom system. And the music made passengers tolerate their congested condition. They conversed and cracked jokes good naturedly. Then came a musical record over the intercom, *Sello Sa Malema* (*Malema's lament*). Suddenly there was emotional rhythmic pounding of the bus floor as passengers joined the music. They stamped with their feet, swayed from side to side in their seats, tried to outsing each other and only succeeded in drowning the record music. It was a scene that threw me back to the bygone days of the conflict. Malema's experience seems to continue to excite the present generation of the Babirwa. Happily in musical ways.

Bobonong had a primary school going up to Standard IV. The local church hall served a dual purpose as a place of worship on Sundays and a multi-class room from Monday to Friday. Though the church hall was unpartitioned, several classes were taught inside the church and others outside, depending on the condition of the weather. One class would be doing its own lesson and so another and another. Three or four teachers each trying to prompt his/her class through a method of rote learning is not conducive to maximum pupil attention; yet such were the circumstances of our learning environment. One teacher would be shouting, 'two times two'; another, 'Class, we are going to do spelling. Can you spell "cat" for me?' And another in the middle of his scriptural lesson would be leading a recitation of one of the psalms, usually, 'I will lift up mine eyes unto the hills from whence cometh my help–' The enthusiasm for teaching by the teachers and for learning by the children was the motive force behind any achievement of those early years of formal education in our village.

I arrived green at school. I had never read any book or written any letter of the alphabet before. My father, not my mother, would read and write Setswana, and he had a library of three books – the holy bible, the London Missionary Society hymnbook and I believe the third one was a Setswana translation of Bunyan's *Pilgrim's Progress* (*Loeto loa Mokeresete*). But my father had never had time to open these to me. Although I was in the habit of opening any one of the three of them to sing my parents' favourite hymns – my illiteracy was total since I could not distinguish the hymn book from the rest. I was as blank as my new slate.

The beginners' curriculum was of course the universal three R's – Reading, 'Rithmetic and Writing. Religion was the fourth. There were six classes in our school, Sub A, Sub B and Standards I to IV. Each class lasted a full year. Promotions from one class to another were not policy and occurred grudgingly. I was promoted once,

7

otherwise progress was slow. Teacher shortage was acute. When I started, Ramathethe, the minister, was the teacher, assisted by lady teacher Sekgola; both unqualified but doing their best to alleviate the shortage and keep the lower classes occupied. Senior pupils were used extensively to teach.

The disadvantaged children were those who started in their late teens. They could not stick school for more than two or three years. They normally dropped out in Standard I when the majority could read and write a letter in Setswana. Perhaps they could not bear to be outclassed by their juniors in age. In a community where age was the indisputable badge of respectability and wisdom it was an unendurable insult to have the young upstarts – and females on top of it – try to discredit and upset the mores of the ancestors – pitting minors' knowledge with their majors in class. So the big boys dropped out and headed for the Boer farms and the mines to prepare for the next stage of life – taking a bride. Neither the pay nor the employment conditions were good on these farms and mines.

Adventure seekers were not deterred. They left barefooted or with hide sandals on their feet and came back from the farms shod in takkies (trainers) and speaking a language they called 'Hollands'. 'Kan jy Hollands praat jong (can you speak Hollands)?' The have-beens quizzed each other and exchanged a few banal words to prove their dubious status identity: the have-not-beens became subjects of good humoured slander in the foreign tongue. Very often that became a challenge to the latter and led to them running to the farms in turn, for their underpaid stint and a smattering of the Hollands taal (language). Other adventure seekers chose to go on contract to the mines on the Reef. They returned speaking 'Fanakalo,' a crude mixture of Zulu and English, full of abusive epithets and baby talk: 'Tata lapa beka lapa (Take here put here)!'

Bobonong was becoming cosmopolitan by proxy from all directions. With the boom of contract labour to the mines the value of reading and writing became obvious. Even the arch diehards could not be blind to how education made communication with distant relatives possible. Villagers could no more resist the wisdom of investment in primary education for children of either sex. Fathers coming back from the mines vowed to send or keep their children in school. The educated did not have to work underground in the mines. They were employed in clerical positions where the pay was higher and the work lighter and less hazardous. School enrolment increased yearly, though dropouts did not cease. With the increase in school population more and better qualified teachers were recruited. In the past we had depended on the local staff who worked with extreme devotion and dedication in spite of their under-qualification. Sekgola, Mafokate, Nkama, Nakedi were the local pioneers. Now came Mokobi and Lesitamang from Serowe – Standard VI and VIII respectively. Our last teacher in Standard IV was Mr Olifant from

Kimberley, a lively young man, fond of music compositions and poetry. One of his songs exhorted the Babirwa children to forge ahead in their education: 'Bakalaka and Batalaote have forged ahead, (you) Babirwa are lagging behind – Wake up Babirwa and help yourselves. . .' We sang it lustily with Olifant conducting vigorously to emphasize the significance of the words of the composition. Olifant was also a linguist. Besides English and Setswana he spoke Xhosa and Afrikaans. Whenever one of his class pupils came to school in some new dress, shoes, shirt etc he would tease the dressed-up: 'Skilpad het 'n nuwe dop gekry (the tortoise has got a new shell).' The class would roar with laughter as they watched the victim try to shrink into his or her shell.

When Olifant arrived it was after the June vacation and I was away at the cattle-post, a hostage of my father's herd. The hired herdsman had been picked up by tax collectors for failing to pay his tax and since I was the only one present when it happened I just had to hang around until a substitute arrived to relieve me. Lacking means of communication and far from the village, it took long to find a reliever and to return to school. When I eventually got back, the next day our class was due to write the external examinations. My 'truancy' was reported to Mr Dumbrell, the school inspector and on this occasion the external examiner as well. The question was whether to allow me to write with others or to disqualify me for my extended vacation. I watched with bated breath as Olifant and Dumbrell debated my fate. My enrolment in the Rand boarding school might hang on being amongst the year's graduands! At some stage I saw Olifant pull a sheaf of papers from one of his desk drawers. Apparently some of the papers were performance records of our class by previous teachers, for I could see Dumbrell's face relax somewhat as Olifant appeared to plead for me to be allowed to enter for the exams. When the results came Serara and I had passed with good marks. Serara Sello, now Mrs Kupe, was my arch rival in class.

In those days, at the height of universal male chauvinism, I did not take too kindly to being relegated to second position in class by a feminist. But the impudent Serara never let me sit on my laurels. One day, half in jest, I threatened her: 'Next time you get number one in class I will thrash you.' 'Just you dare,' she challenged in her screechy little voice. 'You think I'll watch you raise your hand against me? Just you try!' Discretion is the better part of valour. I declined the physical test. It was 'bad' enough failing to prove undisputed mental superiority. Physical humiliation might be an unmitigated disaster. Anyway, what's wrong with this female upstart? It was a joke. Ha! Ha! Ha!

Between me and you, reader, I struck a rock before the racist Dr Verwoerd and Strydom did. In 1956 when the Federation of South African Women led more than 20,000 women to Union Buildings in protest against pass laws, singing: 'wathint'imbokoto uzokufa (you have struck a rock. You'll die)', I knew what they were talking about. I had learned my lesson well. Dr Verwoerd and Strydom never did. They are no more. SS is still climbing her academic and professional ladder. She seems unstoppable. I should have known even then.

Exactly half of our Standard IV class proceeded to Standard V and VI in other schools inside and outside BP. Serara and Kelebaatswe Mosweu went to Serowe, later to Hope Fountain in Rhodesia. Dikgang Manatong went to Kimberley's Gore Browne while I moved to my dreamland – the Rand (Johannesburg and environs). The four of us were pioneers – the first Babirwa contingent to go in quest of education outside Bobonong and outside Bechuanaland.

THE NEW SCHOOL

The prospect of attending a boarding school in Roodepoort near Johannesburg engrossed my mind at the close of 1941. My imagination tilted at new horizons. At thirteen, there was nothing much more to explore in Bobonong. The opportunity to visit new regions was welcome. Exciting new discoveries lay outside the village precincts. The spirit of adventure was gathering momentum. It felt good to be on the threshold of a new experience. Very good. But what was it like out there? I was curious. Impatient. I was dying to be there.

My intelligence about my next port of call was limited. Gabriel Motlhasedi, my cousin who was already a pupil at the boarding school, lived forty kilometres away in Tobane Village. And in the six months he had been there we had not met. Perhaps the new school was like Bobonong which was the only school I knew. What about the town? What did a town look like? What did the 'golden city' (Johannesburg) look like? Bobonong has no cinema up to this day, although a large percentage of the villagers have probably seen films or slides in cities. In those days movies in the village were an unwritten chapter. The nearest thing I saw to a movie was an advertisement of 'Mazawattee tea.' This was in the form of slides showing some black man by the name of Xaba enjoying this relatively novel beverage among blacks. 'Tea is good for us', ran the theme of all the slides. In the background of this novo tea-drinking compatriot were just a few rondavels (round houses) – hardly different from the familiar ones in our village. I wanted to ask people who claimed to have been to Johannesburg what it was like in Johannesburg. But being shy, I never did. Had Mom been to these parts of the world I would have squeezed every detail of information about urban life from her. She was the one person in whose presence my chameleon nature revealed itself. The introvert changed into the extrovert – prying, babbling and blustering. Unfortunately this woman who could bring my other self out of me had never been anywhere further than Palapye railway station. That, however, did not keep my imagination fettered. Disjointed tidbits about town life circulated freely in the village. These could be woven into some imaginative

10

discernible pattern of social existence. From Dad and his short friend, Ra Thuso, besides their recurring theme of heavy cocopans underground and their reminiscences on the loud-mouthed breed of 'chee baases' (shift bosses), I learnt of the heterogenous nationalities employed on the mines. Tsonga, Swahili, Sesotho, Setswana, Chinyanja, Xhosa, Zulu, were some of the languages spoken in the mine compounds in addition to Fanakalo, the special mine lingua created by the white miners. To impress his linguistic abilities on me, Rathuso now and then addressed me in Zulu. 'Ukhulile mfana . . . (Boy you have grown up. Look how tall you are. Taller than I already)', he would remark while he eyed my awkward lankiness meditatively. Sometimes Dad and his friend discussed the mine food: mbunyani (mine whole wheat bread); nchaichai or mageu (fermented potable mealie pap); nyula (mine stew); and so on. These names sounded delicious. I made up my mind to taste some of this mine menu if and when I got an opportunity. Regretfully when I did get a chance to visit Uncle Tumediso at the West Rand mine compound he did not think the mine diet was good enough for a budding scholar like me. He served me ordinary bread and eggs. I was chagrined.

Before I went to the Reef, Uncle Tumediso was one of those who contributed to my nebulous picture of the city. Apparently he was footloose and travelled around to visit friends and relatives in other mine compounds, black residential areas and back yards in 'white suburbs'. From him I heard of mafufunyani (local train), Sedikidiki (South Newclare, a black residential area) and malaeta (mine boxers), who did not abide by Queensberry rules. Sedikidiki, according to Uncle T, was full of 'Russians' (Basotho gangsters), it was congested and crime-infested. The local trains were marvellous products of modern technology. According to Uncle Tumediso their speed was phenomenal; they had no 'engines'; they had no rear, nor head; as a result passengers who found a waiting train on the platform never knew where it was facing or where it was going until they heard an announcement from railway officials; their sirens were melodious, and Uncle put his two fingers in his mouth and emitted a plaintive siren wail in mimicry of 'mafufunyani'.

Malaeta (barefisted mine boxers) were a product of the lack of recreational facilities in the mine compounds. The boredom of the compounds drove miners to organise sports among themselves outside the mine premises. Uncle himself took part in the bare-knuckle fights and brought back home some specimens of the amulets he used to vanquish his opponents. They looked so innocuous. I tried them on and they failed to infuse into my flabby muscles the essential dynamite to knock out my imaginary opponents. Uncle and his buddies were obviously conned by some tricksters who stood to benefit.

It was Uncle Tumediso again who mentioned the 'colour bye' in one of his narratives on urban life. It sounded like some endemic

11

disease that afflicted the cities. The patients were exclusively white. 'Colour bye?' Yes! The whites suffered from it. 'They have the "colour bye"!' I could not conceive what sort of disease it was. Maybe it was one of those diseases associated with so-called civilization. Was it contagious, infectious, curable, incurable? I did not know. It transpired eventually that Uncle T was referring to the colour bar or apartheid as it came to be known later. At that stage it would not have helped even if he had pronounced the phrase correctly. Not only was the phrase strange, the concept was completely strange also. Bobonong was absolutely free of this prejudice. There were no whites except Rabinowitz (Ramaragwana to the villagers, arising from his ample behind). Other whites came on official or trade tours and fled back whence they came before an assessment of their biases could be made and documented in the minds of the village community. Otherwise as far as Ramaragwana was concerned, he was integrated into the community. To all intents and purposes he was a full-fledged Motswana. His colour did not prejudice him in the eyes of the Babirwa. Why would it? They had maswahe (albinos) in the village and nobody thought they were superhuman, non-human or sub-human because of their rare pigmentation or lack of it. Ramaragwana was quite welcome. His local dialect was not yet perfect – so what? He could boast many things in common with other villagers. He enjoyed his indigenous tot, sometimes brandy with his buddies, talked shop with cattle farmers. And since nothing stopped him from having a nyati (concubine), he had a couple in the fashion typical of Setswana eligibles.

The trip to the Reef was uneventful. The company was composed of some of the children of the elite of the region. Gabriel Motlhasedi, my cousin, was the son of Tobane village head man; Kebuileng, Elizabeth and Alice Mphoeng were children of the brother of the sub-chief of Madinare Village, Phethu Mphoeng. The three were going to St. Mary's in Krugersdorp.

It was Krugersdorp that initiated me into the atmosphere of racial tension in the Union of South Africa. Shortly after our arrival on the Reef, Gabriel and I went to do some shopping in Krugersdorp. We were strolling down a lane in the town when two white youths of our age insulted us. Our Afrikaans was poor at this stage but 'kaffir' we knew was not a complimentary form of address. I was a *casus belli* and fists started flying when the little Boers uttered it. No sooner had the fight started than the other party received reinforcements in the form of their bigger boeties. When we realised the odds were against us, we turned heel and went down the street at break-neck speed. The vengeful jeugbond came in hot pursuit. Prospects of a KKK lynching were very real. Luckily an African employee sweeping outside a cafe perceived our untenable situation and took pity on us. 'Come inside here,' he beckoned to us as we hurtled past the cafe for dear life. The moment we slipped inside, he planted himself at the door of the cafe, broomstick in hand and challenged the gang to enter. His Jewish employer in shirt sleeves came to back him up.

'Vhat you vant here? Get avay! Get avay from my shop. Get avay, I say!' he shouted at the clan. We were ushered into the safety of the business premises back yard where we were soon entertained to mugs of tea and buttered scones. In due course our hot pursuers must have despaired of ever getting hold of their insulated quarry. Only when our bodyguards were absolutely certain that our venture into the outside would bring us no bodily harm, did they let us out. It was a hair-raising experience but an eye opener as well. The Jewish cafe owner reminded me of Ramaragwana. I had learnt he was a Jew. The experience did not make me Boer-phobic but it certainly made me alert every time I crossed paths with white pedestrians. One had to be keyed up all the time to sidestep a deliberate shoulder bump, or parry an unprovoked punch. The streets in the central business districts of the towns were not safe for blacks in those days.

Roodepoort, where our boarding school was, was a small but growing town. In fact its size is not obvious because the mining towns constituting the Rand are situated next to each other and boundaries are not marked. There is another thing that enhances the size of this little town. It has two railway stations, Roodepoort West and Roodepoort. Roodepoort West was basically the station for 'natives,' as blacks were officially known. It derived this status from its proximity to the African residential area or location. The location is to the north of the station. Next to the old location – there are two, old and new – is a cemetery. The size of the cemetery tells a story. Either the old location is very old or the mortality rate of the inhabitants of the old and the new locations is very high. So many graves from so few houses! The road to St. Ansgar's passed between the location and the graveyard. It partitioned the living from the dead. At night the road seeemed like an eerie passage. A glow worm on the left – the graveyard side – gave one the creeps and made one trip on spooky obstacles. On the right – the location side – the movement of shadows in dimly lit lanes made one jumpy in anticipation of ambushes laid by social delinquents.

The new location is to the east of the old location. Whereas the old location looks rusty and weary with age and pollution, the new is clean and tidy. Its wire fences glimmer in the sun and severely restrict the gardening enthusiasm of the dwellers. The old was on freehold land. The new is built by Roodepoort municipality and administered by them. This reflected a new trend in land ownership rights for blacks in the urban areas. Roodepoort railway station, the non-identical twin station of the area, is near the new location but serves mainly the white commuters. The white residential area is farther to the east with lush, spacious gardens and bungalows. The contrast with location match-box pondokkies (little houses) is

13

striking. Across the rail line to the south is the central business district. There is the new town hall with its chiming clock. Everything in town looks beautiful and properly maintained. It is a far cry from the other side of the rail line.

I fell in love with St. Ansgar's on arrival. The school is built in salutary surroundings. Its grounds are a vast orchard. A variety of deciduous fruit trees everywhere: apricots, peaches (and I love peaches), apples, pears and plums.

Teacher Masipha was the head teacher of St. Ansgar's. He was the class teacher of Standards V and VI. He was a BA graduate and in 1943 before I finished my Standard VI he obtained his BA (Hons) post graduate degree. Unlike Bobonong, St. Ansgar's had highly qualified teachers. Though the shortage of staff was about the same, the adequacy of class rooms and a properly-set class timetable tended to hide the understaffing. There were only four teachers for eight classes. Each teacher was responsible for two classes. A lady teacher whose name I have forgotten taught Sub A and Sub B. Teacher Dlamini, nicknamed Young Man from his habit of addressing pupils as 'young man,' was teacher for Standards I and II. Teacher Molefe, nicknamed Peacock from his swaggering behaviour, taught Standards III and IV. Molefe used to carry a big English dictionary to school. He was very fond of using long and bombastic words. From him we heard that the longest English word was 'tintinnabulation'. It was not true. There are longer words in the English vocabulary. We did not know at the time. We believed him and envied him for his mastery of the King's language.

Teacher Masipha, head teacher and Standard V and VI class teacher, was the most feared of St. Ansgar's teachers. He never hesitated to dispense rough justice whenever he considered it justified. Location boys (toughies) quaked at the sight of him. During one of our school concerts the location toughies blew out the lanterns, plunged the concert into darkness and tried to create a ruction. How 'Double Decker', as Masipha was known, got hold of two of the culprits, I do not know. The two got the thrashing of their life and exposed their co-conspirators. The concert proceeded agreeably. Double Decker's status was enhanced among the toughies.

Double Decker was a disciplinarian but very kind and devoted to the success of his pupils. In the beginning as I struggled with new subjects, especially Afrikaans which was completely new, D D would taunt and pour scorn on my poor marks. 'This is not Bechuanaland. You must work hard here!' I had come to St. Ansgar's flourishing a first class Standard IV certificate accompanied by a glowing testimonial to my conduct and aptitude. My past school record was being judged a sham. Teacher Masipha's remarks stung and hurt me. They also motivated me. In spite of my outside-class delinquencies I

14

resolved to reassert my image which I did before the first year was out.

The following year it was flattering to hear my class teacher butter me up with poetic words: 'full many a gem of purest ray serene. . .. full many a flower is born to blush unseen and waste its sweetness in the desert air. . .' On top of the poetic compliment, teacher Masipha honoured me by inviting me for lunch in his house on some weekends. His sister-in-law, Constance, who was doing her Standard VI at St. Mary's in Krugersdorp, was usually around over the weekends. As the four of us – his wife being the fourth – sat at table, Decker would ply Connie and me with questions: 'After Standard VI what are you going to study?' 'Junior Certificate!' would come from both of us. 'After JC?' 'Matric!' from me and 'Nursing!' from Connie. He would then turn to me: 'After Matric?' After some silence, imposed by my vaulting ambition mixed with ignorance of the rungs of the educational ladder, I would coyly suggest 'Doctor! I want to become a doctor!' Teacher Masipha liked my apparent eagerness for education and he encouraged me by pointing to himself and a few other Africans who had obtained or were studying for degrees.

At these luncheons, teacher Masipha did not lose the opportunity to spice the educational pep talk with some apposite political flavours. From B M Masipha I heard of Moses Kotane and the up and coming Walter Sisulu for the first time. Kotane was Masipha's hero on two grounds. He fought fearlessly for the rights of his fellow oppressed. Without any formal educational background, he had educated himself to an extent that he could hold his own in political circles where abstract philosophical questions were discussed. Education and politics in Masipha's view were two strands of the same rope that Africans had to use to lift themselves to heights of respectability. At this juncture politics was something remote, abstract and vague. Education as a tool of self-improvement was obvious. My faith in education was deepening. Education and more education. The rest would then follow as day follows night. The naivety of youth!

1942 saw the tide of the war begin to turn. Though some of us had first degree relatives on active service, the carefree nature of our age immunised us from the anxiety and deep concern endured by adults. However rumours – and war time is full of rumours of all sizes, colours and dimensions – circulated unceasingly, some in conflict, in and around our school premises. I remember the night when there was a power blackout in the Roodepoort area. We jumped out of our blankets, ran out of our dormitories, did not stop running until we had crossed the school fence and from an elevation we could see nothing but a dark expanse where normally floodlight changed night into day. There was drama in the air.

We wondered what could have happened. In the morning we were

15

eager to listen to anyone with some explanation. Two explanations or rumours circulated with equal force around the campus. The blackout was a deliberate security precaution. Hitler was alleged to be preparing to bomb the Reef towns. A lit area could be a glaring target for the Nazi Luftwaffe, hence the wisdom of extinguishing the lights. A parallel rumour said the blackout was an act of sabotage. The Ossewabrandwag, the organisation of Van Rensburg and B J Vorster was behind it. The name Ossewabrandwag sounded melodramatic. Nothing could have excited and nourished our adventurist ethos more than a subversive organisation with such a pet name. The boys did not support the objectives of the Ossewabrandwag, only its method of fireworks and conspiracy.

The Ossewabrandwag sympathised with the Nazis and their cause. Although there was discrimination against Africans in the Union of South Africa, the propaganda against Hitlerism was very strong. If neo-Nazis in the mantle of Ossewabrandwag came to power in the Union, the lot of the oppressed would worsen, not improve. That was clear even to youth imbued with the spirit of indiscriminate adventurism.

When B J Vorster, interned during the war for subversive activities under the auspices of the OB (Ossewabrandwag), became the Minister of Justice in 1961 the fear of a worse era under a neo-Nazi dispensation was vindicated. Vorster was the originator of detention-without-trial legislation, which has resulted in over sixty mysterious deaths in detention. Ninety-day detention law was quickly followed by the hundred and eighty days clause, also known euphemistically as the 'witness' clause. It was while applying these draconian laws that every time an underground ANC activist was apprehended Vorster would announce dramatically: We have broken the back of the ANC. This ministerial chest-beating refrain prompted someone to quip: But how many backs has the ANC?

In 1942-43 at St. Ansgar's B J Vorster's future hung in the balance – restricted in an internment camp. Our own future shapeless and uncrystallised – maybe to be shaped by the policies and laws of a habitual subversive.

My father as well as my uncle corresponded with me from Italy and the Middle East. Airmail letters with 'On Active Service' scribbled across the aerogram and post dated 'Sicily' made me the envy of some boys. But the news in the letters was never exciting. All the questions I asked about the state of war were conveniently ignored when my letters were answered. One expected books to be written on events 'up North' yet the men on the stage of history seemed to be performing an uneventful pantomime.

> We are well. How is your school work. Study hard. Your
> Mom complains that you do not write to her regularly.
> Please write. She gets worried when you don't.

And the precious news occasionally would be 'I have asked your mother to send you the pocket money you requested . . .'

PAX

The end of 1943 came too soon. It was time for external examinations and transfer to another school – a secondary school. In spite of all the apparent anarchy outside class, serious school work was not neglected. All the Standard VI pupils hoped to succeed in the exams and each of us sent applications to as many schools as possible. Teacher Masipha advised me to apply to St. Peter's, the Anglican school in Johannesburg.

The influence of peers, however, was stronger than of other groups and in the end my cousin Gabriel and Albert Majatladi, both Catholics, persuaded me to look to Pax or Marianhill, both RC institutions. Three of us were eventually admitted to Pax.

Personally, I would have preferred Marianhill. Although my Afrikaans had improved tremendously, I felt one could do without it. In fact most pupils did not seem to like the study of Afrikaans for one reason or other. Children in Transvaal schools – Afrikaans was a compulsory school subject in the Orange Free State and the Transvaal – felt a sense of grievance because Natal and the Cape Province were not compelled to teach Afrikaans. Despite the growing popularity of Afrikaans as the main ingredient of the new township lingua to be known as 'tsotsi taal (tsotsi language)' and spoken by the urbanised youth, Afrikaans in a school environment was an unhappy reminder of the naked hatred of Africans by Afrikaners, descendants of the Dutch.

The grondwette (constitutions) of the two Boer republics – Orange Free State and Transvaal – stated: 'There shall be no equality in church and state between Whites and Coloureds.' Our teacher quite rightly made it a point to underline the constitutional origin of our woes. It was distressing. When Dingaan's army massacred Piet Retief and his party in Mngungundlovu at the cry of 'kill the wizards!' we generally judged it a fair revenge for all that had gone before in other parts of the country. With the battle of Blood River where the tables were turned against Dingaan's army by the Boers, we felt a grave sense of injustice and a let-down by fate. Boers were invaders. They had no moral justification for retaliation. The massacre was unforgivable enough. But for the Boers to commemorate the event by declaring 16 December a public holiday and to invoke the name of God for it was to cultivate a seed-bed of strife and to place a big question mark before and behind divine justice. A simmering indignation at the apparent helplessness of being born black in South Africa pervaded even our carefree spirit at St. Ansgar's and without rhyme or reason the chant of 'bulalan' abathakathi (kill the wizards)' could be heard on our playgrounds.

Since the Union of South Africa had a white government and it was

17

this government that was responsible for the disenfranchisement of the Africans and all the misery that flowed from it, all the whites without exception shared the responsibility. In their day to day lives, however, a certain section of the white populace stuck out like a sore thumb. The Afrikaners were petty, uncultured, vindictive, bigoted, sectarian, inflated, arrogant . . . Their knack for embittered relations with Africans was not improved by their employment in law enforcement agencies, especially at the lowest levels. They were the petty officials at pass offices, and they formed the core of the beat police. They stopped and harassed every African with their pass laws, including school boys.

One Saturday three of us stood quietly at the corner of Bree and Van Weilligh streets waiting to see a relative who was employed in the vicinity. Suddenly an Afrikaans-speaking young constable on patrol duty approached our innocent little circle. 'Pass!' he hissed at us. Our spontaneous, unrehearsed reaction was to disperse in three different directions giggling our incomprehension of the unwarranted intrusion. He was bamboozled. He did not know whom to chase and made no arrest. He did, however, manage to threaten us: Kaffertjies ek gaan julle vang (little kaffirs, I'll arrest you). Anybody could have noticed that we were school-kids, this cop included. The problem was that we were black school-kids, entitled to carry school passes and therefore liable to arrest and harassment. Admittedly patrol duty can be boring too. The poor constable might have been looking for some sport to break the monotony of the beat. What better entertainment than intimidate someone whose life is already encrusted in fear of his fellow men! What delight to watch him quake, to watch him plead with tears in his voice: My baas, asseblief my baas (My boss, please my boss). Just to escape a night in a police cell.

Unwittingly and subconsciously some of us were being driven irrevocably into an anti-status quo position. Discriminatory laws made one conscious of one's identity or lack of it. Separate trams, separate coaches, separate cinemas, separate entrances at railway stations, separate entrances and separate counters at the same post offices, separate entrances to buildings and separate lifts in the buildings, separate residential areas, separate schools, separate universities, separate places of worship, separate playgrounds, different job categories, different tax laws and different other laws. Everything was separate and different. Parliament spent more than half its time debating the 'Native question', the 'Native problem', the 'Native danger (swart gevaar)'.

Meantime, the 'Native' was unrepresented . . . Oh no, he was. By a white representative in Parliament, and another in the Senate, chosen for his knowledge of the 'Natives'. There was at the time a white man in Parliament, whose name was on the lips of whites and 'Natives', young and old. This was Jan Hofmeyr, J C Smuts' deputy. He was widely talked of as a genius, a child prodigy. He read the Bible at

18

three years, passed matric at thirteen, was Vice-Chancellor of Wits University at twenty-one . . . A Cape liberal – that singular breed of whites who subscribed to Cecil John Rhodes' motto of 'equality among all civilized men . . .' Teachers, black teachers, spoke admiringly of Hofmeyr the liberal, the genius and implicitly the hope of blacks. I was infected by the current gullibility. In my bias I did not even believe Jan Jofmeyr was an Afrikaner. It was difficult to imagine an Afrikaner who projected an attitude other than a racist one towards Africans. If only he could become the Prime Minister, this Jan, we mused. The complexity of politics generally, and South African politics in particular, was still a closed chapter. Thus my innocent heart wished wishes and my ignorant mind dreamed dreams.

My mother died in 1944. I was doing Form One the Junior Certificate (JC), at Pax Secondary School at the time. A letter arrived in the Study Hall where we were swotting for end-of-year exams. 'Your mother is late . . .' Setswapuleng, my aunt wrote. I received the letter long after the funeral. Although Bobonong village had telegraphic facilities, aunt Setswapuleng did not bother to send me a telegram for two reasons. Since no mortuary existed in the village, funerals took place almost immediately after death. Decomposition is a swift process in the tropics, and farewells between the departed and the living take cognizance of that. Secondly, telegrams in those days were believed to convey only the saddest of news, death. Recipients of telegrams usually preferred other people to open and read them to cushion the impact of tragic pain. Readers of such messages invariably resorted to circumlocution to announce the news. The technique softened the blow. My aunt was therefore considerate. She knew of my attachment to Mom, and probably imagined me dropping on the spot at the sight of a telegram. The best way to break the news was through an ordinary letter.

Another letter came from my father up north. 'Your Mom has left us. Do not go home until I return . . .' The end of the war was imminent. That was the talk and the mood and the wish at the end of 1944. But the Second World War was not completely over yet. The senseless carnage was still going on. The end might come in six months, twelve or twenty-four months. Hitler was still kicking his last kicks. Dad was being optimistic in his plans for me. Demob might take some more time too. During this time I was to be suspended between home and the war theatre. It was unfair. 'For vacation, go to your uncle's in Johannesburg . . .' he had advised. I wondered why the paternal decree. Why the ban. Later it transpired the 'precaution' was for my own security. The theory was that with the demise of one parent the survival of the whole family was in jeopardy. Family cohesion had been disrupted, undermined and the vulnerability of the rest of the members especially the children was an obsession.

After Dad's demob I went home in December 1945. Dad informed me there was to be a cleansing ritual to appease the ancestral gods and to fend off witches. The powers, tendencies and whims attributable to the gods and witches have always depressed and tormented me. Why all these absurd and enigmatic forces against innocent people? Was everything that one heard about them true? Fear of the unknown is a short route to blind faith. I feared supernatural powers of the gods and the witches. Because I feared them I believed everything that was said of them. And because I believed I feared even more. It was a vicious psychological circle. Fortunately in the two years I was at Pax I had changed. Catholic church indoctrination had rid me of my fears. I no longer believed in the gods nor did I fear the witches, because I was a true Christian immune from the devil and his ungodly powers.

I told my father so when he suggested the cleansing ritual. 'No! It is all superstition, I do not believe in superstitious practices. I am a Christian. I shall have nothing to do with the ritual.'

During 1945-46 Bechuanaland was blessed with rain. It came down in torrents. Heavily. For days and nights it poured down. Rivers, rivulets and streams overflowed their banks. Ponds croaked with bull frogs and many creatures proclaimed the wet season with their diverse cries. The roads to the railway stations were impassable long after the school vacation had ended. Three to four weeks I was marooned in the village. Fortunately the telegraph office was still operational and I managed to report my predicament to the school authorities.

When I arrived I found my name at the head of the inmates of St Raphael dormitory. I was monitor designate. It was good to be back after the uncertainty of the incessant rain. Fellow students welcomed and teased me: 'The desert man! Marooned by floods or mirages? . . .' I settled down to my final year at Pax. 'Kizito, what are you going to do next year?' asked In-ze-name. 'I don't know,' replied Kizito evasively. 'Do matric and then take the priesthood vocation. How would you like to study at the Vatican? I shall make the necessary recommendations.' In-ze-name had already recommended a school bursary for Kizito. It was an honour for the student although something made him indifferent.

The conversation took place in the school botanical gardens, as we studied flowers and compared their petals, sepals and pistils. In-ze-name was Brother Celeste's nickname. It derived from his lisp. 'In ze name of ze father and of ze son and of ze Holy Ghost . . .' he led us in prayer before commencement of class and at ze end of ze class. Kizito was In-ze-name's corruption of my own name, Kitso. Actually it was a name of one of the Ugandan Catholics who died for their faith and became martyrs and saints in conjunction with Catholic church practice on the faithful who laid down their lives for church and God. In-ze-name saw me as a devout Catholic who might one day sacrifice his life for his religion and be canonized for it. I was converted to

20

Catholicism during my first term at Pax. The conversion entailed no soul searching, I was ripe for the systematised indoctrination of the Roman Catholic Church. The London Missionary Society to which I professed to belong, previously, had neglected some of the Christian rites on me.

But what was most appealing to me was the emphasis the Church laid on the equality of human beings irrespective of colour. This stress I had missed before in the London Missionary Society, probably because in Bechuanaland it did not need to be made since there was no racial tension to talk about. The implicit support for the discriminatory constitutions of the Boer republics by the Dutch Reformed Churches induced me to welcome the theological endorsement of human equality. I have never entertained the inferior or superior status of some groups on the basis of colour, religion, nation or race. The Church touched the right chord in the repertory of my intrinsic inclinations. Certain mysteries of the church remained mysteries – the creation, the incarnation, the resurrection, life everlasting in either hell or heaven – they exercised the mind and lulled it to dull faith. The average man is gullible. All the complex philosophies about life are beyond him and he tends to be a yes-man if left to himself. I am an average man. It was important to me for the church to declare itself unequivocally on the colour question. Otherwise it was redundant and irrelevant in my social life.

I joined the Roman Catholic Church with high hopes. Here was a church that by implication promised not only heavenly but earthly salvation as well.

Pax was originally a teacher training college. It was surrounded by a number of primary schools which it had spawned for practical training of trainee teachers – Paxana, Paxeso, Paxengwe and Paxola. In 1943 the first secondary school class was inaugurated with two pupils. We were the second group to attempt JC in 1944. Our curriculum was poor and inflexible. There was no choice of subjects, apparently due to shortage of qualified staff in certain subjects. All of us did Arithmetic, Biology, Agricultural Science, History and three languages: Northern Sesotho, English and Afrikaans. The eighth subject, Scripture, was a non-examination subject but it was no less compulsory. Some of us felt we had been taken for a ride because until we arrived on the campus we were ignorant of the curriculum and the syllabuses. There was no prospectus to warn one of the impending strait-jacket. Teacher Masipha had advised me to do Mathematics if I intended to study medicine.

The exclusion of Mathematics from the curriculum was a big disappointment. It was clear that I could not accept a bursary at the school if my ambition was to be fulfilled. My plan was to move to another school after completion of JC. It was going to be demanding to start Mathematics at Form IV level but I was prepared to do it if some

other school could give me a chance. To inform Brother Celeste of my
intention and the grounds for declining the bursary would not have
helped me. Celeste was keen to see me a priest. That is why I chose to
keep quiet when I was offered the bursary. Silence in this case was
not consent. It was simply a noncommittal answer. That this was
misconstrued was not my fault.

The three years passed quietly in spite of the Maths grievance and the
desire to enrol in another school. The school programme was planned
in a way that left very little leisure for either boredom or mischief.
Those who could not resist some indulgence in a bit of mischief had
to look to the unprogrammed night. It meant sacrificing one's
precious sleep. But fun-lovers are great innovators and Paxonians
were no exception. As monitor of St Raphael I had to turn a blind eye
every night to the habits of my dormitory's night lifers. At first I never
could imagine the destinations of the night migrants. Later I got to
know that there was a segment that raided the adjacent kraals for
traditional brew. The other segment paid courtesy calls to ladies'
hostels at the nearby Grace Dieu diocesan school. Both these habits
were foreign to my conduct. Gambling was unpractised at Pax.
Perhaps that is where my tendencies to misconduct might have led
me given the opportunity. In spite of my basic disapproval of the sort
of fun pursued by a part of my dormitory I did not report the
goings-on as I was supposed to do.
    It was a mistake to entrust me with the responsibility of maintain-
ing school discipline. It is contrary to my nature to antagonise other
people if that can be avoided. Reports of such habits could lead to
expulsions. That would have been treacherous. So tacitly I allowed
the night prowlers to do their own things. One of the culprits later
became a principal of a school. I wonder whether he would have
become such an important figure in his community had I exposed his
boyish habits at Pax. Pax students were generally politically apathe-
tic; except on one occasion when we staged a spontaneous demonstration against inspectors Doctors W W M Eiselen and G H Franz.
The two educationists spoke Northern Sesotho very well. They were
reputed to have grown up among the Bapedi of the Northern
Transvaal. Dr Franz was the author of a Sesotho prescribed work.
Typical of South African whites who claim to 'know Natives', they
claimed to know not only the culture of the natives, but to know and
have the right to prescribe a cultural pattern of development for the
same people. 'Missionary education was unsuited for them – it
alienated them from their people and traditions. The Native must be
taught in the vernacular. He must be taught his culture and tradition
in the vernacular. Natives cannot conceptualise foreign culture and
technology taught in a foreign language. It is too difficult.' (In the
meantime the propagation of the teaching of Afrikaans in African
schools was in full force).

22

The above sentiments formed the recurrent theme of the inspectors when they took their annual inspectoral rounds. In the past we had listened to this trash with apparent impassivity. In 1946 it was different. The inspectors' welcome was improper. The students, to the last student, remained seated when the inspectors entered the hall. Brother Lucinius (Kgopana) was tongue-tied. Kgopana was a very soft spoken man, whose voice was raised musically once a year at Easter, when he rendered the Alleluia solo accompanied by the organ. Easter Sunday was months ahead and Kgopana's voice was in the freezer. Only when the hot red faces of inspectors glowered at Kgopana in truculent mood was his voice able to thaw to a whisper: 'Stand up!' A prolonged shuffling of feet preceded the grudging obedience to the 'Stand up' order.

It was the only serious insubordination to authority I can remember in my three years at Pax. Dr W W M Eiselen in 1949 shortly after the coming into power by the Nationalist Party government was appointed chairman of the Commission on Native Education. It was this Commission which recommended the reprehensible Bantu Education Act of 1953.

The ANC or Congress was unknown to many at Pax. Two students, David Ramohanoe and William Maleya, were the only two who claimed to belong to the newly formed ANC Youth League. David was the son of the then president of the Transvaal ANC. He came from Alexandra. Willie came from an ANC family in Sophiatown. The two youth leaguers did not carry out any recruitment on the campus to my knowledge.

My black consciousness at Pax was given a shot by Dr Vilakazi's talk when he visited our school towards the end of the year. Dr B W Vilakazi, together with other African intellectuals of the time, was one of those few people I had honestly wanted to meet in life. They were a great inspiration to me personally. From their lowly and 'primitive' backgrounds they had risen to lofty educational heights and given the lie to the racist propaganda that Africans were uneducable.

It was a morale booster of magnificent proportions. One afternoon, without warning, Dr Vilakazi stood before us. On that very spot the inspectors had seen the silent antipathy of the students. Dr Vilakazi's reception was in marked contrast to that accorded our two previous VIP guests. The hall bulged with genuine welcome. The audience was jubilant. I was particularly impressed. The eloquence of the man in a foreign language was impressive. The content of the talk was very inspiring. Listeners generally must enjoy hearing what they want to hear. The gist of the doctor's speech was quotation from Dr Aggrey: Africans are eagles, capable of soaring to unprecedented heights. But for many years they were kept in a fowl run with the fowls and had forgotten or neglected the power of their wings. It was incumbent upon the same Africans to get out of the coop and exercise and demonstrate their inherent capabilities. Still quoting from Aggrey, he alluded to the harmony, the melody, that issues from the black and white keys of the piano. It was an allegoric rebuttal of the theories of race purists.

The real gem of his address was when he exhorted us to be proud of our colour. Our colour had nothing to do with our intellectual or physical aptitudes. Colour prejudice from any quarter should not make us feel little or worthless. It was a beautiful colour. A colour we should be immensely proud of. 'Some of you may know my wife. And those who do will bear me out when I say she is blacker than the blackest of you here. Yet she is not ashamed of her colour. On the contrary she is very proud of it. I, too, am proud of her colour . . .' I confirmed what the doctor told us about his wife when I met her a year later in Sophiatown. Very black, beautiful and unashamed of her colour. Dr Vilakazi beamed every time he looked upon her comely ebony face.

Before the doctor's talk, it is true, I had never felt ashamed of my blackness nor had I ever felt called upon to be specifically proud of my colour. But with the rampant prejudice against our colour by white people in South Africa, I often wondered why the omnipotent, omniscient and omnipresent creator created a colour so hideous and execrable in the eyes of others. These nagging questions and doubts tended to undermine one's religious base and fervour. The portrayal of Lucifer as black also raised the issue of divine justice on the colour question. Lucifer, black. African, black. Remove black and the equation becomes Lucifer equals African or vice versa. Life is full of puzzles. For an African life's puzzles multiply.

The call for pride in one's black colour was therefore a legitimate duty of every black man to redress the dehumanising colour prejudice practised with religious devotion. Dr Vilakazi's exhortation was timely and in context. In a racist society like the South African white society people of colour need to be deliberately conscientised in their youth. They need to have impressed upon them that their colour is not a thing of shame, but a thing of beauty and pride. Such attitude stimulates a man of colour to stand up erect and say: I am black. I am human. I demand my place in the theatre of social life. Life undiminished. I demand it here. I demand it now.

The viciousness with which discriminatory legislation is applied against blacks, and the ferocity with which any contravention of this body of laws is visited upon the offenders, has the potential of creating yes-men, social robots and political zombies among the blacks. During the fifties when the population of South Africa was 13 million, 10 million blacks and three million whites, a visiting black American is reputed to have said: 'Three million oppress ten million? There can't be anything wrong with the three million. There must be something wrong with the 10 million!' He was both right and wrong. There was, and there still is, something wrong with both the

24

oppressed and the oppressors. The oppressed, by allowing themselves to be disunited, unorganised and vulnerable. The oppressors, by uniting and organising systematically to keep the oppressed in perpetual subjugation. The children of God, in word, oppressing the other children of God, in deed.

Of course it is not the fatalism arising out of many years of oppression and indoctrination of the superiority of whites that is responsible for the protractedness of the struggle against colour prejudice and exploitation of man by man, alone. Other material conditions, superior organisation, economic resources, and all the trappings of a repressive state machinery must be acknowledged and assigned their correct influence, but when all's said and done, the psychological factor plays a crucial role in the context of a social struggle. It conditions the mind and strengthens the will to resist. Conscientisation however cannot be a separate and isolated event. It must be an integral part of an ongoing process of organised active resistance. A systematic interweaving of theory and practice. Had Dr Vilakazi stopped where he exhorted us to be proud of our blackness, that would have been a senseless, sterile teaching. Dr Vilakazi urged us to study hard; to aim at improving ourselves so that in turn we could play a vital role in the upliftment of our people. This may not seem a direct and revolutionary route. Nevertheless education was then, and is now, an important vehicle of progress in every facet of social life. To me education was about everything: the light to illumine the night of toil and suffering, the shield to ward off further assaults against our dignity and an instrument to forge ahead towards the status of merited equality. Nothing annoyed me like the intellectual superiority of whites. If they were so sure of their mental superiority why did they not have integrated schools where the hypothesis could be put to a living test? I itched for such an opportunity. Oppressive societies know the power of education. Consequently they neglect or manipulate the education of the oppressed for their own benefit. Education among the oppressed and exploited masses is a privilege, not a right.

The year 1946 raced to a close. External examinations were around the corner. Side by side with preparations for examinations I was busy trying to find another school for the coming year. I was through with Pax. No allurement could detain me further. I sent off applications to Inkamana, Marianhill and Roma College in Basutoland – the three were Catholic schools and as a good Catholic I wanted to continue at a Catholic school. Marianhill and Inkamana refused me because my school, Pax, was to start a Form IV class. The principal's office had obviously intercepted my applications and decided to act to counter my plans. I was grieved. Roma College apparently did not feel obliged to accede to my school's recommendation. In a clever move they sent application forms and a prospectus to Bobonong instead of Pax. Meantime, until I got home, I was worried that Roma had not responded to my application. I was ignorant of the clever move. I had also made two other applications. One to the Union of South Africa government requesting a bursary. The second one for the same purpose went to the Bechuanaland administration. The Union government declined to sponsor me on the grounds that I was an alien.

Back home I found good and bad news waiting for me. The bad news was very bad. The local administration had replied to my bursary application by sending forms for completion to my father. Dad found one condition objectionable: that which stated that after completion of my studies I would have to work in Bechuanaland for five years. Work in Bechuanaland? For five years! How much can they pay my son, the misers? No, that specific condition was unacceptable! Dad then proceeded to scuttle the application unilaterally. It was a tragic decision by Dad. My ambitions lay in ruins. My father could no longer afford to pay my fees at Senior Secondary School. Between the time of Mom's death and his demob his cattle had been whittled away by cattle rustlers or they had simply gone astray in the absence of a conscientious herdboy. The few he still had could not keep me at school for one year let alone two years. His rejection of the government bursary was due to misinformation, prejudice and self-conceit.

The good news would have been excellent had it not been vitiated by the bad news. Roma College was looking forward to enrolling me as their student. Someone had recommended me as a diligent, disciplined student. We, Dad and I, calculated the cost of enrolling at Roma. It would be beyond Dad's means, especially as he had already taken a new wife. After much agonising we agreed that one way was to go and seek employment in Johannesburg. It was hoped I could save some money and go back to school after one or two years. Alternatively I could register with a correspondence college and try to qualify for University entrance. The plans of mice and men . . .

CHAPTER TWO

Colour Stigma

SOPHIATOWN AND ALEXANDRA

One street ahead a man approached from the opposite direction. Either he was drunk or he was bent on mischief. His walk was abnormal. He lurched from one side of the street to the other. The heat of the January sun beat on the paved street mercilessly and melted some of the bitumen. People kept indoors. Edward Road looked virtually deserted. Except for a group of boys who sought shade under a shop verandah at the corner of Morris Street and Edward Road, the only other man who braved the hot sun was a black uniformed policeman a few yards in front of me.

As the man from the opposite direction drew nearer I recognised him as Mike, alias Mbutani, one of the leaders of the Berlin gang. Mbutani blocked the policeman's way and said something I could not hear. My heart missed a beat as I sensed trouble. Before I could make up my mind what to do – whether to double my tracks or to draw a right angle – the poor constable was reeling from a flurry of blows from Bra Mbutani. His police helmet fell to the ground. Blood gushed from his face. His uniform was a bloody mess. Handcuffs still dangled from his side, looking limp from disuse at a critical moment. The knobkerrie, the standard black policeman's weapon, lay next to the helmet in a mark of discomfited solidarity. I walked past quickly lest Bra Mbutani, although he knew me, should in his bloody mood turn against me for sheer sport.

From both sides of the street people came out of their pondokkies to witness one of the regular street scenes in Kofiefie (Sophiatown). None of the onlookers attempted to intervene. It was the law of the gangster-ridden townships. Mind your business. Keep out of other people's trouble if you do not want trouble. To underwrite this law and underscore his inviolability, Mbutani pulled out his contraband revolver, pointed it to the sky and fired a few 'hands off' shots. Bang! Bang! The spectators retreated instinctively into their shacks, exchanging whispered information about the big shot, Bra Mbutani.

Sophiatown, 1951. I was a visitor from Alexandra township where I then resided. Up to 1948 I was a resident of Sophiatown. I was to be back in 1954 and then back to Alex in 1957 when I ducked the forced removals to Meadowlands. I shuttled between the two townships, because they shared many common features. Their two main differences were at the time: Sophiatown had some street lights whereas Alexandra was unlit. Hence the name Dark City; Alexandra was twice further from Johannesburg than Sophiatown and it had a population more than double that of Sophiatown.

Mbutani and Vivian (Bra Dladla) were leaders of the Berlin gang in Sophiatown. They were mortal enemies of the Young Americans, another gang in the area. The two gangs effectively divided Sophiatown into two war zones. Toby Street to Meyer Street was more or less the undisputed area of the Young Americans, while Ray Street to Johannes Road belonged to the Berliners.

I knew Vivian fairly well. He dropped out of primary school some time in 1947. While I lived at 71 Morris Street, Sophiatown, we met frequently along the streets that later constituted his domain. We cadged around for 'jockeys' at dice games when both of us were unemployed. If I was lucky enough to win I gave him a shungu (tip) and vice versa.

The post-war boom was getting under way. Employment opportunities were improving for those who were not fussy. The building construction companies appeared to lead the boom. Skilled artisans as well as unskilled labourers were in demand. The urban youth and those like me who boasted a modicum of education shunned muscular work like building work. It was moegoe work (a job for country bumpkins). We were the tsebanyane (clevers), cut for white collar work.

At the pass office the Boer clerks tried to push every workseeker into muscular work. The combination of the economic boom and the influx of workseekers from the 'Reserves' led to the construction of an extension of the pass office on a site along Market Street, a short distance from the old pass office. Pass seekers and job seekers walking the short distance from the old to the new pass office had to run a gauntlet of touts and pass fixers. Business in pass trafficking was lively and profitable. The pass office petty officials and their agents squeezed the jobless, the moneyless, passless pass carriers of their last penny. Hungry pass and job seekers stood in long queues to have their urban workseeker status legalised. Often they were turned back on a mere technicality which they hardly understood. In desperation they borrowed money from their working relatives, not to buy food, but to buy pass-fixers. To stifle their hunger they girded – literally – their bellies with strips of rags and came back with the rewarding support of the pass-fixer. Market Street pass office was rotten. After some years the stench was sniffed by the higher echelons in the Union Buildings – the administrative headquarters – and the reaction was to tighten the screws on the pass legislation to the 'better' detriment of pass carriers. Official statements on the introduction of the euphemistic 'The Native (Abolition of Passes and Co-ordination of Documents) Amendment Act' would have the public believe that it was partly meant to foil 'pass consultants'.

The South African Institute of Race Relations in its Annual Survey for 1954-55 wrote:

Since influx control measures were tightened, pass consultants and forgery gangs have conducted flourishing business in the proclaimed areas. Some Africans bewildered by the complexities of urban legislation and unsure of how to present their cases to overworked (sic) officials at registration offices have been willing to find someone with more leisure to assist them. Others who are illegal entrants to the urban areas are prepared to pay large sums for documents authorising them to remain. It was said that pass consultants were charging as much a £7-10s a fine for their services.

The victims of pass consultants were invariably peasants from the rural reserves. Driven by poverty arising from land hunger, they flocked to the towns to seek employment. In urban areas they discovered job opportunities were restricted not only by the relatively slow industrialisation process, but by the application of influx-control regulations which in great measure were being applied arbitrarily and fraudulently by petty officials. Urban Africans, the 'clevers', were a different kettle of fish. Some could pull strings with official acquaintances both black and white; others simply defied petty official instructions to quit the prescribed areas.

Vivian, alias Bra Dladla, was one of those who refused to be endorsed out of their place of birth. Initially he had been lucky to find employment locally with Albert, the Chinese shopkeeper in Annadale Street. Besides working as delivery hand, part of his duties was as a look-out for the police of the gambling and liquor squad. Albert, like the majority of shopkeepers in Sophiatown, was engaged in some illicit deals. He sold liquor to the Africans in contravention of the law. He also ran a numbers gambling game called Fah-fee. Contraband dealers, to carry on their business relatively unmolested, did two things: bribed the police or used several means to avoid detection. One of the means was employing sentinels. Such sentinels had to be conscientious and vigilant to make their employers' business viable if not lucrative. Vivian, a veteran of street gambling where gamblers were forever on the alert for police surprises, was ideal for the job. 'Arah! Arah rai!' he would shout a warning at the approach of the police.

I do not know how he lost his job. But lose it he did. Loss of employment meant one thing: the pass office and its long queues terminating at counters manned by arrogant petty officials. A work-seeker's permit was valid for three or four weeks depending on whether one was born in the area or on the previous employment record in the area. The permit was renewable but not for indefinite periods. Irrespective of one's residential status, to be unemployed was dangerous. It still is. One could be endorsed out of his place of birth due to lack of employment in the place.

Bra Dladla was warned at the pass office: find employment or else ... He stopped visiting the pass office to renew his work-seeker's permit. 'Boere is laf (Boers are silly),' he remarked as he announced his decision not to go back to the Native Affairs Department (pass office). Sophiatown became not only his home, but his world. It was risky to stray into town without a valid pass. So Vivian confined himself to Sophiatown and adjacent townships, Western Native Township and Newclare. It was this restriction imposed by the psychological terror of the pass laws that changed Vivian to Bra Dladla and elevated him to the top of a vicious gang that terrorised lone police and law abiding residents and fought a bloody gang war with the Young Americans, another product of the social system and its ghetto dynamics.

Bra Dladla became a household name in Sophiatown. A name to dread or to revere. 'Cherries' (girls) in shebeens and the streets sang: 'Ek mngca ou Dladla tussen die manne, no one pazamisa (I love "old" Dladla among the men, nobody must interfere).' It became a hit as his notoriety grew. Neutral youths joined those who were neutral on the side of Bra Dladla to whistle the provocative tune. 'Ek mngca ou Dladla.'

The pass laws are a humiliation to African dignity, a scourge to their economic opportunities, and a shameless badge of slavery.

Passes – permits, reference books, identity documents, passports, whatever the official form of the moment – are a nightmare to Africans in South Africa. Nightly, they dream of raids in their homes for passes, dream of being stopped in the streets for passes, dream of queueing up at the pass office for passes. These dreams come irrespective of whether one is employed or unemployed. Pass dreams, unlike other dreams, come true. The raids and harassment through the pass laws are inescapable. A pass carrier has no place to hide. In the fifties I heard a story of one man who hid in a wardrobe to escape a pass arrest. His kid was about three and beginning to detest the ways of the police while apparently untutored in their skillful use of information. She sucked her thumb, rolled her eyes towards the mother and hopped on one leg ecstatically as she loudly proclaimed: 'They will never get my dad. Mom has locked him up in the wardrobe.' She wailed when the police unlocked the wardrobe with her mom's key and dragged the half suffocating dad out of the wardrobe into a waiting troop carrier outside. 'Kwela, kwela (Embark)!' The troop carrier roared away to dump the poor man in a police station and, who knows, maybe to his death on a farm prison where brutal torture was practised on the helpless victims of the pass system.

Besides dreams, talk in the townships centred around the passes, and the entire machinery that enforced them. The Native Affairs Department, in the image of the pass office, arbitrarily determined one's entitlement to a valid urban pass. One had to study and become expert at the ways of petty officials running the pass office. If one's case was 'tenuous', addressing the petty officials in Afrikaans might help. A servile wringing of the hands and 'ja-my-baas (yes, boss)' strategy might help. Other ways would be to lie about some of one's particulars or forge the document. In the forties and the fifties forgery of the pass document was easy and some of us who could read and write English practised it to help some potential victims.

Bribery, as I have already indicated, was rife. The upshot was that the influx-control regulations never worked and will never work as long as loopholes exist in the system, as they will always do, and as long as corrupt officialdom remains, as it will always do. The influx of Africans to the urban areas will never become worse than it is or it has been in the past, if influx control regulations and passes generally are abolished. Unjust repressive laws never achieve anything except to perfect skilful circumvention and diehard defiance.

There was a time when liquor was prohibited to Africans in South Africa. Policy makers and their cohorts pontificated on the irresponsible drinking habits of Africans and how if afforded the privilege to buy liquor they would abuse it to the detriment of the economy at large and the community morals at largest. That theory was given a resounding lie when the prohibition was lifted after many years of raids, arrests, fines and general harassment in the name of 'Native responsibility and sobriety'. In any case, why discriminate between racial groups living as an integral community whatever the policy makers said and however the disintegration (desegregation, if you wish) policy was pursued?

The pass office and its personnel were a good course to study for a pass bearer (supplicant). The ancillary course was the study of police movements. Police raids followed a routine, more or less, a routine of time periods and place. Moreover there were police stations which were more active than others on pass raids: Newlands, Fordsburg, Marshall Square, Hospital Hill, Norwood, Wynberg. One had to know them, their period of activity and their target areas. One had to be smart to survive and to avoid turning a police cell into a permanent place of abode. It was not always easy, because occasionally routine might be de-routinised and one might fall foul of the police innovation. That is if one's pass was regarded as not in order. The trouble, of course, is that a pass was never a hundred per cent in order. A hundred per cent valid pass had to prove that one was employed, had permission to be employed in that particular prescribed area, one had a residential permit where one was living, one had paid poll tax; if one was visiting, that one had not been in the visited area for more than the prescribed 72 hours; besides all these it was a crime not to carry it on one's person otherwise the charge was 'failure to produce'; a valid pass on one's person would not help 'a Native' if he was in the central business district or white area during curfew hours, unless he had special permission.

In Johannesburg curfew commenced at 11pm. In other (smaller) towns I believe it was earlier. Then watch your behaviour when

31

confronted by police for a pass. You might be hauled in for 'obstruction' – obstruction of the police in the course of their duties is a serious crime. In South Africa this crime has a very close affinity with the application of the pass laws. Thrice I was charged with obstruction: The first time was when the white policeman who was studying my pass asked 'What is your name?' and I retorted, 'Can't you read? My name is in the document.' I slept in Jeppe Police Station for three nights – obstructing the police . . .

The second time, a black constable demanded my dompass. Now this constable was in mufti and I did not know whether he was a genuine policeman or just a rogue. So I demanded his pass for identification. He called his white colleague who was also stopping other people and demanding their passes. 'Baas,' he addressed his colleague, 'this one is demanding my pass . . .' Obstruction. I spent a night in Wynberg Police cell.

The third time, I was getting off a bus at the terminus in Noord Street. It was in the morning. I was late for work, delayed by long queues nine miles away in Alexandra. When we alighted, police were waiting. 'Pass.' I gave them my pass, which was quite in order, and I started running to make up for time lost in the queue. The policeman was still studying my pass and when he realised I was not waiting for him to finish his intellectual exercise, he blew his whistle and the force came after me. I got some rough handling. The charge? Obstruction.

By sheer luck I spent half the day in Hospital Hill police station. The unwritten law of the dompass is: Don't argue, don't react when your dompass is demanded. Oblige. Produce. Otherwise, 'obstruction', and you might swap your clean blankets for lice-infested ones for a couple of nights. The pass laws are a wicked design enacted and imposed by an evil and insensitive regimen. People talked about the passes, dreamt the passes, cursed them, forged them, suffered under them, 'bought' them, queued long hours for them and carried them submissively in their pockets and produced them at every street corner, bus terminus, railway station and deep in the sanctuary of their homes.

As a regular victim of the pass laws I hated them intensely. The disenfranchisement of the Africans was responsible. People with the vote would not put such a piece of legislation on the statute books, let alone tolerate it. Blacks were voiceless. Without a voice one is dumb. Dumbness is the foretaste of doom and misinterpretation. People endowed with voices claim to know what you need, what you want. Your likes and dislikes are misinterpreted and distorted. You might gesticulate or go into tantrums, those with the voice normally turn stone deaf to such abnormal language.

Every Sunday I attended the eight o'clock mass at the chapel in Bernard Street. I received holy communion and prayed for many things, things whose possession or dispossession would improve my piety and my chances of salvation. The priest prayed for all sinners, the congregation, the Pope, and those in power, the government – the government that disenfranchised the blacks and gave them passes. I prayed with the priest and believed the government might change heart. Like all humans, the government was human; they could sin. Like all humans who sinned they might confess and repent. After all, weren't they white and ipso facto more Christian than I? They were the evangelists. The missionaries who taught us to love our neighbours as ourselves. Straying sheep. They will repent. And there shall be rejoicing in heaven.

Outside of the chapel the police were active. They raided illicit beer brewers, overturned the beer pots and smashed the empties to forestall future brewing where the brewer could not be identified with the brew. Where the brewer was caught red-handed she/he was dragged out to join the sheepish line of those apprehended in the street, on a doleful march to the police station. A sample of the brew was taken in this case and the bulk was spilled. Monday was a busy day. Courts handed out sentences and imposed fines. Poor people. Without a regular income, they devised means for some income and paid for it in fines.

Every Sunday after church it happened. I saw it happen. The arrest of beer-brewers. The arrest of pass offenders. The arrest of shebeen queens and kings. In the chapel, the glorification of God in hymn, the soothing word from the priest's sermon and my own devout and silent prayer for the things I cherished, gave me hope of a sublime life. Two steps from the chapel doorstep the sublime turned into the hideous. Arrests. Arrests and harassment of the black-skinned. Arrests carried out in the name of a Christian government in a Christian country.

Doubts began to torment me. Doubts about the Christianness of the white Christians. Why did they pass oppressive laws against their fellow men and apply them harshly? What about the clergy? Why were they so silent on these discriminatory practices?

The literacy rate was low in the townships. Someone with JC was considered educated by township standards. The educated, whether old or young, could shed light on the myriad laws and procedures that applied to the existence of Africans. I became a confidante and advisor to some neighbours and acquaintances. 'I will be endorsed out of Johannesburg, if I report to the pass office for an extension of my workseeker's permit. I was warned the last time I was there, that if I do not find employment by a given date I would be kicked out of Johannesburg. What do I do?'

'Tell a lie. Tell them you have been doing a temporary job with du Toit and show them two shillings as monthly levy from him. They will give you an extension,' I would advise. It usually worked. The lie and the two bob sacrifice. The beneficiary came back beaming. 'I do not know how to thank you!'

33

Others, usually women looking for domestic employment, would also come: 'A missus in Bellevue is prepared to employ me, if I can produce a reference. Can't you help me?' With a smile I would scribble a few lines to say Cynthia worked for me (a fictitious name at a fictitious address) and I found her to be hard-working, polite and unspoiled. Cynthia, smiling coyly, would come back to express her gratitude.

Sometimes it would be my neighbour Nkosi planning to organise a Sunday stokvel (small-scale party): 'Can't you get me a bottle of gin to sell at my stokvel? I really need money to send Nontombi some pocket money.' It was no problem. A piece of decent paper and pen, fictitious white customer's name, cash and the co-operation of a flat cleaner or nurse-girl in uniform and the bottle would be secured.

Word spread that I was resourceful. My clientele grew and my honorary services were much appreciated by the beneficiaries. Friends warned me: 'You are courting trouble. You'll be arrested for forgery.' I refused to listen. People were suffering. It was my way to sympathise and show solidarity. Disgusted, they gave me a name: 'Sibotshwa (jailbird or prisoner)'.

Disillusioned with fruitless weekly worship in the chapel I drifted into dice throwing and card gambling. I still went to church services over Easter, Ascension Day and Christmas. In spite of doubts gnawing at my breast on religious relevance and the role of the clergy and their white flocks on social matters, I still gave church doctrine the benefit of the doubt. Since my early youth, religious mysteries had always frustrated me. They were impenetrable. Mysterious mysteries. My inherent outlook was religious nevertheless, despite my incomprehension. Or was it because I did not want to be regarded a fool by playing a Thomas? As a little kid I asked my mother one day: 'Mom, who created the earth?'

'God,' answered Mom unthinking and grinding her corn on the grindstone. I had heard it before somewhere. I wanted elaboration. 'And who created God?' I pursued. 'Nobody!' said Mom.

'Did he create himself?' I prodded Mom, whose monosyllabic answers were unenlightening. 'Maybe,' came another short reply. 'How?' I quipped in the same style. 'Shut up and stop asking stupid questions!'

I shut up and stopped asking stupid questions. The fact that I could not fathom these mysteries made me feel stupid. It made me profess my faith unquestioningly. There were moments when the mind strayed into the controversial arena of mysteries again. It had to be checked. 'In-ze-name' was enraged one day when one of our class tried to conduct a searchlight on the mystery of the creation during scriptural lesson. 'Only a fool says there is no God!' In-ze-name pronounced with pious indignation while he fingered his rosary in obvious prayer for the fool or in supplication for forgiveness of his

34

fractious temper. As a Christian one had to believe, not question. Basically I did, in spite of nagging scruples. I really had no quarrel with the mysteriousness of religious mysteries. My concern was with the flagrant hypocrisy of the Christianising Christians, the crusaders for the brotherhood of man – Christian brotherhood.

Sophiatown inhabitants seemed to bear their miseries stoically. There was no political agitation I can remember at this stage, although a court case arising from the 1946 black miners' strike was going on. Yes, we had heard of the strike and the shooting of the strikers. Students from the Reef had been quite vociferous about the shooting of the strikers. I recall a group of us cursing Smuts and his government as the train passed the mine dumps near George Goch. The mine dumps were an embodiment of the hard labour of the Africans underground. They were also a reminder of the huge profits the mining companies reaped out of the sweat of cheap black labour.

But to the Smuts government, a black strike was intolerable. It could ruin the profits of the magnates and cut off tax benefits to the government. Without the enormous taxable income from the mines the state machinery and its wheels of repression would grind to a halt and kaffirs might get out of hand. Yes, a black strike was anathema to the ruling clique. It might generate repercussions difficult to contemplate. We pointed at the dumps and swore. The confessional could handle subsequent remorse.

Until the adoption of the 1949 Programme of Action the ANC had not yet assumed a mass character. It was an organisation which operated through annual conferences, deputations and petitions. ANC leadership was of course aware of the immediate and long term grievances of the black nation. These were the subject of their deputations and petitions. However lack of mass mobilisation had shortcomings. It excluded potential activists and unwittingly allowed the energies of these to be dissipated in negative social activities. Mass campaigns are a source of inspiration to those struggling for any cause and very much reduce a sense of frustration engendered by inactive helplessness. Finally mass organisation serves to project the extent and urgency of the demands to the government and the public at large. The oppressor cannot ignore the impact of mass organisation. He will always try to make some adjustments – negative or positive. Whether the response is negative does not matter. The feedback achieves the same result – intensification of the struggle.

During this short period of my stay in Sophiatown one man tried very hard to influence me politically by giving me a weekly left-wing paper, *The Guardian*, to read. I felt very embarrassed by this wooing. Whether through intuition or from information, I suspected the paper to be a Communist paper propagating Communism. My knowledge of Communism was zero except the injunction of the church: Communism is a Godless creed. Have nothing to do with it! At school we were advised, nay persuaded, nay ordered, not to read any literature without the imprimatur inscription on it. Our history books had to be approved or published by one of the church organs. As a result of this indoctrination I was extremely careful of what I read. Every time, after I had received this paper from my friend, I quickly dumped it into the rubbish bin the moment his back was turned, without even bothering to scan the paper headlines. The mere touching of the paper made me cringe from a sense of betrayal of my Christian principles, a sense of flirtation with the devil. I threw *The Guardian* into the rubbish bin, replaced the lid firmly and washed my hands in the tub. It happened weekly. I had the guts neither to tell the man to stop giving me the paper nor to read it.

All around was misery: the misery of arbitrary arrests; the misery of poverty; the misery of disease; the misery of illiteracy; the misery of helplessness. I felt it. I resented it. Not the ANC. Not the Communist Party. But the oppressive discriminatory laws agitated me against the misery. The white government was the agitator.

The human spirit, the collective human spirit, never succumbs to misery. There is some inherent resilience in the human spirit that refuses to be crushed. Sophiatown was not all misery and gloom. Misery, yes. Gloom, yes and no.

The arrests of beer brewers and shebeeners did not stamp out illicit brewing or shebeening. Shebeens flourished in Sophiatown. The major ones took on glamorous names: 39 Steps; Falling Leaves and Back of the Moon. The last was honoured in song by the patronisers: 'Top shebeen in Joburg is Back of the Moon . . . Back of the moonlight . . .' The 'cherries' sang the song, twanged their fingers, wriggled their hips and shuffled their feet in rhythm with the music. All done with grace and beauty and a carefree spirit.

Shebeens were social outlets. In shebeens people met to socialise, to carouse, to chat, to ventilate their common grievances and make light of them by entertaining one another with white man's liquor. We were prohibited from drinking or selling it. The shebeens sold it. We bought it and drank it in an atmosphere of conviviality. Shebeen patrons were men about town. Men with money to spend and to spend liberally. 'Fill the table and count the empties,' was a popular style of placing an order. It meant one was loaded and in a mood to demonstrate one was not a penny pincher.

The free spending in shebeens seemed to belie the abject poverty characteristic of the location inhabitants. If an outsider could drop from the sky into 39 Steps, Falling Leaves or Back of the Moon, he would not believe the descriptive account of misery outlined above. No, here, the ouens or mujeetahs (wide guys) dressed expensively and contrasted the imported labels on their clothes – Mayfair slacks, Chester Barries, and so on.

They challenged each other to guesstimate the cost of each other's

36

apparel, from the shoe to the hat. Where did these guys get all this money they were throwing about in shebeens and spending so lavishly on clothes? Some were 'professional' gamblers. They lived by gambling and won by hook or by crook. A handful might be illicit diamond or gold smugglers. Others were 'business partners or shareholders'. Still others might be railway truck lifters.

'Business partners or shareholders' were the commonest breed. Almost any black worker employed in a business where there was something saleable to the township dweller, if he was a 'clever', did not hesitate to filch from the firm he was working for. Sophiatown creaked with stolen property. There was no manufactured product that was unobtainable through the back door, except perhaps motor cars in those days. Food, liquor, clothes, cutlery, household appliances, furniture items, they all sold like hot cross buns at give-away prices. Every line was fast selling. Demand far exceeded supply at those prices.

These back-door transactions were protected by a wall of conspiracy against the law. Every township dweller was either involved or at least knew about the widespread racket. But mum was the word. The underpaid black police palms were greased to make them toe the line of the whole township. Corruption was rife. The white police were not immune from it, otherwise shebeens would never have survived.

'Business partners' did not apologise for their peculations. On the contrary, they felt they were having their own back on their exploiting employers. As far as they were concerned they were taking what they were entitled to. If they were said to be defrauding anybody, they were defrauding the defrauders. They were just trying to get square with their creditors.

Blacks are not born thieves and criminals. In South Africa many come up against a system that gives them two options: obey the law and common ethics and perish; or disobey the law and ignore dictates of conscience and survive. Many opt for survival one way or the other and by so doing risk the sanctions of the laws that force them to turn to unethical standards of social interrelationship. The property owning class, mainly whites, who do not appreciate the penury and the general misery of blacks, cannot easily reconcile themselves to this shameless pilfering in their places of employment. Let the point not be misunderstood. White workers are not saints. Although they have less compelling grounds to go into 'partnership' with their employers, they do, nevertheless. The difference is that the black worker has no guilty conscience about it; whereas, the white worker, because he cannot justify it, must do it knowing that exposure might lead to social scandal. Black workers are free from such moral inhibitions. Railway truck robbers were the main ouens. They operated in broad daylight in the streets of the central business district while everyone was watching except the police.

In the thirties and the early forties South Africa experienced a unique social problem, 'the poor white problem'. A hundred years after the Great Trek (1836) of the Boers, there was another Great Trek by the same people from the farms to the urban areas. The soil was no longer yielding enough to sustain the run-away population. The aftermath of the great depression was still being felt everywhere. Boers and boereseuns (sons) abandoned the farms to try their fortune in the towns. Thus the poor-white problem appeared at the top of the agenda of government programmes. It was intolerable that in mineral-rich South Africa, a country blessed with cheap labour, whites had to be poor. The South African Railways and Harbours (SAR&H), a public corporation, was entrusted with the sacred duty of creating employment for the poor-whites. It mattered not how underemployed they might be, they had to be employed by the SAR&H. They were illiterate, the majority of them, so SAR&H was the ideal employer besides the mines. But the mines were owned by private companies and their profits came first. SAR&H operated on public taxes. It did not matter if they made losses as long as the poor-white problem was being eliminated.

Lucky poor-whites were employed as supervisors of black labour, and in spite of their comparable poverty they could console themselves with the social status of being addressed as 'baas'. Others, because of the shortages of blacks to be supervised, did the same menial tasks which blacks did, pick and shovel stints. Others worked as delivery hands of railway consignments to businesses. Normally the delivery team comprised a driver of the railway wagon/trailer and the security hand. These were the teams that fell pray to deft lifters of railway goods. The lifters were organised in gangs of three or four. They carried out their operations with a great daring and skill. A few times I watched the gang operate. It was their operation at the corner of Market and Von Weilligh Streets that left me gaping and ecstatic. A railway delivery wagon stops outside Kirsch & Stein. The driver, consignment papers in hand, jumps out of his driver's seat and enters the business premises to announce the arrival of the company's order. The security hand sits on the open wagon, and flicks his sjambok playfully. A black guy clad in a khaki dustcoat parks his delivery tricycle next to the wagon. He whistles 'Stormy weather . . . Don't know why there's no sun up in the sky . . .' a popular tune in those days. Two other guys appear on the scene. One starts a conversation in Afrikaans with the poor white. He likes it. To be addressed in Afrikaans and to be called 'baas'! The second man on the other side of the wagon draws the attention of the baas by taunting him. 'Baas, hoekom is jy so lelik? Here jy is so lelik soos 'n aap. (Boss, why are you so ugly? Lord, you are as ugly as a monkey)'. Needless to say the trick worked perfectly. The security hand, whip swishing, goes in hot chase of the decoy. In that short interval, two boxes from the truck were gone.

38

It happened every day. Tactics employed were varied from time to time and from situation to situation. The lifters were doing good business. Blacks witnessed the operations and minded their own business. Whites were often beguiled by the audacious and cool manner of the gangs and hardly suspected any foul play. Most whites still believed that Africans were docile creatures, innocent children, incapable of sophisticated methods of robbery. The argument was the same. The exploited were justified in exploiting the exploiters. And they had never heard of Karl Marx. These categories of township money spinners patronised the shebeens, vented their grievances, boasted of their exploits and enjoyed their dubious dividends. It kept the morale of some sections high.

Another morale booster to the ghetto dwellers around this period was the boxing prowess of black Americans, Joe Louis in particular. The brown bomber as Joe Louis was popularly known was the hero of the oppressed masses in South Africa. Every victory he scored in the ring was a victory for blacks everywhere. The celebrations in the shebeens extended for weeks. Talk everywhere where blacks were gathered revolved around Joe Louis, the pride of the downtrodden. Sugar Ray Robinson was another of our heroes.

In 1948 I moved from Sophiatown to Alexandra Township. I liked Sophiatown very much but I had to leave in search of my independence. Sophiatown was full of all degrees of relatives. In varying degrees they felt I was a minor requiring some guardianship. It was ridiculous. I believed I knew my mind and was entitled to my idiosyncracies without interference. The move to Alex was an assertion of my majority at 20 years.

Dr Malan and his purified Nationalists also came to power in 1948. Zulu choristers, derogatorily known in the townships as 'ngomabu-suku (night songsters)' sang 'Uyinja hulumeni we Malani uyinja hulumeni (You are a dog of a government, Malan, a doglike government)'.

The new government was unpopular with the hoi polloi. The literate blacks read the newspapers, clucked their tongues, shook their heads at what they read and predicted trouble between the white government and the oppressed. The illiterate heard the cluck of tongues, saw the shaking of heads and begged to be informed about the distressful happenings. Snippets about the grand design of apartheid disciples circulated widely in the buses, trains, townships and factory floors. They were magnified and twisted. A hitherto unknown uneasiness and a sense of vigilance pervaded the ghettos. Politics became top of the agenda in general conversations among the ghetto dwellers. Predictions, both optimistic and pessimistic, were aired at random. No doubt during the general election campaign preceding the Malanites victory the blacks had felt more threatened by white political power than ever before. Apartheid sounded ominous and unspeakable. In fact apartheid was just a new slogan for the old concept of the colour bar. This new slogan expressed the old white-domination policies in a new aggressive and unambiguous language. The 'colour bar' was a vague and obscure phrase. Apartheid – apartness or separateness – was forthright, sincere and unmistakable. 'Kaffer op sy plek en koelie terug na Indie (Kaffir in his place and coolie back to India)' was a no-nonsense talk. Kaffir substituted for Native as a semi-official term for African; Baas substituted for white male in the same way, and Communism substituted for liberalism. New common nouns for old common nouns and new abstract nouns for old abstract nouns. The new nouns took on a new function, an adjectival function. They were descriptive. Derogatorily descriptive.

Africans, more and more of us and more than ever before, recognised our dark forbidding fate. It was during this year that my disillusionment with the version of white Christianity grew and oppressed me more than all the oppressive laws oppressed me. It was bad enough to read the hair raising cries of the Malanites: 'Ek staan op 'n kaffer se nek (I stand on the kaffir's neck)'; 'koelie terug na Indie (coolie back to India)'; and 'Hotnot op sy plek (Hottentot/Coloured in his place)', and so on. But to learn that one of my Catholic brothers at my *alma mater* endorsed apartheid was shattering. Brother Rogatus, my Afrikaans teacher, was reported to have applauded the coming into power of the Nationalists of Dr Malan. Previously I had embraced the categoric rejection of the colour bar by the Catholic church. True, in the process of time I had discovered that what the church preached was not exactly what it practised. But for a monk, a faithful who had answered such a high Christian vocation like Rogatus, to openly support a social system that viciously discriminated against other children of God was the last straw. I cross-questioned my informant about the authenticity of his allegation against Rogatus and he assured me it was verifiable if I wanted to. I did not proceed to verify it. His account of events and the earnestness of his explanation convinced me. To me, Brother Rogatus was not just an individual, he was representative of the white Christians and the whole white electorate. It was the era of outspokenness. The Afrikaners typified it and the normal hypocritical white Christians were following suit. Rogatus was a symbol.

Some phenomena might remain mysteries: God, the creation, etc, but the attitude of whites, their double dealing, their racism and untrustworthiness, was now crystal clear except perhaps to the pathologically blind. I scrupled no longer about going to mass on Sundays. That was the status of my religion when I arrived in Alexandra at the end of 1948.

JOINING ANC

The streets were unusually quiet. It was Sunday night. There was

40

nothing unusual in the quietness of a Sunday night, because the hectic weekend normally took its toll of the inhabitants of Alexandra and they retired early to bed to regain some of the dissipated energy for the blue Monday at the factory floor. What seemed unusual was the conspicuous absence of the 'unemployable' loiterers at shop verandahs where they normally hung around smoking their dagga zolls (marijuana joints), occasionally pouncing on lone night wanderers and turning their pockets inside out.

The shop verandahs at the intersection of Selborne Road and Sixteenth Avenue were favourite meeting places for the mischievous dagga-smokers. However, this particular group knew and respected me. I was always hailed with 'Hey-tah, bra Mike', which was a revered passport of safe conduct. Tonight I could see from afar that the shop verandahs were deserted. The Dark City was awash with soft moonlight. Probably it was the moon that had chased everyone from the streets. As someone who was acquainted with the dark streets I was afraid of the lit streets. Light was good at night, it made one see lurking shadows from a distance, but it also helped lurking shadows to see one from a distance. My every step therefore twitched with nervousness and tension especially in view of the desertion of the verandah posts by my friends. Heart pounding, I advanced to my pondokkie at 51 18th Avenue. To calm my heart I struck a match to light a cigarette. Just then, a blow from a blunt instrument landed on my hatless head. The beautiful full moon seemed to undergo an instant eclipse. The hitherto unnoticed stars twinkled in my eyes. Many unseen hands started to rummage in my pockets. Money, watch and cigarettes were quickly removed from my person. 'Why are you assaulting me?' I asked an irrelevant question with my initial recovery of breath. In reply another blow with the same instrument landed on one of my shoulders. 'Baleka (run),' I was ordered. Alexandra was irrational and unpredictable. Baleka. Where to? How?

I could not run, I was still groggy from the blows. Moreover, where could I run to? If at this corner, where for years I had been greeted so affectionately, I could be assaulted in broad moonlight, where could I run to? Orange Grove? Forest Town? Lower Houghton? Parkview? Where? These were all white residential suburbs. There, these commonplace muggings were unknown. The streets in those suburbs were patrolled by a vigilant and motivated police force. The night curfew confined Africans to Alexandra, Pimville, Sophiatown, Newclare, etc, where they were harassed by the pass raids and set against each other by the menace of unemployment. Anyway it was not my nature to run from my people. I walked slowly down to number 51 18th Avenue, feeling the blood trickle down my face.

I knocked at Cousin Botshelo's door. After ascertaining that it was me, she got out of bed growling against the interruption of her sleep. She opened the door and gave a mighty scream on seeing my bloody face. 'Yoo, they have killed my mother's child, Yo-oo!' she wailed.

Neighbours rushed out of their rooms to view the standing corpse of Botshelo's mother's child. Improvised first aid kits floated around and the bleeding was soon under control. As soon as cousin Botshelo satisfied herself that I had risen from the dead, she fixed her big rolling eyes on me reproachfully. 'I have always warned you not to roam around at night. You don't listen. Where did it happen?'

In Alexandra such attacks took place anywhere and at any time. It was not the first time I had had this sort of experience. One night a panga barely missed my belly. The assault was unprovoked. Another night a knife slashed an 11-inch vent through my new jacket. No provocation at all. It was a miracle I was unharmed personally. One Friday night (pay day) a sharp knife was placed against my jugular vein, while a muscular arm viced my neck and many eager hands emptied my pockets. I stopped wearing a hat after two expensive ones had been snatched from me at a bus stop. One night I came back to my rented room to find my wardrobe cleaned of its contents. Many years and wages of a bachelor's extravagance had stuffed the wardrobe with commodities of exotic labels.

I could not claim to be the unluckiest of the countless victims of township hooliganism. On the contrary. Many died violently every day. Others were maimed for life. Alex was crime-infested. Decent folks deliberately risked long terms of imprisonment by carrying unauthorised lethal weapons for self-defence.

Mike Ntuli was my friend. We lived in the same yard. When I arrived from Sophiatown disillusioned with white Christians and the church, Mike and Eliazana, the cripple, dragged me, reluctant, back to church, the Holy Cross Mission Church at 3rd Avenue. Mike was a likeable guy. He was decent, responsible and well-brought up in the Zulu tradition. His steady employment enabled him to look after his senile father and his schoolgoing brother and sister. He was in his early twenties.

Mike killed a notorious scarfaced thug with the thug's own knife, after the thug had stabbed Mike's younger brother and his friend. He had tried to intervene. The knife was raised against him. He snatched it and plunged it into the owner. He died. It was murder. Murder unpremeditated. But murder all the same. One would have imagined that all the circumstances would have been taken into account. But no. The favourable evidence of eyewitnesses and his employer's glowing reference did not count for much. Ten years, hard labour! It was sad. Criminals went unpunished. The decent folks, unwitting victims of unjust laws and perverse social circumstances paid dearly for fateful events not contrived by them.

In the mid-fifties, a gang was born in Alexandra and was christened Msomi gang. Alexandra had always been notorious for gangs. It was an old breeding ground of vicious groups. But Msomi gang will go down in the history of the township as the thoroughbred of gangs.

Widely-travelled and well-read people compared Alex to the Chicago of Al Capone when Msomi gang was in full stride.

Msomi gang was a typical product of Alexandra. It derived its name from a notorious murderer in Natal province, around this period, who used an axe to chop and kill his victims. Msomi the axe-killer or Ndoda (man) Msomi as the township jesters and stylists referred to him. Msomi was obviously a psychopath with a natural urge to deprive people of their lives. The people who inherited his name and his gruesome deeds could not be classified as psychopaths. I knew some of them before they became what they became: Shadrack Matthews, 'Ginger', Boy Mokone, 'Funny Face', Noah, Ntaka and others. Most of them were decent guys who became helpless victims of the pass laws and lack of employment opportunities. Shadrack Matthews was a small businessman who struggled to earn his living by honest means. He was also an active member of the African National Congress (ANC), the oldest and most influential liberation movement in the African continent. It was ironic that this idealistic man founded an organisation like Msomi. What happened was that the original objectives of the organisation were overtaken by forces beyond the control of Shadrack.

Shadrack had conceived an organisation that could defend its members, initially the taxi owners, standholders and business people like himself, against the extortions and molestations of another gang, the Spoilers. Police protection was never forthcoming to the law-abiding citizens of Alexandra. The police in South Africa are there to protect property and true property owners, the whites. Not pretenders to property ownership – the township standholders whose properties were mortgaged to the last grain of sand, and the poor people who were struggling against odds to meet the interest payments on their mortgages. Shadrack knew, and everyone knew, it was useless to expect protection from the police. So Shadrack conceived a self-reliant body to fight the gangsterism of the Spoilers.

The organisation was soon infiltrated and eventually hijacked by elements with narrow self-interests and a lust for revenge against the Spoilers. Some of the original members withdrew one by one when they noticed the new direction and the new name of the original body. Shadrack found himself a hostage whose ransom was his own life. He had created a Frankenstein monster. As erstwhile colleagues, some of us tried to advise him to pull out. No. He could not, unless he wanted to be a dead man, a minute after pulling out. He was right. The gang was very strong. It had managed to disperse, eliminate or win over some of the Spoilers. Even the white police, 'Machine Gun' and de Bruyn, the two most feared pass raiders in Alex, had joined them. The gang had also become extreme and ruthless. Protection fees were payable not only by former enemies or their sympathisers but by former business colleagues of Shadrack Matthews. The two white police and probably others in higher places shielded the gang, for they shared the spoils of the whole racket.

'Machine Gun' and de Bruyn were alleged to have played one of the most sinister roles of the gang. If on their routine police duties they found a revolver on a non-Msomi inhabitant they took him to the police station, charged the arrested man an admission of guilt fine and of course retained the revolver. The same revolver would be sold to another non-Msomi through an unknown Msomi intermediary. The unwitting buyer would later be raided, fined for possession of the revolver on admission of guilt and the whole racket went on and on, with the gang making money from fines and sales of one article. Decent folks easily fell victims to this racket because the need to defend oneself was paramount in the fear-ridden ghetto. People were prepared to pay any price for a revolver though they knew that they risked arrest and long terms of imprisonment. The option of a fine was also welcome. Gaol was a frightful aspect. The police were not interested in sending the 'trapped' to court because they stood to lose much. The money-spinning weapon, and the lucrative game of pitting black against black and procrastinating the unity of blacks proceeded unhampered.

The reign of Msomi gang lasted close to five years. People outside Alexandra could not understand how Alexandrians could live in Alexandra. Some top Spoilers emigrated from the township, fleeing from their rivals. They sojourned in some of the big towns, Durban, Cape Town, Bloemfontein, Port Elizabeth, etc, and hoped for better days when they could return to Alexandra. The bulk of the population had nowhere to go or like me they felt in principle there was not a better ghetto to run to. The South African ghettos were the same. They were breeding grounds for crime and mutual terrorism. They all had the potential for internecine conflict. So we all stayed and gambled with our lives as outsiders were fond of saying. I was very lucky not to cross paths with Msomi in all the five years except on the very last day of their reign. It was my daily hope, since the Msomi terror began, that some of them as former acquaintances might spare me. However the gang had grown big not only in its terror scale but in numbers. The new members especially those known as 'young Msomis' did not know me. At the same time they were more vicious and responsible for the callous excesses in the catalogue of the gang's terrorism.

One Friday night I boarded the last bus from the city to Alexandra at 10.45 pm. Of all days Fridays in Alexandra recorded the highest crime figures. Not only in Alexandra but in any ghetto, Friday was the busiest day for any gang. Friday was pay day and the sweat of some of the employed could be enjoyed by some of the unemployed, at knife or gunpoint.

At the last but one stop in Alexandra, a group of young Msomis rushed into our bus brandishing knives, pangas and revolvers. 'Protection fee! Protection fee!' The gang ordered every passenger to

44

cough up for the gang's coffers. Right at the back of the bus I sat petrified, knowing my run of luck had terminated. Women screamed and opened their bags for the gang. The men plunged their trembling hands into their pockets and turned them inside out to save their lives. My turn was coming and I sat there sphinxlike, my thought processes frozen and every nerve in my system numb. I was saved by some miracle. Before the gang could reach my seat, the police, who obviously had been lying in ambush for the gang, jumped onto the moving bus, real cowboy style. Unprepared for this, the gang offered no resistance. Their weapons were confiscated and they got a typical police handling. That Friday was the only day I witnessed the police fulfil their duties to the Alexandrians, self-interest aside.

Actually the scene did not convey any message of a new development in Msomi busting. The whole thing was an isolated event, not a link in the chain of police investigation as far as I was concerned. Shortly before there had been a public outcry in the press about the heinous deeds of Msomi. The press pointed out that the inhabitants feared to report the acts of the gang: there was no assurance of police protection since the local police appeared to be involved. It was clearly the allegation of police implication that changed the attitude of the police hierarchy.

I sighed a sigh of relief after the dramatic police rescue. Otherwise I went to bed ignorant of the news of the decade. The good news came the following day, a Saturday. I was in a bus again back from shopping in town. For the nine miles from the bus rank in Noord Street to the first stop in Alex I buried my head in the morning newspaper hardly conscious of my fellow passenger next to me. He might be a Msomi or a Msomi sympathiser and an innocent look at him might cost me an arbitrary protection fee. The newspaper I was reading had nothing of last night's events. I did not expect it. I had heard of journalists visiting war zones to report on frontline action. Alexandra was a different frontline where the combatants belonged to the same camp and did not generate much interest to attract journalists.

When I unburied my head from the paper to look furtively around and ascertain that I was back in Alex, my fellow seat passenger whispered in my ear: 'Did you hear?' 'What?' 'Ou Shadrack mang (Shadrack has been detained).' 'What for?' I asked stupidly. It was hard to imagine Shadrack Matthews arrested for his role in the gang. The gang was above the law. They were the law. They dictated the township life and remained unaffected by their own dictates. Their actions could not boomerang against them, there was a strong safety catch. Collusion with the police. 'Waar voor (What for)?' 'Vir die Shandies (for the thingummy). Die Mzos (The Msomis),' my friend explained to me. The news was deafening. I heard but there was something unassimilable about it. I sat there speechless while some of last night's events were recounted by my informed friend. Then I remembered the bus drama of the previous night. Yes, from the conduct of the police last night it could be true. It transpired that my friend had all the details including the fact that the police who carried out the raids and the arrests came from outside Johannesburg. Apparently the entire Johannesburg force was suspected of contamination.

An event of some great magnitude had taken place in Alexandra. I felt it within me. I smelt it. The air was saturated with its fragrance. I saw it on the faces of the residents. I heard it in their voices. Relief replaced the fear, the resignation, the tension, that pervaded the social atmosphere in Alex in the immediate past. On this Saturday, people laughed and raised their voices in conversation. Conversation that related and analysed the horrid deeds that had characterised the township existence. For the time being the carnage had been halted and the image of the police improved to a cautious degree.

In the complex web of South African political and administrative fabric, Alexandra was a step-child of step-parenthood. In common with the other ghettos it was beyond the pale. As a black freehold title area, nine miles from the centre of the city, it was something of a no-man's land, a reservoir of cheap labour, and a dumping ground for superfluous and redundant labour. A population of more than 100,000 was crammed in its one square mile. Under the municipal bye-laws Alexandra did not fall under the jurisdiction of the Johannesburg Council. The white suburbs adjacent to it however were part of Johannesburg and administered by it. Alexandra was presumably run by the Alexandra Health Committee, a body without a source of income, without proper authority and without a semblance of power to run a viable local administration.

Alexandrians, because of the anomalous relationship with the Johannesburg City Council, were discriminated against as far as black employment opportunities were concerned. The Native Affairs Department, later the Bantu Affairs Department, commonly known as the 'pass office', screened work-seekers for influx control purposes. Redundant work-seekers were sent back whence they came. Rural migrants back to the reserves to go and watch, hollow-eyed, their meagre pieces of land deteriorate annually and decline to yield a livelihood for themselves and their families. It was a sentence of slow death. Residents of Alexandra were also screened and sent back to Alexandra to gravitate into social cannibalism – preying on their luckier brothers and sucking the sweat of their brows. The laws of survival justified it. Who could blame them?

In 1954 I changed employment while a resident of Alexandra. The euphemistic 'Abolition of Passes and Co-ordination of Documents Act' had been passed by the all-white parliament the previous year. In spite of what the title of this Act claimed, passes for blacks were not abolished by its passage. On the contrary, the pass laws were tightened, entrenched and extended to African women for the first time.

At the pass office after half a day in the slow moving queue, I had eventually exchanged my old single-sheet pass document for a multi-paged document with my photo on the inside cover. The dompass – 'dom' for stupid – as it came to be known – was a comprehensive document divided into a number of sections detailing one's identity, tax payment, residential permit, employment address and employer's monthly signature. I had already paid 10 shillings for this dompass and the man who issued it warned me: 'If you lose it you'll pay double the amount, £1 for another one.' Many blacks saw the introduction of the dompass as a fraudulent racket. One paid for it regardless of whether or not urban rights were to be granted to one. It was a forced sale.

Armed with my new dompass I now crossed into another queue where hopefully I would be registered as an employee of the company whose letter of employment I bore. I pushed the prospective employer's letter and the dompass under the bars of the counter, hardly anticipating any objections. The man behind the counter glanced at the letter without reading it and lifted his eyes, and popped what one would consider a routine question: 'Waar bly jy? (Where do you live)?' Had I answered, 'Sophiatown', he probably would have asked me a few questions to test my knowledge of Sophiatown. I knew I could pass any question on Sophiatown with distinction. But as I foresaw no danger from answering truthfully I answered, 'Alexandra'. The man's rubber stamp fell with a thud on the dompass. 'Gaan werk soek in Alexandra. (Go and look for work in Alexandra)!'

I opened my mouth to protest. No word came out of my dehydrated vocal cords. I stared at the man with sheepish eyes. 'Next,' he bellowed, to get me out of the way. Completely stunned I groped my way out of the queue maze of woe-begone faces, many of whom awaited a similar fate or worse. My rubbery legs carried me outside the ruthless and ruinous building. My mind was foggy. Work in Alexandra! Where? What part, precisely? Had I been able to make an utterance I would have shouted: 'You are mad. You don't know where Alexandra is. Sanitary bucket workers are under-employed there. Putco, the bus company will not take me. I have no light vehicle driver's licence, let alone a heavy duty licence. The police will not take me, they are aware of my 'undesirable' associates. So where in Alexandra shall I find employment?' I crossed the street, my black pride dishevelled and harassed. I cursed the laws that so humiliated me, I cursed the racist law givers, their ancestors and their progeny to eternity. I crossed another street. A car hooter got me gyrating. I had crossed against the red light. Pasop! Beware!

My normally sluggish mind ticked at an accelerated pace. This was a matter of life and death. Denied employment rights in the city it was

47

hard to say what would become of me. Up to now I had managed to keep out of crime for livelihood, thanks to regular employment. Though the wages I was receiving were starvation wages, it had made survival possible. Strong influences had always existed to drive me into anti-social paths. In spite of needs, fanned by some former friends who had in despair gravitated into lawless ways of earning a livelihood, I had prevailed against the strong temptation. In 1950 I lost my job through what I considered unfair employment practices. I was very much disillusioned. The job insecurity agitated my mind and prompted me to search for alternatives. Self-employment avenues were limited. Where they existed the commonest, since it required minimal capital, was hawking, but I had no aptitude for it due to my introvert nature. Frustration and aimless drifting eventually got me into 'professional' gambling. In gambling one must have luck and/or wits. In 1950 I had the luck and I made friends who had the wits. Gambling earned me money to spend lavishly on day-to-day essentials, and to spare. For 10 months I led this life. It was precarious and dangerous. There was no guarantee that my luck would hold for ever. Nor were the wits of my friends and their loyalty guaranteed. It was dangerous because it also implied that to evade pass arrests as an unemployed African I had to resort to illegal practices to maintain my pass 'in order'. It was a slippery path. Some friends and relatives prevailed upon me to quit gambling and look for regular employment. I did.

Four years later much water had flowed under the bridge. I had been in regular employment for over three years. I had joined the African National Congress (ANC). Gambling or any dishonest means of livelihood would be inconsistent with my newly assumed role and dignity. That is why my normally sluggish, cool grey matter was sprinting and aflame.

Ah, don't inform the secretary you have been endorsed out of the city to Alexandra! Show her where to sign. Pretend the Native Affairs Department has registered you as employee of the Imperial Fur Co (prospective employer). She won't know. How many secretaries in Johannesburg bothered to acquaint themselves fully with the myriad details of the dompass, except perhaps the Boer girls who imbibe them from their police boyfriends, flaunting their braggadocio to impress how they make short shrift of passless Africans? Pauline McGuiness was married, very English, ignorant and politically naive. She probably believed Queen Victoria was still on the throne and that South Africa was still a British dominion, where the much vaunted British sense of fair play and justice prevailed. Most unlikely to have a Boer boyfriend let alone bother to study the dompass regulations.

Once an idea takes root in the fabric of the mind it revitalises mortal flesh. From the listless wanderer of a few minutes ago I felt my step grow firmer and more elastic. Just as Pauline was powdering herself for her lunch date I walked into her office, artificial smile on my lips, dompass in my hand and opened at the relevant page: 'If you just sign here Mrs McGuiness . . .' 'So you are fixed?' queried Pauly, cheerily fishing for her goldcapped pen from her bag. With a flourish, Mrs McGuiness' signature was in the dompass. For the next three years Pauly signed it where it indicated the employer had to sign. Police stopped me, paged through the document, satisfied themselves that I was employed because of the firm's rubber stamp and secretary's signature, satisfied themselves on a cursory glance at the Alexandra stamp that I had somewhere to reside and satisfied themselves that my tax payment was up to date – I made a special effort to pay my tax promptly to enhance the look of validity of my dompass. For the three years I took pains not to taunt the police whenever they stopped me for my pass. I produced the pass with a grin and just stopped short of rubbing my hands in obeisance and gratifying them with 'my baas'. When I had to change the job in 1957 for another, I was anxious there might be trouble. The pass office kept records and there was bound to be a discovery of my illegal employment. However, I was prepared to plead innocent of the fraud. The Imperial Fur Co was likely to take the rap for that one. I had saved some money for a lawyer if it became necessary.

At the Albert Street pass office I was attended by a carefree, genial young Boer clerk. After going through my records he burst out laughing: 'Hemels, jong, jy het onwettig by hierdie plek gewerk. (Heavens, man, you have been employed illegally at this place). Jy is 'n skelm. (You are a rascal).' He shuffled around indecisively for a while, then cancelled the unwarranted stamp and registered me with my new employer. He warned that my former employer was going to be in big trouble. He looked quite amused and so little-concerned, however, that I could not believe he would initiate the trouble. Boers can be human too.

Alexandra was not only a seedbed of social crime, it was also a seedbed of political revolution. It was logical. Its squalor, acute unemployment, overpopulation, and dereliction by civic authority epitomised the disproportionate share of the racial oppression it bore. Under the community surface of indifference, resignation and defeatism smouldered a fire of hope and political resentment. The Nats, as the new regime was known, interpreted their unexpected landslide victory as a mandate to reshape South Africa in their own image as quickly as possible. Commissions were appointed to look into certain norms and practices and recommend blue-prints for changes in line with party policies. In some areas, commissions were not considered a necessary prelude to desirable change. Legislation was introduced in parliament as a matter of urgency. Two such laws were the Immorality Act which prohibited carnal relations across the colour-line and the Mixed Marriages Act which prohibited inter-racial marriages. The latter was passed in 1949, within a year after the Nats assumed political power, the former in 1950.

Seretse Khama of the Bangwato in Bechuanaland married Ruth Williams, an English lady, in the same year the Mixed Marriages Act was passed. It was a traumatic event in the politics of South Africa. The authors of the Mixed Marriages Act were hysterical. The oppressed masses in the ghettos were ecstatic. This external social event became a major political event within South Africa. The couple were banned from entering South Africa lest they corrupt those in the country by their 'immoral' example. The British government came under a scathing attack for apparently condoning what had taken place.

One might wonder what the goings-on in a neighbouring country had to do with the policies of another country. Actually they had a lot to do with them. To start with, the 1909 South Africa Constitution Act which created the Union of the four provinces (the Cape, the Transvaal, the Orange Free State and Natal) had left the door open for the incorporation of the three High Commission Territories (Bechuanaland, Basutoland and Swaziland) which remained under British jurisdiction. The condition for incorporation was the consent of the inhabitants of these territories. In the past the chiefs in these territories had been wary of incorporation. Nevertheless, successive white governments in South Africa, presumably encouraged by the view that the economic dependence of these territories would eventually bring about a change of attitude in favour of incorporation, continued to work for and flirt with the idea of swallowing up these dependencies.

Now, obviously, if the future subjects of an apartheid regime were allowed to develop along lines in conflict with their future status, the trend presaged unhealthy political relations in the future greater Union. Even if it were assumed – a remote assumption in the minds of the Nats at this stage – that these neighbouring starvelings were to be foolish enough to reject incorporation ultimately, their behaviour could create undesirable precedents for the Union 'Natives.' Psychologically, they would be ruined. They might start thinking that the white sex pastures were for them too. If they met the 'natural' rebuff which would greet their impudent advances, they might be tempted to resort to rape! The Khamas' example was bad. It had to be condemned with all the force of hysteria. It was.

The Nats were right. The psychological impact of the marriage was beyond all reasonable expectations among the ghetto dwellers. It was amazing. One might have been misled into believing that ghetto-blacks cherished the idea of marrying whites. Such an idea would have been a misconstruction of the greatest magnitude. The Africans were quite happy with their Ma-Dlaminis and Ma-Mofokengs. They were not contemplating any mass divorces and mass inter-racial marriages. But they were extremely delighted by Seretse's marriage. They were against the obsession with racialism, the denial of personal liberty and the regimentation of emotions through legisla-

50

tion. The marriage of the Khamas was a challenge, a defiance, an omen of the sinister schemes of the racists. So the marriage was welcomed and celebrated in all the nooks and pondokkies of Alex and all the black ghettos.

The people sang: 'Seretse has married a white. Boers hate him . . .' The composition, in spite of its monotonous refrain, became a hit. Gallo, the record company, clambered on the bandwagon and cut a single which kept the phonographs whirring. The Khamas' pictures flooded the Johannesburg picture market. Picture framers made a roaring business. There were few rooms in the townships which did not have the Khamas' picture adorning one of the walls. In spite of the controversy the marriage generated in the Bangwato reserve, in Johannesburg the event was an exultant occasion among the blacks. The shrill outcry of the white press, the Afrikaans press in particular, and the white parliament, was matched by the boisterous enthusiasm of the ghetto dwellers.

It was one of the most vivid expressions of the rejection of apartheid I have ever witnessed in South Africa. Seretse became a symbol of resistance against apartheid. He became a hero overnight. I loved his *demarche*. That is what I thought it was.

1949 also saw a resurgence of a new spirit of rededication by the oppressed African youth in South Africa. The African National Congress Youth League formed in 1944 piloted the Programme of Action at the annual conference of the ANC. Hitherto the ANC had been a moderate organisation seeking changes through constitutional procedures – petitions, deputations. Moreover, the organisation could not be strictly defined as a mass organisation. The suffering masses were not drawn actively into struggle and the leadership of the organisation devolved upon the elite, the educated, the men of independent means. The adoption of the 1949 Programme of Action brought a new character of militancy, mass activity and wholesale participation of ordinary people in campaigns of resistance against oppression.

Among the objectives of the 1949 Programme of Action was: 'appointment of a Council whose function should be to carry into effect, vigorously and with the utmost determination the programme of action. It should be competent for the council of action to implement our resolve to work for:

(a)   the abolition of all differential political institutions, the boycotting of which we accept, and to undertake a campaign to educate our people on this issue and, in addition, to employ the following weapons: immediate and active boycott, strike, civil disobedience, non-co-operation and such other means as may bring about accomplishment and realisation of our aspirations;

(b)   preparations and making of plans for a national stoppage of work for one day as a mark of protest against the reactionary policy of the government.

The Programme of Action of 1949 was a new departure in the history of the ANC. It ushered in a new era, a decade of militant forms of struggle, it was farewell to deputations, petitions and ineffectual protest. The Programme of Action was confrontational. It called for sacrifices on the part of the liberation movement.

A national stoppage of work for one day was organised for May Day 1950 by the ANC, the Transvaal Indian Congress, the Communist Party of South Africa, and the African People's Organisation (APO). Eighteen people were killed on that day, shot by the police. Half the casualties occurred in Alexandra. It was a high price extorted by the trigger-happy police. The whole day they fired wildly and indiscriminately. The May Day work stoppage was followed shortly by another work stoppage on June 26 to mourn those who died on May Day. Since then June 26 has been celebrated annually by the ANC as Freedom Day.

Events moved rapidly after the first shots from the arsenal of the Programme of Action. The major event was the Defiance Campaign of 1952. The targets of the Defiance Campaign were six unjust laws: the Pass Laws, Stock Limitation Regulations, the Separate Representation of Voters Act, the Group Areas Act, the Suppression of Communism Act and the Bantu Authorities Act.

The Defiance Campaign received a lot of publicity internally and internationally. More than 8,500 volunteers all over the country defied the unjust laws and served varying terms of imprisonment. It was called off in 1953 following the passage through Parliament, in the first session of 1953, of the Public Safety Act (providing for declaration of a State of Emergency and rule by proclamation) and the Criminal Laws Amendment Act (providing for vastly increased sentences, including up to 10 lashes, for future acts of defiance). The psychological impact the campaign made on the masses was tremendous. Ordinary men and women, who had nothing to lose but human dignity to win, joined the ANC in droves. It also scared the privileged whites: 'The Natives are becoming cheeky', they remarked.

I also joined the ANC in 1952, on impulse. Over the years I had thought much about the aims of the ANC. They were laudable. But, how? How were these aims to be achieved? Certainly not by mere espousal and expression! Something needed to be done! Defiance campaign was the right action. Arrest us! Kill us! Eat us if you will! The way you destroy human lives you must be cannibals! C'mon eat us! That is how I interpreted the mood of the defiers. It was my mood. Frustrated, angry and reckless.

In spite of this mood of self-immolation, becoming a volunteer in the defiance campaign was easier said than done. I shall volunteer tomorrow, I told myself. Tomorrow was postponed to another tomorrow and another tomorrow and another tomorrow to another

52

tomorrow. Defiance campaign went on. My admiration for the defiers increased. As my admiration for defiers increased my resolve to hurl myself into the fray declined. I was beginning to acknowledge my faint heartedness to myself.

One night I went to see a film at the Good Hope Cinema in town. The last bus to Alexandra was at 10.45 pm and I had an hour to idle in town, window shopping. The sound of singing voices came from one end of the street. It floated challengingly in the streets as it drew nearer to me. 'Asikhathali noma siya botshwa, sizimisel' inkululeko . . . unzima lomthwalo . . . (We don't care whether we are arrested we are dedicated to freedom . . . this burden is heavy . . .)' A solid phalanx of defiers singing a defiant song marched past me to their rendezvous with certain arrest. Before I knew my mind I had fallen in step with them, singing the revolutionary song and feeling some perspiration of conflict-anxiety ooze through the pores of my skin. 'Unzima lomthwalo (This burden is heavy),' I sang lustily, bringing up the rear of the defiant phalanx.

This was a typical impulse. There was no premeditation. Even as I sang with the volunteers I did not pause to look back, to see what was to happen to my rented room. I stayed alone in the room. I had a few possessions – some utility furniture and an extravagant bachelor's wardrobe. With the key in my pocket and nobody likely to know my whereabouts until I appeared in court, the unoccupied room was likely to be a godsend for the township burglars. This prospect was real, but inconceivable in the overwhelming circumstances.

Fortunately or unfortunately, depending on the prism through which one viewed the process, I was noticed by the group and soon the leader decided to investigate me. Who was I? Did I know what they were doing? Where did I reside? I was Mike. I knew they were defying unjust laws. I resided in Alexandra, I answered. 'Go back to Alexandra. See the volunteer-in-chief of your area and register as a volunteer. You will be assigned to a group and the group in due course will be instructed when and where to defy.' So just past Mayibuye Restaurant along Von Weilligh Street I was turned back to go and follow the procedure of disciplined defiance.

Sunday I was at Freedom Square in search of the volunteer-in-chief for the area. I doubt whether I found him, but I did manage to pay a subscription for ANC membership. I was never called to join a group of defiers. I do not know why. Perhaps I did not adhere to certain instructions properly – about meetings and certain schedules.

The honour to be among the newsmakers had defied me. My membership of the ANC lapsed temporarily when I failed to renew it by paying a subscription fee. It was not lack of loyalty or devotion. It was a combination of oversight and lack of organisational discipline.

An interesting feature of the liberation struggle in South Africa is that it is 99 per cent fuelled by government policy and only one per cent by agitators who are themselves the products of the government's reactionary policies. Education policy in South Africa had never been satisfactory to black aspirations. African education had always been differential, unequal, neglected and shamelessly underfinanced. But the policy objectives within the framework of missionary education were never so arrogantly proclaimed and defined by the previous governments. Henceforth education for Africans, known as Bantu education, would fall under a special ministry of the central government – the Bantu Education Department – and be systematically controlled to conform to the government policy of grand apartheid. Churches were to transfer their schools to government or lose government subsidies. Moreover the burden of education would rest squarely on the shoulders of the Africans themselves. Meanwhile, the fruits of 'Bantu education' would fall into the laps of the authors and designers of this system of education, through indoctrination and the submissiveness of its subjects. Blacks were asked to pay for their own oppression. For the first time I understood as never before that white privilege was set to entrench itself in perpetuity. The naive scales I wore before, of a belief that with the growing of literacy among the Africans all barriers to social equality would be removed, dropped from my eyes as ripe fruit falls from the tree. The Africans were destined to be hewers of wood and drawers of water for all times. Unless they resisted.

In spite of my unplanned truancy from school, deep down in my heart I continued to cherish higher education. I still dreamt of a windfall that would see me back in school. The threat of 'Bantu education' shattered the dream. One alternative remained for blacks to salvage their dignity and ward off impending doom at the hands of privileged society: protest, organise and resist.

I can still feel the surge of anger swelling within me as I read the parliamentary debate on the second reading of the Education Bill. I folded my newspaper and confronted my friend JH: 'I say, JH, do you see what the Boers are trying to make of us? Slaves for eternity!' 'Agh, man, Malan-hulle kan gaan shee. (Malan and company can piss off)', replied JH in typical ghetto style. My first serious attempt at agitation flopped. Assuming M and company did what JH said they could do or did the other thing as well, what then? Would we not wallow and drown in their by-products?

I renewed my membership of the ANC because of the Bantu Education Bill. It never lapsed until the organisation was banned. My final decision was a cumulative process of many years. In the past the inclination to protest politics was motivated by anger and frustration alone. Now the motivating factor was sober consideration – naturally, still coloured by all the previous emotions.

There was widespread agitation against the Bantu Education Act. The ANC contemplated a boycott of schools, but in the end boycott of schools was found to be unsustainable and impractical. That however

54

did not stop the opening of cultural clubs in Alexandra and the East Rand to cater for children who had been affected by the introduction of Bantu Education in schools. The Alexandra Cultural Club run by M Molewa served the affected section of the community very well until the 1960 State of Emergency closed it through the detention of Molewa.

All the churches which ran the mission schools, protested strongly against the closure of their schools (except the Dutch Reformed Church). Not that the churches were ordered to close their schools straight away – no, they were given options that were not real options. The government simply told the churches: hand over your schools or lose subsidies. Most schools did the obvious. The Catholic Church, endowed with better resources and more sensitive to the moulding of young minds, faced the challenge. It was a great sacrifice for the Catholic teachers. Thanks to their spiritual motivation, they bore it stoically.

One might be wrong, but I venture to opine that the attitude of the churches towards the apartheid regime has never been the same again. It was a gradual orientation, but it has taken an angle I could never have anticipated in my days of disillusionment with the Christians and the churches. The South African government is its own enemy.

Campaigns against Bantu Education were soon followed by others. The Congress of the People (COP) which adopted the revolutionary Freedom Charter in 1955 and led to the marathon treason trial of 156; the Union Buildings anti-pass demonstration by 20,000 women in 1956; the Alexandra bus boycott (three months) which spread countrywide in sympathy; anti-pass and anti-Bantu Authorities campaigns which culminated in violence in Sekhukhuneland and Zeerust in 1957-58; burning of women's passes in Lichtenburg; the militant anti-pass demonstrations by women on the Reef in 1958; the highly successful and emotive potato boycott of 1959. Alexandra was host to the first Africa Day rally in 1959 – O R Tambo, Deputy President then, inspired the huge rally by stating: 'The stampede of independence has started. And no power on earth can halt it.'

Ghana's independence in 1957 was the first domino. Could black South Africans remain exceptions? Freedom in our lifetime was the slogan of this hectic period.

Alexandra was not all crime and politics. Between the two extremities existed a large area, neither black nor white. An expanse of grey area populated by the majority who hankered after life, simple, jolly and unencumbered by man's inhumanity to man. There was hardly an Alexandra homebound or townbound bus that did not ripple with mirth induced by one humorist or another. Jokes centred around the 'baases', their 'missuses', the gods and Christian God. None of the anecdotes could be said to be flattering to the subjects. The nine-mile ride was never tedious.

Over the weekends the sounds from gumba-gumba parties made juniors cavort in rhythmic abandon. But the insatiable night-lifers frequented Magida-sibekane (face-to-face dancing). Magida was on the high rise of 18th Avenue. The music – a cacophony of an assortment of drums, horns and percussion – could be heard from one end of the township to the other. The whirligig lasted until sunrise. The man who ran this dance-theatre 'Magida' (Khumalo was his real name) had a colourful history. He narrated it personally when I got to know him closely. He became a big time armed robber because of pass restrictions and lack of employment. The long hand of the law grabbed him and deposited him in prison, the notorious Barberton Maximum Security prison. He outlived the barbarity of the place. It was after his release from this stint that he invented the noisy weekend entertainment. The place was not such a great moneyspinner as many assumed, but it kept Magida's head above the water together with his big family, besides giving the patrons raucous entertainment. We recruited Magida to the ANC in 1958 during the big women's anti-pass demonstration. From then Magida's business went down. The ANC was calling. Leave everything and follow me.

The dingy, gangster-ridden squalid Alex cannot be evaluated fully. The first South African black international soccer star came from Alex, 'Danger' Makatalala. He was invited to join some Netherlands soccer club. It was a feather in the cap of Alex soccer spirit and skill. One of the outstanding black golfers was an Alexandrian, 'Mangena'. In music, Alex has produced international artists like Hugh Masekela and Caiphus Semenya. There have been other musicians of less international repute but quite high on the national scale – the flautist Ntemi Piliso, the penny whistler, Spokes Mashiyane and the jazz musician, Zakes Nkosi. In politics Alex has not been found wanting. Moses Kotane the foremost African Marxist was from Alexandra. Alexandra was the first urban home of the internationally famous imprisoned black nationalist, Nelson Mandela. The Secretary-General and the Treasurer General of the ANC, Nzo and Nkobi, both hail from Alexandra. Alexandra was a cauldron of black aspirations and talent, and a mirror of black frustrations. I was nurtured in the township.

SHARPEVILLE AND AFTER

Chief Luthuli, the President-General of the ANC, burned his pass on Sunday, 26 March 1960 in Pretoria. He was staying there while giving evidence for the defence in the marathon treason trial, which had started in 1956. It was a signal for the pass burning campaign which flared up immediately thereafter.

The pass burning in March 1960 was precipitated by the Sharpeville massacre on 21 March 1960. Alexandra Township seems to have been more prepared for the event. A calculated, well-planned and

56

well-timed ANC campaign to culminate in the burning of passes on a yet undetermined future date had been in progress. The campaign was initiated by a resolution of the ANC annual conference in Durban at the end of 1958. By the beginning of 1960 the Alex ANC region was already on a short fuse, agitating for the burning of passes ahead of the National Executive schedule. It was therefore logical that the precipitate pass burning would be more extensive in Alex when the signal eventually came. It was. Bonfires illumined the Alex night skies.

Shortly after the Pan-Africanist Congress split from the ANC at the beginning of 1959 they had also adopted resolutions against the pass laws. However, their demonstrations were to be organised on different lines. Demonstrators were instructed to leave their passes at their homes and present themselves passless at police stations. In Johannesburg there was no mass support for this approach and only a number of PAC leaders responded to their own call. They were arrested vowing no defence, no bail and no fine. In Sharpeville the response to the PAC call was massive. The trigger-happy police observed this spectacle. It was absolutely orderly and peaceful. They did not like it. Their fingers itched. Without warning, the order was given, 'Fire!' They fired. Sixty-nine people died and hundreds more were wounded. It was genocide. Events moved quickly afterwards. Huge demonstrations in the Western Cape. National Day of mourning. Pass burning. State of Emergency. Banning of the ANC and the PAC. The declaration of the State of Emergency did not come as a complete surprise. A few days before its declaration there was widespread rumour and speculation about it, and many activists simply skipped the country or went underground to avoid the wide net. Many suspects, active and dormant, were detained under the State of Emergency. As I was an unknown quantity, the State of Emergency spared me, but not before a false alarm had me on tenterhooks.

The false alarm came from Wynberg police station where many ANC comrades were detained. Apparently Sergeant Ramashala of the Security Branch was intrigued by my absence from the detained crowd and could not refrain from asking concernedly: 'Where is Dingake? Where is Dingake?' The comrades believed I was in danger. They smuggled message after message: 'Vamoose! The police are looking for you!' Some intuition told me, no, stay put, it is a false alarm. However, I took some elementary precaution by moving house.

Sergeant Ramashala was one of those black security police, whose life's ambition was to impress their white baases with their hard work, diligence and conscientiousness to an extent that they made white security officers look like traitors to their own regime. Ramashala's investigative predisposition was unparalleled in Alexandra. He tended to be reckless with his life in fulfilment of his duties. A heavy boozer, who preferred lone missions and assign-ments, he frequented shebeens and visited homes of ANC activists at any hour he chose. He took full advantage of ANC policy of non-violence, by intruding at private meetings and by generally provocative behaviour in every contact with known members of the liberation movement. He knew every single activist in Alex as no other security policeman did. When he discovered I was not among the detainees he was confounded. He must have sensed an out-rageous dereliction of duty on the part of his superiors. Anyway, his superiors knew better. I was not on their list.

Ironically, Ramashala was not the only one who 'wished' for my detention. A close comrade, whom I shall call F, also could not understand my freedom in the wake of the State of Emergency. Comrade F confronted me and my friend Peter: 'Why are you two not detained?' How could we know? We had not compiled the list of detainees. It was puzzling. Some who on record were detainable had not been detained. Yet others who had long kept aloof from the struggle had been detained. Privately I thought my friend Peter had all the credentials for a State of Emergency candidate. Suspicion against him could be said to have some ground; against me, suspicion was groundless. Peter was chairman of one branch in Alexandra. He was deeply involved in the Zeerust disturbances in 1958 and served a jail term arising from them. He was a fiery speaker at our weekly public meetings and was fond of taunting Ramashala and Dunga. I was different. I consciously avoided taunting the police and was generally decent to the point of timidity before them. Although I was a branch office bearer I kept a low profile at public meetings because my soft voice always cracked when I tried to speak loudly. We could not always afford megaphones. Moreover I really preferred other people to speak, they did it better.

In the wake of the intensification of the struggle the security police have cultivated, exploited and manipulated with perfect skill, any tendencies to mutual suspicion among fellow freedom fighters. A thousand and one ways are open to them to foment intra-organisa-tional suspicion and mistrust. By deliberate lies and practical insinuations, they sow internal suspicions and dissensions, and turn freedom fighter against freedom fighter. Comrade F's curiosity and frankness did not disguise the reality of the era the liberation struggle was entering. Dirty tricks from the police. Chronic mutual suspicion among freedom fighters.

In the aftermath of pass burnings and stay-at-homes, the police stepped up their activities. They arrested many people and charged them with a variety of crimes — vagrancy, arson, public disturbance and a host of others. The new situation of illegality presented a challenge to the few activists who had escaped the net. The structure of the organisation had to be maintained in new form. There was to be co-ordination of the organs of the ANC on regional levels as well as on the national level. There were fewer and less experienced hands to tackle the job.

Unbeknown to me, I was one of those appointed to what was known as the Emergency Committee. The abnormal times called for the suspension of normal procedures and practices. The democratic elections gave way to executive appointments in a hierarchical order. The task of operating the ANC underground was formidable after years of above ground existence. The State of Emergency threw the whole country into confusion. Confusion existed everywhere. The government was confused. They spoke with many discordant voices, especially after the attempted murder of Dr Verwoerd, the prime minister. Sauer, the most senior minister after Verwoerd, declared that the 'old chapter' was closed. He was publicly rebuked by Eric Louw, the Minister of Foreign Affairs, who stated that any policy change towards a new dispensation in South Africa could only come from the hospitalised 'gauleiter'. International investors panicked and confusion reigned in their ranks. The State of Emergency was declared to make South Africa politically stable and attractive to foreign investors. It achieved the opposite. Could South Africa be still regarded as safe for investment? A fever of disinvestment gripped foreign investors. The government had to clamp down hard upon the panickers. Heavy restrictions were imposed on the repatriation of foreign capital.

Within the liberation forces there was much confusion. After the successful day of mourning, anonymous leaflets flooded the townships calling for interminable stay-at-homes. Loyal members of the organisation, lacking close contact and guidance, swayed with the wind. The Emergency Committee had to work round the clock to bring about relative stability in the unfolding process. It was not easy. Black organisations which had not been banned and others who claimed to represent the interests of the oppressed tried to cash in and fill the vacuum left by the ban on the PAC and the ANC.

What was interesting was that the majority of ANC members who joined other organisations did not do so out of disillusionment or rejection of the ANC. They regarded working through other avenues without prejudice. On investigating further, one invariably came up against the disinclination of people to operate underground. It is natural. Underground work is hard, demanding and pregnant with hazards. Only the truly dedicated, selfless and disciplined cadres are suitable for the underground.

Besides the onerous work of the underground, some of us had to work in the capacity of 'welfare officers' – identifying, tracing and organising aid for the dependants of the detainees. We had to organise legal defence and fines for those who were arraigned in cases related to the emergency regulations. At work it was hard to find time for lunch. We flocked to the Defence and Aid Fund offices to report

59

needy cases and accept the necessary assignments. For the few surviving activists there was no idle moment. Sometimes the hard work and the poor cooperation from branch and area contacts made one yearn for the confined spaces of the State of Emergency victims.

One can rightly say that the State of Emergency period was the crucible in which one's mettle was tempered. Some fell by the wayside, never to come back. Others withdrew temporarily to reassess their commitment and their stomach for the unpleasantness of the liberation struggle. One friend of mine, JM, impressed me with his honesty. 'Mike,' he confided, 'things are bad. I have cold feet. Please do excuse me. From now on I shall not be involved in the struggle. I do not think I can withstand detention.' I was very much touched by this honest and simple confession. Very few human beings acknowledge their weaknesses or admit their deficiencies with such candour. I praised him for his confession and assured him I would hold no grudge against him nor regard him with contempt.

The State of Emergency also showed some of the black security police in a new light. A couple of weeks after it was declared a prominent security officer resigned from the police force. Sergeant Dunga had impressed the treason trialists with the accuracy of his evidence. Whereas the majority of the police and the informers who gave evidence for the Crown distorted and embellished their testimony, Sergeant Dunga reported speeches and events as they occurred at ANC meetings. People in the movement referred to him as intelligent and honest. One day after a public meeting in Alexandra, Sergeant Dunga had approached me to complain about the hostile attitude demonstrated by members of the ANC, towards himself and the other members of the police force. Said Dunga: 'You should not hate nor worry about us because you know who we are. You should be worrying more about the informers in your ranks. They are the danger to you and the struggle, not us.' My efforts to wheedle those informers out of him failed. But I still believe he had a point.

When the rumour of Dunga's resignation started circulating, like true revolutionaries, we were sceptical about the genuineness of Dunga's move. It was a police trap, we thought. He was being groomed for more sophisticated intelligence police work, we believed. The authenticity of the resignation was not improved in our minds, even by the article Dunga wrote in *Drum* magazine outlining his African socialist principles. A big question mark still hangs over Dunga's resignation. Some believe he did resign for the reasons he is alleged to have resigned for.

According to the underground grapevine, Dunga was said to have resigned because, upon the declaration of the State of Emergency, the white security police had departed from a previous norm of confiding in all the members about impending raids. For security reasons the black police on this occasion had either been instructed not to go off duty or those who were not on duty were simply instructed to report for duty without divulging the purpose of special duties. Some black officers in the townships ventilated their bitterness at this lack of trust and discrimination, since the white officers were appraised of the sacred duties. Dunga resigned in disgust over this mistrust and discrimination. That was the speculation I heard and chewed on. Two more cases of black Security Branch officers' sympathies during the Emergency come to mind.

On the basis of the false alarm initiated by Ramashala, I had deposited my meagre furniture and other effects with a family for safekeeping while I found 'secret' accommodation with some buddy. Indeed I tried hard to keep the address secret. In the mornings I left under the cover of pre-dawn twilight. From work, in the evening, I arrived under the cover of dusk. I was convinced the police would have difficulty finding me, because at work too I had organised an 'escape route' if it became necessary.

I returned from work one evening to find that a Security Branch man had been to my hideout. According to my room-mates he was black and sympathetic. Somehow there had been a leakage of our planned distribution of an underground leaflet. The police had got wind of it and were geared to frustrate our efforts. The policeman I shall call Sergeant B (the black security police officers were sergeants, it was their highest rank at the time), had come on a mission to tip me off about the impending raid. 'Tell Mike, we are coming to raid this place tonight. He must take precautions.' The denial of my stay at the place did not dissuade Sergeant B. 'The Special Branch know he stays here. It is useless denying it. Please warn him.' I was warned when I arrived. It would have been unwise to pooh-pooh the forewarning. So I gave the police a wide berth. They arrived and turned the place upside down in my absence. That was the story I got two days later. Sergeant B's image changed in my eyes. My inborn hunch, that the police force was composed of individuals and was not a monolith, was given a boost.

Before the State of Emergency was lifted there was another incident to corroborate my earlier experiences. This time two black security men surprised me at work. Blushing and apologetic they asked for my pass. 'You know I burnt it,' I answered rather aggressively. 'Are you busy?' they continued their coy interrogation. 'Yes I am,' I told them. 'You see, we have been instructed to check whether you have a pass or not, and if you have not got one we are to take you to the Grays (Special Branch Headquarters). Since you are busy,' one of them said looking at his friend, 'I think we'll report that you were out when we called. The second thing, we want to warn you, that if anything happens that can be connected with the ANC on June 26, you shall be held responsible and detained.' (They meant I would be one of those held responsible). My queries as to the kind of things they expected to

61

happen for which I could be held responsible yielded no results. 'We just wanted to warn you,' was all the tangible fruit of my efforts. The observance of June 26 in 1960 was not such as to provoke repercussions even from the petty police officialdom. So our token declarations of 'dubious' existence were ignored by retributive man gods on this occasion, in spite of the forewarning.

Shortly after June 26 the government started releasing some detainees until the state of emergency was completely lifted at the end of August.

The State of Emergency had been a severe setback to the struggle. The liberation struggle had not been crushed. But it had been arrested and imprisoned. Shortly before the State of Emergency and the ban of the two mass organisations, the morale of the activists and the masses had been very high. 'Freedom in our lifetime' sounded a graphic and realistic slogan. Led by the ANC, the masses chanted it along with other popular slogans of the liberation movement. The PAC predicted freedom in 1963. The masses were taken up. The ban and the State of Emergency undermined the mood of enthusiasm, disrupted the trend of mass political involvement in the fight against oppression and triggered minds in search of novel solutions to the political problem of the country.

One could sense a sharp polarisation of the mood of the oppressed. A small but vocal section began to advocate violent methods with a new vehemence. In the past, part of the small section had held reservations on the policy of non-violence, but the policy had been staunchly defended on unshakeable grounds. After the State of Emergency and the ban the grounds on which the policy of non-violence rested showed cracks and leaks. During the State of Emergency, incidents of a violent nature were sporadic and numerous. In Alexandra, Putco buses, symbols of inefficiency and exploitation, were popular targets of molotov cocktail hurlers. Arsonists attempted to burn down one of the Dutch Reformed Churches. One appreciated the hatred against the Dutch Reformed Churches. They were the spiritual fathers of apartheid, the guardians of its development, its entrenchment and its glorification. Submission of blacks to white domination was the crux of their evangelising mission in the black community. In the white community, superiority of the whites was their sermon. Their creed was that whites were children of Seth, the blessed, and the blacks were children of Ham, the cursed. All children of God, yes, but some favoured by divine benevolence and others outcasts, judged and condemned by the Godhead above and dehumanised by white brotherhood on earth.

It was natural that the frustrations endured through the imposition of the State of Emergency should be vented in violent ways and visited upon symbolic targets. The current political theme in the ghettos during the State of Emergency was: peaceful protest has been banned. What next? Those who advocated formation of new legal organisations to carry on where the banned ones left off, were cross-questioned. What if the new organisation or organisations experience the same fate, as must happen, shall we become a nation of Sisyphuses, pushing heavy stones uphill and watching them roll down again to be expected to start all over again ad *infinitum?* The idea was preposterous to young bloods feeling the pinch of oppression and watching revolutionary trends further north. The young talked of violence and pointed to Algeria. That was one side of the mood coin.

There were others who were overcome by despair.The State of Emergency proved that the white government was powerful and determined not to let go its privileges. These privileges were created by legislation enacted by an all-white parliament. Moreover they were safeguarded and defended by state power influenced by international monopoly capital and controlled by rabid white nationalists. The public media, controlled by vested interests, eulogised measures aimed at enforcement of law and order. The 'right wing' press and the 'left wing' press agreed unanimously. Law and order. By all means. 'Chaos' cannot be tolerated. It is a feature of South African white politics that in any political crisis eventuated by black resistance the Verkramptes, the Verligtes, the Nationalists, the Liberals, the English-speaking and the Afrikaans-speaking elements converge. They come together and, oysterlike, close ranks. The Native, the Bantu, the African is the mortal enemy. The government does not stifle black opposition. Only a certain kind of opposition that not only questions but threatens white privilege and racial discrimination.

The perception drove many into a mood of fatalism. Others motivated by personal aggrandisement and opportunistic bent opted for the barren, fraudulent and unviable 'Bantu Homelands'. The Bantu Authorities Act, the legal foundation of Bantu Homelands, had been resisted countrywide by hereditary leaders, the chiefs, and their people in the rural areas. Chief Mabe in the Western Transvaal – he was banished into exile, Chief Abram Moiloa in the Zeerust District – he had to flee into exile, Chief Mopeli of Witzieshoek, now Qwaqwa – he was banished to the fringe of the Kalahari Desert and died there; Chief Sekhukhune of Sekhukhuneland – he was sent into exile; in Natal the peasants were up in arms against dipping tanks and stock culling; in the Transkei, mainly Pondoland, discontent was simmering beneath the surface soon to erupt into violence which was put down by brutal repression conducted under a localised State of Emergency.

The Native Administration Act of 1927 empowered the governor-general to rule by proclamation in the 'reserves' if it were necessary. He was the Big Chief of all the chiefs and had the power to install new unhereditary chiefs if they were amenable to co-operation, and to depose old hereditary ones if they were obstreperous and unco-operative with government. The Bantu Authorities Act of 1951 underwrote the old Act and introduced new, sinister perspectives of the bantustans. Thus set in the era of yes-chiefs and phony independence. Black South Africans never accepted so-called independence in the bantustans, they were coerced and bludgeoned into it by government violence and intimidation and their ignorance was gainfully exploited by the handpicked stooges.

During the State of Emergency and afterwards there was this interplay of buoyancy and depression, there was this interaction of events, people's non-violent methods of protest versus violent methods of repression by 'granite apartheid' policymakers. Compromise and confrontation clashed for prominence in the new unfolding scenario in the liberation struggle.

The situation was fluid. The release of national leaders provided a new impetus. The ex-detainees oozed incredible confidence. It was difficult to understand their optimism. The general euphoria of the pre-State of Emergency situation had been interrupted by the State of Emergency and arrested by onerous struggle underground. The experience was sobering to some of us who, for the first time, lived and worked practically under conditions of illegality. The task of organising and maintaining an underground machinery was an uphill battle. Activists had to learn new methods and acquire different techniques of operation. Not only that, we had to change ourselves to adapt to new conditions. Strict discipline became the keystone of the work of liberation movements. Organisational procedures underwent a dramatic change. The traditional democratic process was an unavoidable casualty. Annual conferences or any other conference as provided for in the constitution of the organisation were suspended. Democratic elections of national leaders and office-bearers became a thing of the past. It was part of the new spirit of discipline to accept the suspension of this crucial concept of the freedom struggle without reservations. Yesterday's freedom fighters changed into dedicated revolutionaries overnight. It was not easy and the morale of the masses was ailing.

Then came the ex-detainees, triumphant and confident. Public morale picked up quickly. The leaders were back. Expectations, vague and untranslatable, were in the air. Political magicians had arrived.

An All-in African conference was soon sponsored. The sponsors invited organisations and prominent individual Africans regardless of past or present political affiliation. Police intimidation and old mistrust undermined what might have emerged as a powerful revival of a lawful extra-parliamentary movement for the rights of the oppressed majority. Some members of the organising committee were arrested and charged with incitement. (The charges were later

64

withdrawn). The Liberal Party withdrew from the project except for Julius Mali who decided to stick it out as an individual. Former members of the PAC also withdrew from involvement pleading one thing or the other. In the end the former members of the banned ANC were left to carry the can together with a number of non-political organisations.

The All-in African Conference was held in Pietermaritzburg and was addressed by Nelson Mandela, whose ban ironically had lapsed and had not been renewed. The underground machinery of the ANC had gone all out to organise for the conference. It was an important test and the ANC passed it with distinction. Nelson Mandela electrified the conference in his address with his fearlessness and outspokenness. The spirit was high at the conference. Fists raised in the air and arms in piston-like motion, delegates sang the new revolutionary tune: 'Amandla ngawethu nobungcwalisa nabo bobethu (Power is ours, so is justice)'. Our power lay in our unity, determination and hard work. 'Amandla ngawethu (Power to the People)' became the new revolutionary slogan of the liberation movement. Gradually, it overshadowed the old slogan: 'Mayibuye i'Afrika (Come back Africa)'. The slogan caught on like wildfire. Back in Alexandra and Soweto, in stokvels, parties and shebeens, carousers raised their fists, pumped the air and heaved their shoulders in stylish rendition of the new revolutionary piece: Amandla ngawethu. It was exhilarating. Instinctively, activists gazed upon each other with the eyes that said it all: the yearning for freedom and the spirit to attain it, are unkillable twins.

The conference condemned the apartheid government for the Republic of South Africa Constitution Act which legislated for the establishment of a republic without consulting the black majority. It also resolved to embark on a campaign of non-cooperation if the government did not respond positively to the demands of the conference, namely, withdrawal of the decision to make South Africa a republic without consultation with the voteless majority. Nelson Mandela was appointed secretary of the Action Council which was formed to implement the resolutions of conference.

In conformity with the new conditions of semi-legality of black opposition Nelson Mandela went underground to start a life of an outlaw, thereby deserting his wife and small children for a principle, a principle of human equality.

The decision by Mandela to go underground epitomised the new mood of uncompromising resistance. It foreshadowed, intensely a future of sacrifices. The mood was also a reflection of the mood of the government, a mood of intolerance, nervousness, insecurity and consequent brutality. Chief Luthuli, the President-General of the ANC, used a popular slogan: Let your courage rise with danger. The white supremacists were becoming dangerous. The oppressed were reacting with courage. The general work-stoppage to protest against

65

the Constitution Act was scheduled to take place at the end of May 1961 to coincide with the declaration of South Africa as a republic. The work-stoppage was for three days – from May 29 to 31. The National Action Council, led by Mandela from underground, campaigned vigorously for the success of the general strike. Slogans were painted countrywide condemning the declaration of the minority republic. Leaflets and pamphlets were distributed on a nationwide scale to draw the oppressed into the campaign. Most English-speaking white South Africans were opposed to the republic for sentimental reasons. Severance of ties with the British monarchy was something the English jingoists could not tolerate lightly. For a brief moment the Natal province held the country and the world in suspense with threats of defiance and secession.

In the atmosphere of conflict between white sentiments and interests, the opportunistic English press gave the campaign by the National Action Council unaccustomed publicity. Nelson Mandela was interviewed from time to time and his statements about the objectives and the scale of the campaign were given good coverage. The English press was not motivated by any sense of altruism or the principle of freedom of speech. No. They were motivated by pure self-interest. They were playing a political game of forging 'alliances' of convenience. As the day of the referendum approached and as the Natal secessionists began to waver, and as the day of the general stoppage of work loomed ominously nearer, the English press reports became less enthusiastic and subtly sceptical of the idea and likely success of the general-strike action. During and after the strike the reports became more subjective and more inaccurate. The alliance of convenience was gradually eroded and finally jettisoned.

From the organisers' point of view the strike was a big success considering the conditions under which it was organised. The wide publicity of an inappropriate interview with the Secretary of the National Action Council a few days before the strike might also have served to confuse the working masses. The Secretary, in reply to a question as to whether the strike would be voluntary, had replied in the affirmative. The press of course went to town on this, interpreting it as meaning that there was no moral obligation on the part of the toilers to support the strike. They even went as far as to imply that there would be no picketing whatsoever.

The picketing reference almost threw the activists out of gear. After a brief heated debate on to picket or not to picket, the Alexandra activists went into action on the eve of 29 May. Car scraps, discarded corrugated irons, boulders, rubbish bins, anything with obstructive properties was hauled onto the roads to make them impassable or less passable to police traffic. We were wrong. The army was called, not the police. It was a barometer of the intense organisation that had gone into the campaign. The government was taking no chances.

Shortly before the referendum the government had legislated for 12-day detention without trial to enable them to deal with would-be mischief-makers. The army came to the townships to disrupt the disrupters of law and order and carry out mopping-up operations on the evening of 29 May. After the back-breaking task of moving deadweight across the streets I sneaked through fences to my pondokkie and slumped into bed. Dog tired. I was awakened by my landlady in the small hours of the morning. 'Mike, Mike!' Bang! Bang! 'Mike, get up!' I jumped out of bed in a somnolent stupor, bewildered at the frantic knocking. 'Mike, wake up! The soldiers were here looking for you!' It did not make sense. I groped for matches, lit a candle, and opened the door for the landlady, to hear the story of the army that searched for me and was outmanoeuvred by a lady and bamboozled by the unfamiliar ghetto terrain. It was sheer luck the army missed me; luck plus the landlady's conniving sympathies. My rented room was attached to the main cottage although it had a separate door at the back. The army men knocked at the front door and produced my picture and a slip of paper with my misspelt name. The landlady denied any knowledge of the name and allowed the men to look in the front rooms of the cottage. They satisfied themselves that the person they were looking for was not in the cottage and left to awaken tenants in the rented shacks, hardly suspecting any other part of the main cottage. It was shortly after the troop carrier had roared its emptyhanded departure that the landlady came banging at the door. 'Clear your room of any incriminating papers, they might come back,' she advised. Together we cleared all undesirable literature and carted it across the street to a respectable friend of the landlady. Incriminating stuff safely across the road, I handed the keys to the landlady and went into hiding for the three days of the duration of the strike.

A number of prominent activists who did not have this luck were captured by either the police or the army net. They spent 12 days in detention. It was the beginning of the detention without trial era, the epoch of the abolition of habeas corpus in South Africa. The rule of law was suspended. It is still suspended.

The South African army was increasingly being used to maintain law and order in the townships. The day following the declaration of the State of Emergency, the army was very much in evidence, patrolling the streets and driving people to work or into their homes. The May 29-31 stay-at-home provoked another show of force from the army. Government intolerance to peaceful opposition was becoming more and more transparent. It was clear the gloves were off and the mailed fist was on show.

It was in response to the sum of all the harassment, the bannings, the detentions without trial, intimidation by both the army and the police and numerous acts of institutionalised violence culminating in Sharpeville, that Nelson Mandela in reviewing the government

67

reaction to the demonstrations against the republican constitution concluded that the old chapter was closed. Clearly the mood of the oppressed was changing. Government violence, intransigence and intolerance was breeding a parallel counter-reaction from the liberation movement. The end of 1961 saw the emergence of Umkhonto we Sizwe (MK). It was an accurate translation of the frustration and despair at the relevance of the non-violent policies which the liberation movement had pursued with such religious fervour for over half a century.

Notwithstanding the mood of impatience, the resort to violent methods did not follow lightly. The matter was debated long and hard. There was no arguing that the oppressed died violently under the white government laws and the state machinery regardless of their passivity. But it was also clear that counter-violence would bring more violence on a larger scale. The escalation of violence was likely to go on and on until it engulfed the whole country and every living being, innocent and guilty. It was a grim prospect. Those who took the decision however were fired by the spirit of patriotism, their devotion to human dignity and the love of their fellow humans. Better to die on one's feet than live on one's knees.

History would be the judge. Its verdict would rely on historical facts. The guilty party would not escape the sentence. In absentia or posthumously.

THE TRAGEDY OF RIVONIA
Nineteen-sixty-two was a good year for the underground of the ANC. The organisation consolidated its underground structure and its work. The newly formed MK was growing and giving the government and its agencies many anxious moments. Acts of sabotage increased in number and intensity. More leaders of the liberation movement joined Mandela underground and reinforced prospects of keener opposition. It was the year MK started recruiting volunteers for external training in sabotage and guerrilla warfare.

The response from the youth was unprecedented. The organisation was inundated with applications for training abroad. Although not all known former members of the ANC were members of MK, the ordinary man in the street was not aware of the distinction between the political nd the military structures of the underground. On a number of occasions I was approached by senior citizens of Alexandra who had known me as an office bearer of the ANC and presumed I was now a member of the underground: 'M'tanami (My child), my son is unemployed and gravitating towards delinquency. Won't you take him for training so that he can come back and fight amabunu (Boers)? Please, m'tanami. We are tired of amabunu and I don't want my boy to go and rot in gaol for stupid crimes . . .'

Such requests were both inspiring and embarrassing. To promise attention to the request would be tantamount to public acknowledge-

68

ment of one's role as an underground functionary responsible for recruitment. It could be misleading if one was in the political wing as I was. Moreover, it could be dangerous, since it was fraught with security implications. Complete denial of association with the recruiting machinery also had its disadvantages. It could have a demoralising effect on sympathisers and potential supporters. The strategy I adopted was to deny any connections while promising to investigate. Arrangements to contact the potential recruit could then be made with the machinery responsible. Generally, people never believed these dissembling procedures. There was an occasion when I was confronted by an angry brother-in-law of someone who had skipped the country. 'Bra Mike, how can you send S away for training when you know he has two small children to support?' The man was fuming. My attempt to challenge his hunch or source of intelligence did not make him retract his allegations. He was convinced I knew about S's disappearance and he did not like it.

These were some of the characteristic problems of clandestine organisation. How to ensure contact and collaboration with the people without exposing oneself to police intelligence? To crown the good work of the year the ANC organised its first conference since the ban. For security reasons, as well as the need to co-ordinate the external and internal work of the organisation, the conference was held in Lobatse in Bechuanaland. Delegates came from all over South Africa and abroad—London, Egypt and Dar es Salaam. Travel restrictions across South African borders were not tight at the time, but the police did their utmost to disorganise delegates to the conference from centres within the country. Delegates who had unintentionally left their passes at home were stopped on the way and held in police stations until the conference was over. Our delegation came across a police roadblock at the Lobatse borderpost. The priest collar and gown I wore to disguise our destination and mission became an embarrassment when a security officer who knew me well shone his torch in my face and exclaimed: 'Ah, dis Dingake! Van wanneer af is jy predikant? (Ah, that's Dingake! Since when are you a minister of religion?)' The story got into the *Vaderland* (a Johannesburg Afrikaans evening paper) on Monday to say some well-known ANC members were disguised as ministers of religion on the way to the conference. Although the majority of our delegation were identified by the police at the roadblock we were not stopped, because we carried our passes.

Nineteen-sixty-two was also the year Nelson Mandela toured African states to drum up support for the liberation struggle in South Africa. The year also saw the passing of the 'Sabotage Act' to counter the wave of sabotage that was engulfing the country. In Johannesburg a massive protest demonstration against the Sabotage Act was organised during the lunch hour. It was impressive and dignified. A six-to-eight-deep column of blacks and whites marched down Eloff Street and Pritchard Street to the Cenotaph. At the intersection of the two streets where the procession took a right turn, a black photographer stood on an upturned 44-gallon drum taking pictures of the procession, click, click! While he was thus training his camera, and focusing with all the absorption of a visual artist recording an historic event, one of those two-legged epitomes of apartheid kicked the drum the cameraman was standing on. The photographer crashed to the pavement. His camera flew across the street towards the OK Bazaars. As the outrage of the despicable act stung the marchers, a white journalist, camera slung around the neck, got hold of the sneak and bloodied his nose in retaliation. Other journalists helped their bruised colleague to his feet. The dignified procession marched on, undiverted by infra dig side attractions. To the Cenotaph. To commemorate the funeral of habeas corpus in South Africa.

B J Vorster shortly thereafter began to wield his enormous powers under the Sabotage Act ruthlessly, as well as other powers (particularly those under the 90-day clause) that have brought South Africa to the permanent status of a police state. A number of prominent leaders, among them Walter Sisulu, Moses Kotane, Jack Hodgson, Helen Joseph and Ahmed Kathrada, were placed under 24-hour house-arrest. Walter Sisulu who was the key organiser of the Lobatse conference was not home when the police tried to serve the severe ban on him. According to the press, the police could pin the notice of the ban on his door and the ban would be as good as served on his person in legal terms. And a minute's absence from his house could then be regarded as contravention of the house arrest order. Walter Sisulu hurried back home to comply with the iniquitous order. The 24-hour house arrest was challenged successfully in court. The success was shortlived. The government reimposed the bans in slightly modified form. Walter Sisulu broke the ban and went underground. In doing so he was also risking the estreatment of his R6,000 bail in one of the many political cases he was facing then. He relates the story of how his son, Max, then a teenager, reacted to his departure for his hiding place. 'There goes the people's money . . .' commented Max disapprovingly.

The year also saw the arrest of Nelson Mandela after his successful tour of the African continent. The police armed with the draconian laws, their espionage network and their anti-subversion training, were beginning to show their true colours. The first mass detentions under the 90-day clause took place on 24 June 1963. The detentions were obviously aimed at the pre-emption of any 'subversive' activities of the underground ANC anticipated for June 26 (Freedom Day). The 90-day clause of the General Law Amendment Act empowered the police to arrest and hold any suspect for 90 days, and gave them the discretion to release or re-detain the suspect for a further period of 90 days. The law courts could not intervene. Among those detained on June 24 was Bartholomew Hlapane. Within 18 days of the arrests in June, the Rivonia arrests took place. Liliesleaf Farm in the Johannesburg suburb of Rivonia was the underground headquarters of the liberation movement. Altogether 12 people were caught in the raid, very prominent leaders of the movement.

Rivonia was a traumatic event. It was a big shock for the voteless masses who daily prayed that amabunu should never find Sisulu's hiding place. In the trains back home they expressed bewilderment at their unbroken spell of collective misfortunes. 'S'enzeni (What have we done)?' they asked in perplexity and searched each other's black faces for an eternally evasive answer. Who sold Rivonia? This question was generally unasked but uppermost in many minds. The few who asked it speculated wildly on the basis of press rumours and maybe rumours from Congress sources alarmed by the growing laxity of security in the ranks. Who sold Rivonia? When the raid and the arrests took place, like everyone else, I was curious. Who sold Rivonia?

I was in the habit of tapping information from released detainees, about what happened during their detention. Although members of the liberation movement were under strict instructions not to make statements to the police in detention, some of us who had read literature on torture methods knew the directive, 'Don't talk' was more of a propaganda slogan in the era of the 90-day clause. It was a relic of the past, when the rule of habeas corpus still applied. It is true that some detainees refuse to talk in detention and pay with their lives or their health. Many make involuntary statements, but statements nevertheless, with adverse repercussions for the cause. There are a few exceptions who for reasons best known to police interrogators are spared harsh interrogation. My curiosity about the inside of detention was not born of suspicion of other comrades but primarily out of anxiety as to my prospective behaviour if I ever fell foul of the 90-day clause. It was a way of mentally conditioning myself for the eventuality.

Just before the Rivonia arrests a few detainees who had been detained before the big swoop of June 24 were released. The experience of one of the first released detainees was humdrum. Certainly poorer than my several experiences as a pass offender. He had refused to talk. The second man I interviewed was Patrick 'Giraffe' Mthembu (he was assassinated in the late seventies). 'Giraffe' was released after Rivonia. When I first heard of his release, I reacted impulsively: 'He has sold out,' I blurted out. Pat was a member of the High Command of MK. He was among the first MK officers to be trained abroad. The training in the People's Republic of China had made him too big, swollen-headed, reckless and irresponsible. Before he left for China he had inspired me with some of his good qualities. He was broadminded, tolerant of personal criticism and never

71

underestimated the enemy. Now, he came back with a vice-grip handshake that made one stand on one's toes and squeal with pain. Having made one feel one's metacarpus creak, he proceeded to announce that he was back and the Boers were going to be diarrhoea cases. That sort of behaviour and other pompous attitudes undermined my former confidence in him. Hence my outburst. But after composing myself I thought 'Giraffe's' release might be an organisation-busting stratagem by the security police. They would know his release would cause consternation and suspicion. That would suit them gorgeously. In this light I revised my initial suspicion.

To show my cameraderie I visited 'Giraffe' for a chat over his detention. While Hilda, 'Giraffe's' wife, prepared me some tea in the kitchen, 'Giraffe' related his story. It was in the form of two complaints: Brian Somana who was released about the same time with 'Giraffe' was scandalising his name, complained 'Giraffe'. Brian was saying Patrick Mthembu was a sell-out who had made statements to the police and had led them to the Rivonia hideout. How Brian knew all this was an open guess. Patrick Mthembu however protested his innocence at the allegations. Brian was a liar, he counter-charged. Said 'Giraffe': 'I pray Arthur Goldreich and Harold Wolpe will be safe from the police hunt, so that they might testify to my innocence one day.' (Arthur and Harold had just made the great escape from Marshall Square police station where they were held after their arrest at Rivonia). According to 'Giraffe', he was in on the secret of the escape plan and if he were an informer as Brian alleged, he would have alerted the police, especially in view of the fact that the escape plan had to be postponed at one point. I was one of the very few who had prior knowledge of the escape. And I was aware that Patrick was authentic on that point. Of course that alone did not exonerate him from all liability of possible co-operation with the police on other facets. Some sell-outs have an ambivalent conscience. Anyway that was Patrick's first complaint.

The second complaint was that his colleagues in the High Command were ostracising him. They even refused to pay him his functionary allowance on the pretext that there was no money. They were lying, according to 'Giraffe'. He knew there was money to last for the year when he was detained. He had only been detained for under two months.

Pat was bitter. Embitterment can be an active source of irrationalism and unscrupulousness. To forestall what I believed was formulating in Pat's mind and emotions I pleaded with some of his colleagues to reinstate his allowance. I was ignored. Pat was redetained before the start of the Rivonia trial. He gave evidence in the trial. He was one of the few who used to be in and out of Liliesleaf, but whether he sold Rivonia was not investigated during his cross-examination. The mystery of who sold Rivonia was not brought near denouement by Patrick's evidence. The consensus of opinion among Rivonia trialists was that Patrick had not been a hostile witness, whatever that implied.

Bartholomew Hlapane was released from detention during his second term of 90-day detention. We had been very close before his detention. It was natural that I should be among the first people to welcome him back from his harrowing experience. I recall how incoherently he tried to relate his ordeal. Close on 180 days in isolation is nobody's cup of tea. The one thing he was eloquent on was Comrade Alfred Nzo's fighting spirit in detention but his praise for Nzo sounded like he was a very poor contrast. From where he sat chatting with me Barth looked like a broken man. It seemed every bone in his body had been minced. Mentally too, he was a ghost of himself. He admitted it: 'Comrade, I need to see a psychiatrist. Please arrange one for me.' I reported Barth's state of health and his specific request to the responsible committee.

Underground processes take time. By the time I reported to Barth that a psychiatrist was ready to see him, Barth had changed his mind. He was all right, he informed me. He had been attended by Dr Kazi. Dr Kazi was not a psychiatrist but a general practitioner. Barth's wife, Mathilda, was unhappy with Barth's somersault. More than ever, Barth needed a psychiatrist. Barth suffered from frightful nightmares by night. He talked in his sleep and twisted restlessly in bed. By day he suffered from hallucinations. He perceived non-existent objects. 'No, Barth needs a psychiatrist,' argued Tilly. Barth was adamant. He could do without one. Kazi had done him good. You can take a horse to the river . . . Whatever the validity of Matilda's observations, Barth was recovering his coherence in speech. He began to tell me about some of the memorable events in detention.

After his arrest, Barth was detained in Langlaagte police station. He was kept in isolation. On or around 8 July 1963 he was transferred from Langlaagte police station to Rosebank police station. He noticed on arrival that the cell he was placed in was occupied by someone. The occupant was not there when he arrived. Later in the day Brian Somana was brought in. It transpired he was the legitimate tenant of the cell. Brian explained to Barth where he had spent the day. He had been taken to Rietfontein Hospital for his tummy-ache. (Rietfontein is a TB hospital.) His tummy troubles started when he was forced to eat hard mealie-pap in detention. His was a delicate tummy and did not agree with pap. Pap gave him indigestion, tummy-ache and other related upsets. Amabunu were kind enough to take him for medical examination. And while he lay on his aching tummy and his back, with the MD hovering over him with his stethoscope, he overheard amabunu, the police escorts, discussing plans to raid Rivonia in a day or two. Brian confessed he did not know Afrikaans very well (he did not know Rivonia well either) but he was sure amabunu were saying something about a 'communist hideout' and the impending raid.

(Police security measures apparently were a sieve, at this stage, with leaks drenching the entire police force including casual police escorts). Brian was anxious about the safety of the comrades hiding in Rivonia. He wanted to save them. He had a plan. His wife was due to visit him the following day (a rare privilege under the 90-day detention). If Comrade Bartholomew Hlapane could give him a name, preferably two names – in case the one first named is not easily traceable – of persons who knew Rivonia, he could ask his wife when she visited to raise the alarm through these knowledgeable personages.

Well, the security of the liberation movement was at stake. Bartholomew co-operated with two names. He was, after all, the key contact between the men in Rivonia and the activists outside Rivonia. He knew them all; those who knew Rivonia, those who 'knew' it vaguely, and those who did not know it. Brian was one of those who 'knew' Rivonia vaguely. He had been allowed to drive some people on a couple of occasions to Rivonia. For security reasons, however, his passengers had always been transferred from his vehicle to another before they arrived at the true destination. Brian's knowledge of Rivonia was thus vague and limited. He needed somebody's co-operation. Somebody who knew. Who better than the man who utilised him for halfway passenger transportation!

The following day Brian's wife did not come to visit as the Boers had promised. Very unpredictable people, the Boers. Untrustworthy scum. The two, Barth and Brian, resigned themselves to the impending doom. They had been moved to help. They tried. Their circumstances frustrated their attempts. Pure agony, to see the approach of disaster and at the same time to feel the full weight of helplessness in its inexorable face. On 11 July, disaster struck. The struggle was flung back many years. The privileged whites who had been anxious about their privileges while Sisulu's whereabouts were unknown, rejoiced and celebrated their luck. None knew better than Brian and Barth how lucky they were. The whites. Had Brian's wife visited . . ! Brian and Barth had a vision of Rivonia. They were powerless and hamstrung. They could not even prophesy its imminence. Poor guys, denied even the role of Cassandras.

The underground suspended Bartholomew from organisational activity for a period of six months. This was not due to any expressed suspicion against him. It was a normal security precaution based on common sense. Once the police showed a public interest in an individual by detaining him, it meant they had been watching the individual closely. The release from detention could not be construed as evidence of future police indifference towards the ex-detainee. On the contrary, the release could be a signal for closer police surveillance. As an old friend I was instructed to keep the informal social contact level active and to report any observation worth reporting.

It was in the capacity of an informal contact with Barth that I raised the idea that he should consider going into exile. I was convinced in my mind that the next detention would break Hlapane completely. His whole physical and mental state was tottering on the brink of total and final collapse. Barth refused to entertain the idea. It sounded preposterous to him. Exile? Whatever could he do in exile? There were too many people in exile already! What about his many children and his wife? Who would care for them? No! Except for the argument about the maintenance of his family, which will continue to plague revolutionaries with dependants, his other arguments were ridiculous. Actually even the one of who would look after his family when he was in exile was baseless on deeper analysis. Who looked after his family for six months while he was in detention? Who would look after them if he collected a 12-year or life imprisonment sentence? These were obvious posers. How would he answer them? I did not put these questions to him. Barth's attitude was worth pondering and reporting. At the end of the suspension period, when Barth's reinstatement was reviewed, Barth's attitude about leaving the country was a subject of passing reference. Those who had reservations about Barth's immediate reinstatement reserved them. I was one of them.

If underground work during the State of Emergency was tough, work after Rivonia was tougher. The Rivonia arrests gave the government and the police a major breakthrough in their fight against the struggle of the masses. The police had gained the upperhand in the contest, and they seized this initiative and clung to it with bulldog tenacity.

While 'Rivonia' might have been discovered through the treachery of an informer, hypothetically it could have been the result of a combination of two factors: routine police intelligence and poor security precautions by the liberation struggle. December 16, 1961, the day of the violent inauguration of Umkhonto we Sizwe (MK) caught the government with their pants down. The escalation of acts of sabotage sent jitters through the main organs of the state, shook them out of their traditional complacency. On the other hand the inauguration of MK brought a new spirit of 'derring-do' and readiness for extreme sacrifices. The successful sabotage operations of 1962-3 created extreme over-confidence with its dangerous corollaries of recklessness and complacency. Regions, areas, streets and cells, through their structures, exhorted the membership to observe some elementary rules of security: change venues of meetings, be punctual at meetings, don't discuss your role in the organisation with other members of the organisation who are not working directly with you, be careful whom you talk to and what you say, etc. These elementary principles were broken daily. The non-observance of the rules could never be regarded as deliberate and conscious. It was all the result of emotional fervour overwhelming common sense and mutual trust generated among the membership by the wave of spectacular achievements of MK. The optimistic side of the mood was good. The incipient complacency and recklessness produced by such a mood however was dangerous.

Shortly before the swoop of 24 June, 1962 there were reports of one area in Soweto where the MK cadres were recruiting youth openly for training abroad. The involved cadres denied the allegations when confronted by senior authority, but the allegations were not invalidated by the mere fact of denial.

There was a more serious incident of negligence of security precautions a month preceding 24 June. The High Command had organised and directed regional commands to send recruits for training abroad. At 9 pm or thereabouts, while I lay on my bed trying to sleep, there was a loud knock at the door, reminiscent of police knocks. I was still a bachelor at the time, the house I stayed in was not in my name, and I was relatively new in it. To all intents and purposes I was in semi-hiding. And the house was ideal. The loud knock shattered my feeling of security. For a brief moment I toyed with the idea of jumping through the window and making my escape from the imaginary police. 'Who is there?' I shouted with a sudden change of course of action. I was relieved to hear 'Giraffe's' voice. He was in the company of 11 other men. 'Comrade Mike, we have run out of accommodation for trainees. Can you accommodate these overnight? Tomorrow evening they will be on their way to Bechuanaland . . .' Eleven men crammed in a two-bedroomed house. Not bad in terms of sleeper density. In Sophiatown and Newclare that same number could be crammed in one room. Sleepers learned to economise space by lying in opposite directions – feet against heads – on the floor for the young ones, while two adult couples might share one bed and conserve space by piling on each other and making bad worse in the long term. In terms of security considerations this was crazy.

How do you keep 11 complete strangers from the prying eyes of the neighbours you cannot vouch for? What made the undertaking untenable was that the toilet, like all Soweto toilets, was detached from the house. Eleven bladders activated by numerous cups of tea brewed out of sheer boredom would not help to reduce unwanted ups and downs in the yard and the equally undesirable exhibition. 'You are mad!' I cut Patrick short. 'Accommodating these men here can only serve to put me in jeopardy. Why didn't you ask me to help organise accommodation beforehand? I would have found a safe place!'

In spite of my extreme displeasure I was eventually persuaded to take the 11 for the night. And for the Sunday. I left early in the morning for a meeting and a few appointments. Before I left I urged my visitors to take precautions, not to expose themselves.

During the day I had also received disconcerting information relating to the trip to Bechuanaland. One of the comrades at the meeting I attended that Sunday morning had reported a similar incident. He was standing in a bus queue at the bus rank in Diepkloof (one of the Soweto townships), Friday afternoon, when a man driving a Combi, shouted to his friend as he drove past the bus rank, 'Sondag ons ry Tanganyika toe (We are driving to Tanganyika on Sunday).' From the description I knew the man was the regular who drove recruits across the border to Bechuanaland.

The two related but separate incidents convinced me that the police would have advance knowledge of the trip. The Johannesburg afternoon paper *The Star* carried an article reporting the interception of a convoy of vehicles carrying recruits near Rustenburg the following day, Monday. To survive, it was clear the organisation had to change its style of work and practise disciplined underground methods. It was too late. Priorities were askew. June 24 and July 11 followed quickly after the convoy fiasco. On July 18, a week after 'Rivonia' I came home at 8 pm to be warned by my neighbours not to hang around the house. 'The police were here looking for you!' 'Were they? What did they want?' 'They were led by a man in handcuffs.' 'A man in handcuffs?' 'Yes, one of those men who were leaving for Tanganyika . . .' Gracious me!

It was a double shock: the police looking for me; my neighbour knowing that the men had been on their way to Tanganyika. There was no doubt that my neighbour had seen the men. They were the most conspicuous bunch around for a long time. But somehow in my naivety I did not think he would have associated them with excursionists to far away lands. My, my! One good thing out of these revelations was that I could now trust my neighbour and entrust him with some assignments for my security. The first and foremost thing was to vacate the house, clear all my belongings, furniture, crockery, cutlery, books and the tiniest scrap of paper from the condemned house. I could do it with the help of my neighbour if he monitored police checks which he undertook magnificently. I was delighted the police had not left some of their number watching the house. If some ANC cadres were bunglers, they obviously had their counterparts in the police force. But there was no doubt that the police would be coming to try their luck. After clinching the deal with my good neighbour, I left to organise a rescue team. We set aside the following day and night as an observation period of police movements to and from the house. Comrade Kate Molale who died in a car accident in Tanzania in 1980 (may she rest in peace) was in charge of the miniature Dunkirk.

The 24 hours established a police check pattern. They arrived at the house, knocked at the door, swore 'bliksem (blast)' because there was no response, knocked at my neighbour's door. 'Bang! Bang! Jong bly hierdie bliksem se donder hierso? (Boy, does this damn-blasted man stay here?)' My neighbour answered: 'Yes, he does. But he is a bachelor, you see. And most of the time he stays with his girlfriend in the backyards in town. Over the weekends, however, he never fails to come home.' The police were not local police. They were Pretoria police. They enquired where the Township Superintendent's office was and left. At the Superintendent's Office they found the house registered in Anderson Tshepe's name. Tshepe had left for Bechuanaland, and his family and I continued to pay rent in his name. So unless the police caught me in the house or found something to identify the occupant of the house they would not have known I was the wanted man.

The third day, the rescue forces led by Kate cleared the house in a well-planned, well-timed and perfectly executed operation. Two trucks under cover of darkness carried me and my entire household effects to safety. Someone kept contact with my dear neighbour to monitor the final scene of the drama. Over the weekend police impatience prevailed. They broke into the house to find it an empty shell except for the camouflage curtains. It was a narrow shave.

Just before the Lobatse Conference in November 1962, a body known as the National Secretariat was formed. This was a shadow committee of the National Executive of the ANC. Its objective was to understudy the National Executive Committee in order to step into its shoes in case a catastrophe overtook the NEC. I was one of the members of this committee. Overnight, the Rivonia raid transformed the National Secretariat from the role of executive to that of legislator-decision taker. Once again morale hit rock bottom and some stalwarts quaked at the sight of the bare fist of the police.

The security police, perceiving the fecundity of their torture methods, applied them intensively. Looksmart Ngudle died in the hands of the police, the first man to die under the 90 day law. An inquest into his death was held. The police lied without shame. The judicial officer, obviously programmed to believe the lies, believed. The police were exonerated in spite of the weightier and more plausible evidence of the detainees. A pattern was set from then on. Death in detention. Inquest. Police lies. Judicial officer's gullibility. Exoneration of the police. The pattern has not changed. It will not change as long as the South African security laws remain on the statute books. Police intimidation reached unprecedented heights. The few who stuck it out seemed to be the core of the lunatic fringe. Relatives and other Batswana acquaintances implored me: 'Run home! Can't you see the boat is sinking? Go, man, go! Don't be a fool!'

Running home to Bechuanaland was easier said than done for me. For 16 years I had worked and lived in Johannesburg and many of my friends did not even know my Bechuanaland connection. The principle of saving my skin was anathema to my sense of African solidarity. I took pride in the fact that chiefs of the High Commission territories, among them Khama III of Bangwato, were members of the

House of Chiefs in the first constitution of the ANC. These chiefs had seemed more foresighted than many of their subjects who kept aloof from the struggle of the oppressed in South Africa. Although the majority of them earned their livelihood from employment in South Africa and received their education from there, they failed to perceive the economic and de facto political integration of the region. The counsellors of flight to domestic haven apparently had not read and studied an article in the *Optima* (an Anglo American Journal) by Dr W W Eiselen towards the end of 1958. Eiselen's article had been prompted by the £1 (one pound) a day campaign by SACTU (South African Congress of Trade Unions, a member of the Congress Alliance). In reply to this campaign and the clause of the Freedom Charter that says 'The people shall share in the wealth of the country', Eiselen sought to place the contribution of the economic cake in South Africa in proper perspective. He argued that those who advocated the sharing of South Africa's wealth with the 'Bantu' must understand that this wealth basically derives from the South African mines; that the mine labourers in the majority come from across the South African borders, Swaziland, Basutoland, Bechuanaland, Nyasaland and Tanganyika. The policy of sharing the wealth of South Africa therefore implied that it must be shared with all the 'Bantus' from the above-mentioned territories. This could not happen since these were foreigners. The logic of Herr Dokter's analysis appeared to disqualify the South African 'Bantus' by virtue of the fact that they were in the minority (in those days) in the mines. It was an attenuated argument for apartheid by an intellectual giant and architect of important aspects of apartheid.

There was another reason for sticking with the oppressed of South Africa. As soon as the Nationalists came to power it became clear they would not tolerate the independence of the High Commission territories. That is why Seretse's marriage unleashed all the venom of Afrikaner abuse and condemnation. At that juncture, however, one could not foresee the destabilisation threat. The concept of independence for the territories was still shrouded in an ambiguous outlook designed by the South Africa Constitution Act of 1909. This act brought about the Union of South Africa, a constitutional dispensation that excluded the black majority in South Africa and, imbued with characteristic colonial spirit and superior race arrogance, entertained future incorporation of the three High Commission territories of Bechuanaland, Basutoland and Swaziland. The incorporation ostensibly was to take place after consultation with the chiefs of these territories. In the programmes and blue prints of the successive white South African governments, the eventual incorporation was a foregone conclusion, a *fait accompli* of the near future. How could anyone reject the material benefits that would accrue by the mere act of annexation; employment in the gold mines by the able-bodied and the limited missionary education! Employment in the mines was full of hazards, permanent disablement, death and disease, but it was employment all the same and ensured one some form of subsistence while one was able-bodied. 'The natives would be grateful'. There was no employment opportunities in their countries. They would join the Union. It was a matter of time.

Except for the very few who had independent means of livelihood in the form of livestock, the majority of the population of these territories were forced by the economic circumstances of their countries to depend on South Africa and be grateful for it.

I was also one of those who were dependent and grateful. But I was consciously grateful to the ordinary South Africans who did not own the means of production and were exploited, particularly the discriminated against, oppressed and voteless black majority, who by their thankless sweat had raised South Africa to its economic status in Africa. There was no better way of expressing this gratitude than by active solidarity in their dark hour. Besides this theoretical consideration there was the practical aspect of economic and physical integration of South Africa and the High Commission territories. Dr W W Eiselen had highlighted it inadvertently in his *Optima* article.

At the beginning of 1964 I was asked to go into hiding in order to carry out the work of the organisation relatively unmolested. The security police were beginning to take an interest in me. The movement did not want to indulge them with an easy quarry. Neither did I. A full time functionary role held unromantic prospects. I knew it. Did my fiancee know it? Here would be an extreme test.

CHAPTER 3

Kidnapped

DETENTION

The black, green and gold colours of the ANC flag fluttered on the screen. The cinema audience got to their feet as the tune of Nkosi sikelel' iAfrika (the African national anthem) came over the loud speaker. The mixed audience resumed their seats at the end of the anthem. I have no memory of the movie although I watched it from beginning to end. The prelude was entrancing. It blurred my vision. The flag was not ANC but TANU (Tanzanian African National Union). I heard that later.

O R Tambo invited me to a parade of cadres of Umkhonto we Sizwe recently returned from a military academy in the USSR. He made the briefest speech that expressed succinctly the anger and the determination to settle scores with amabunu. He spoke the language of the ordinary man for the ordinary man. Only yesterday the men who took part in the military parade here, in Mandela camp, were advocates of non-violent methods of struggle. Now here they were far from home demonstrating their martial tendencies. I choked with conflicting emotions. Belligerent and pacifist.

The following night, in my Mwananji apartment, I was just preparing to retire, when there was a knock at the door. 'Boet Mike, Boet Mike, Vuka (Get up)!' I jumped out of bed at Maud's commanding voice. Outside a car was waiting to carry us to a party. There were five of us in the car. One passenger a high ranking member of Frelimo and the rest of the passengers, ladies, from South Africa – one a fiancee of the Frelimo official. The party, I was unofficially informed, was a ceremonial inauguration of guerrilla operations in Mozambique. Eduardo Mondlane, the President of Frelimo, had been expected from Europe but unfortunately he was held up somewhere and failed to arrive in time for the party.

It had taken the ANC almost 50 years to espouse violence as a method of struggle. Frelimo, apparently learning from our experience – the futility of talking the oppressor out of power – decided to make it hot for Portuguese colonialists from the start. Angolans had already resorted to armed struggle in 1961. Frelimo was off to a flying start. In South Africa, Rhodesia and Namibia, preparations were advancing. Southern Africa was proceeding headlong towards a conflagration. Nkosi sikelel' iAfrika (God Bless Africa), our prayer, for many years remained unanswered. Too late now. It was the fire.

Event followed event. All historic and stimulating. Mwalimu Julius Nyerere had irritated the West by importing Chinese instructors for his army. The first contingents of this Eastern trained army were

81

graduating and I had the honour to attend the passing-out parade. Mwalimu, and his Vice-President, Karume of Zanzibar, inspected the parade. It was an impressive ceremony. Though my ignorance in Swahili was absolute, I had no wish nor need for Mwalimu's speech in Swahili to be interpreted.

The four events above marked the highlights of my four week stay in Dar es Salaam. My colleagues in the National Secretariat had asked me to undertake a mission to the exile headquarters of the ANC, to report on the internal state of organisation as well as to discuss new structural arrangements to co-ordinate the internal and external wings of the liberation movement. I had left Johannesburg on August 1964. On that day, a Saturday, the *Rand Daily Mail* of that morning had published a smuggled letter from Ivan Schermbrucker in detention describing his torture. I remember Ivan making the point in the letter that to call on detainees not to talk was unrealistic because the security police torture methods were extremely effective. My mandate was to return to Johannesburg and submit a personal report and here was Ivan scaring the wits out of me! The mind could not stop to puzzle the dilemma: to return or not to return.

Independence in Tanzania was less than four years old and already the government was showing full commitment to the liberation of the rest of the continent. The liberation movements of Southern Africa, all had offices in Dar es Salaam and Mbeya in the south of the country in certain cases, and they all enjoyed the unstinted solidarity and hospitality of the government and the people of Tanzania. The ANC acknowledged their hospitality in song: 'When our freedom comes along, we shall need you, we shall love you for the things you have done for us, Oh Tanganyikans, here we are far from home . . .'

The attitude of the government of Tanzania to neo-colonialists was also frank and unambiguous. In response to the objections of the British and United States governments to Chinese instructors for the Tanzanian army, Mwalimu had made a few telling points: that the people of Tanzania had attained political independence and had the right to exercise it; that they were a non-aligned country and military assistance from a socialist country was but a small legitimate step towards the expression of non-alignment; that his inherited army had mutinied, and it had not been trained by the Chinese but by the British; that the British in fact had no cause to complain since they monopolised the education system of Tanzania. I was informed that one expatriate commenting on Mwalimu's speech blamed Karume: 'It was those communists in Zanzibar . . .' Was the white South African government any different or worse? They too blamed the communists for the struggle for freedom and independence. They too claimed to 'know what was good for the Bantu'. An African who tried to be independent-minded was a 'cheeky Bantu', probably misled by communists and liberals. Did the African have his own mind?

I returned from Tanzania very much inspired. Whatever happened

I had set foot in an independent African country. Moreover one that abhorred racialism. Here in independent Tanzania there was no sign of discrimination in reverse. The people were culturally assertive and nationalistic: 'Are you an Englishman?' was a spontaneous question if you happened to speak English to them. Otherwise 'inter-racial' conflict was non-existent. One would need the genius of the inventors of the colour bar to invent it.

Back in Bechuanaland I found the local security police-cum-immigration officers extraordinarily interested in me. They were aware of my nationality so they watched me from a distance. But even at that distance their presence was uncamouflaged. Everywhere I went they hovered in the background. I had my suspicions why I was being watched so closely. With their refined intelligence, gleaned from both the local sources and international connections, they would have known I had no designs against the Bechuanaland administration. Yet they shadowed me everywhere. I wondered to what vote they charged the expenses incurred in their surveillance. A futile poser at this late stage. It was pertinent though, since I spent five weeks in Bechuanaland. However I had a strong hunch that the Bechuanaland intelligence in this case worked a quarter of the time on their own behalf and three quarters of the time on agency obligations.

My hunch was confirmed when I arrived in Johannesburg in late October. Johannesburg was saturated with news. News. News. Bad news. Bad news and scary gossip. A sum was on my head. That was pretty awful. Almost all the members of the Committee I worked with were detained. The exception were two members: one had skipped the country while I was away and another had not been taken in. It was gloomy. The day following my return to Johannesburg one of my detained colleagues, Bartholomew Hlapane, was released. He immediately got in touch with Kipps, the one safe member of the depleted committee. 'Has Comrade Mike come back?' asked Hlapane with suspicious interest. 'No, he is not back,' replied Kipps, lying and wary. The two, of course, together with other members of the Committee, were officially the only persons who knew about my mission.

Kipps was to be praised for his white lie. A day after my return Hlapane is suddenly released and on the scent! The police in Bechuanaland had definitely tipped off the South African security police. They deduced that since I was missing from Bechuanaland I had slipped back into South Africa and they alerted the South Africans. I pumped Kipps' hand: 'Well done, comrade. Barth has to be watched!' To watch Bartholomew effectively meant protecting other key personnel who were exposed, such as Kipps himself. So I suggested that he leave his employment and go into semi-hiding. Kipps was one of the few members with potential whom we had taken steps to keep in the background in the legal days of the ANC. Now these reserves had a major role to play. Unfortunately police methods were winkling many of them out before they could prove their true mettle.

Hlapane got wind of my presence in Johannesburg by some comrade who still trusted him. He went back to Kipps, disgusted, probably after passing the intelligence windfall to the police: 'Why did you lie to me about Mike?' he stormed at Kipps. Kipps defended himself by admitting that he had learnt of Mike's return after meeting Barth and he understood Mike was in Johannesburg for only two days and had returned to Bechuanaland for some unfinished business. Not to worry. He was coming back. Barth's feeling of being double crossed was assuaged. He went back to the police to report. These goings-on leaked out to me during my interrogation. My original suspicions against Hlapane in 1963 were vindicated. Suspicion on BP police role was also vindicated. They alerted the South African police about my disappearance from BP and my possible presence in South Africa.

Before I left on the mission to Tanzania, underground work was hard but liveable. Back from Dar es Salaam it became unbearable. Whereas before I had been in hiding, which was tantamount to self-imprisonment, now I was in hiding and on the run. A weird paradox. Most of my colleagues were in detention and had been tortured mercilessly. To save themselves from eternal torture and harmful disclosures, they presented me as the key functionary who knew all the answers. They were quite right in the assumption that I would stay out of the country and out of reach. Theirs was the correct strategy under the circumstances. Unfortunately they did not realise they were dealing with a programmed traffic robot that flashes green, amber and red, traffic or no traffic. So I came back. I had been mandated to come back and report. It did not matter that I had one colleague to report to, I came back. To report.

On hearing of my return, the detainees sent one frantic smuggled message after another: Run back whence you came. Amabunu will castrate you if they lay their hands on you! Yes, I was going to run back whence I came but I wanted to tie up a few things first. Nuts! There is nothing you can tie here; your arrest is only going to help untie more things. Run!

The police were hot on my heels with Barth playing the tracker hound. His car, the legitimate property of the organisation but now his by possession, sped from one Soweto township to another. Everywhere he went Bartholomew tactfully raised the question of my whereabouts. Some might have seen me the previous day and others the previous year, all of them were genuinely in the dark about my permanent abode. Simply because I had none. The police did not depend solely on Hlapane, they studied my dossier(s) carefully and made some deductions about my social friends and relatives. All of them were raided. Children were awakened in the middle of the night, wardrobes ransacked, and old correspondence read without permission and then tossed provocatively all over the floor. Those who demanded search warrants or tried to demur were silenced with a stern look or a threat: 'Hou jou bek, of ek sluit jou toe! (Shut up, or I lock you up!)' Many of these friends and relatives had not seen me for months, even years. Police harassment aroused a lot of concern for my safety. The cry of 'run' reached a crescendo when Piet Beyleveld gave evidence in the trial of Bram Fischer and others. In his evidence Piet mentioned my name several times. The publicity given to this evidence plus the unabating police raids on innocent relatives and friends affected all men of good will. 'Run whilst there is time and place. Run!'

My colleague and friend Kipps was picked up by Captain Swanepoel. Swanepoel was on a routine patrol, probably with a prayer in his heart to get hold of Kipps or Mike. Swanepoel had never met Kipps. The two did not know each other except by name. Swanepoel stopped Kipps and demanded his pass. 'So waar is god', there he was. One of the two wanted men. The Captain emitted an Afrikaner cry of elation and performed a short jig. 'Ons het hom! (We have got him)!' Swanepoel danced more on searching Kipps. There was a letter addressed to Mike Dingake from my cousin in Bechuanaland delivered through the channels of the ANC. It was an innocent letter except that it deeply implicated Kipps. How was he to deny knowledge of my whereabouts?

The day Kipps was taken we had an appointment for one o'clock. At one o'clock when he failed to appear at the rendezvous, I sensed trouble. Between us, we had developed punctuality to a religion, a religion we practised with all the fanaticism of the devout. Unpunctual behaviour on the part of either of us was a warning signal. Half an hour after the appointed hour I had given up Kipps and moved from the venue of our meeting. It was not enough to move away from the meeting place; I had to move out of my current hideout. If you hide from the police you must be prepared to be on the move all the time. I was on the move. On the run.

The police of course worked on Kipps. He informed me after his release. I do not know what things he told the police but I know he did not reveal my previous hideouts. I believe his exceptional wit must have enabled him to run rings around the police. It was an impressive performance by Kipps. His arrest, his interrogation, his role after release and his flight from the country were all dramatic. Shortly after his release in February 1965, both of us left the country. Johannesburg was getting too hot for me. Moreover, not only friends and relatives screamed 'get out'! The ANC, inside and outside, instructed me to leave. My asset status could rapidly turn into a liability if I were detained.

Bechuanaland was preparing for elections when I arrived back home.

Four parties, the Botswana Democratic Party, the Botswana People's Party (Matante), the Botswana People's Party (Motsete), and Botswana Independence Party (MPHO), were contesting the elections. The most interesting reaction during the run-up to the elections was that of some farmers, predominantly Afrikaners along the Tuli Block. They feared the more radical parties: BPP (Matante) and BIP might win the elections, in which case they expected unpleasant relationships – confiscation of their property and who knows what else. It was all nonsense. None of the parties had proclaimed any hostile intentions against other groups. But projection is a common disguise of conflict and anxiety. By ascribing one's own motives and attitudes to others, one feels justifiably threatened where no threat exists. And it was not surprising the Afrikaners in Bechuanaland would feel jittery, not because of what the prospective independent government of Botswana threatened to do to them, but because of what they knew the South African government was doing to the Batswana and all Africans. The BDP was considered moderate and a few adaptable Afrikaners joined it. Apparently some supported the BDP because, after all Seretse Khama was married to a white woman and was evidently free of racial prejudice or, hopefully his marriage made him an honorary white and he would apply apartheid against his fellow Batswana. That view seems farfetched, but not after listening to the story of one Van Z of Lobatse. Van Z attended a BDP election rally in Lobatse which was addressed by Seretse Khama. Oom Van Z applauded many points made by Seretse during his speech but when Seretse started expressing himself on South Africa's apartheid policy, Van Z could not stomach it. He turned to Van Z Junior: 'Seun, nou praat hy kak; kom ons loop! (Son, now he is talking shit; let us go!)'

Eventually, the Van Z's of Botswana not only left the election rallies in a huff, they left Botswana for South Africa, or sent their children to schools in Rhodesia and South Africa. Among them were English speaking Van Z's. Shortly before the elections, Dr Verwoerd, a shrewd politician he was, had secretly lifted Seretse and Ruth's ban to visit South Africa. He had also assured the Afrikaners of South African citizenship, whether they held or qualified for Botswana citizenship or not. Clearly the government of Dr Verwoerd envisaged some uncordial relations between Botswana and the Boers. It took steps to ensure continuity of comfort and privilege to their own blood.

Whereas in Johannesburg the security police hunt for me was hearsay from those who were arrested, raided and generally harassed in my name, in Bechuanaland, especially in Lobatse where I settled, police surveillance was first hand, intimidating and ubiquitous. Both the Bechuanaland and South African security police were involved, working independently and jointly. Bechuanaland police went on the first shift. Early in the morning they were noticeable, cycling round the yard I was staying, in twos or threes. Later in the morning when I walked to town, three, sometimes four, overtook me on the way, each greeting politely as he cycled past: 'Dumela rra' or 'Dumela Mr Dingake'. Outside the post office a known South African security officer of the rank of lieutenant parked his car and sat reading what appeared to be a magazine. Every time I went to the post office this man sat in his car; waited and watched. I complained to Mr Higgins – Chief Immigration Officer-cum-security officer – about the provocative shadowing by his men and the alien post office sentinel. As far as his men were concerned, it was for my own security, according to Mr Higgins. 'I can dispense with it if it is for that reason,' I informed him. 'And what about the well-known South African police officer who patrols the streets of Lobatse brazenly and parks his car strategically outside the post office?' 'Yes, I know he is a Special Branch man, Mr Dingake, but what can I do. He comes here on a valid passport.' Mr Higgins' argument was baseless and dishonest. The validity of the man's passport was not in question; obviously he was no fool to expose himself to instant expulsion if he was on sacred duties of operating an intelligence network in a foreign land. What was in question were his bona fides. Was he in the pay of the Bechuanaland security police or the South African security police? Mr Higgins did not listen to my arguments; the man had a valid passport so he had a valid reason to make a mockery of the security of Bechuanaland. Some queer relationship seemed to exist between the two security forces. Subservience and domination interacted, resulting in co-operation detrimental to the interests of the country and the refugees.

Higgins was an interesting man. Unlike his counterpart in Francistown, Innes-Kerr, he never sought any confrontation with me. He acknowledged my citizenship and was always courteous, where Innes-Kerr could be abrupt, discourteous and name-calling. Innes-Kerr once called me a 'renegade' to my face when we had one of our unfriendly verbal exchanges. A renegade Motswana. Not Higgins. He was subtle with insinuation. Funny, he irritated me more than the open and frank Innes-Kerr. One afternoon he (Higgins) rang me. 'Mr Dingake, we have an ANC refugee here; could you come and meet him.' I got mad. He was mischievous. He knew very well who was responsible for refugees arriving from South Africa. I was unconnected. But Higgins wanted to have a dig at me, to embarrass me. He was trying to imply that in spite of my apparent aloofness from refugee involvement I was one with them. He was not deceived: that was the message of the provocative telephone call.

Unemployment was the scourge of our stay in Lobatse. Soon after our arrival from Johannesburg, my wife had mixed news for me, a blend of good and bad. She was expecting our first child. I stopped smoking. Cigarettes like all luxuries were a heavy expense item and I smoked like a chimney. Our meagre savings had to be allocated frugally to last us through part of the nine months. Someone gave me advice: buy goats and sell them in town. Apply for a small livestock licence from the Botswana Meat Commission. I did that. Somewhere mid my sentence in Robben Island, I learnt from someone that one of the headlines in British newspapers reporting my arrest was 'A Bechuanaland Cattle Farmer Detained'. It was typical newspaper sensationalism. I did not have a cow to my name by the time of my arrest. Only a few goats for speculation.

On 24 November, the day my daughter was born, I received a phone call from Tennyson Makiwane, the ANC chief representative in Lusaka, suggesting that I visit Lusaka. There had been a similar suggestion before which I had declined on the argument that I could not leave my wife alone in her state. The suggestion seemed reckless on two grounds. Telephone communication was unsafe in South Africa. It was equally unsafe in Bechuanaland. Bechuanaland was in all respects a satellite of South Africa. Secondly, Tennyson expected me to travel through Rhodesia which had just declared unilateral independence. For many years we had known an unholy alliance existed between South Africa, Portuguese East Africa and Rhodesia. Travelling through Rhodesia could be courting disaster. I felt the decision could not be taken lightly – could Tennyson think about it and consult others in view of my strong reservations.

A week later a telegram, couched in cryptic language but expressing slight impatience at my delay, arrived. I discussed the telegram with my wife. We both felt uneasy. What made us fearful was that after nine months in the country, the dual police surveillance had not abated. Instead it had intensified. And in Rhodesia there was the cloud of Smith's UDI.

In the end, however, my sense of loyalty to the South African freedom struggle prevailed. I argued with myself and my wife that Smith's UDI would not affect me. After all I was a Motswana holding a Bechuanaland passport and a British subject entitled to British protection and justice. The worst that could happen on my way through Rhodesia was for the Rhodesian authorities to deny me passage to Lusaka by declaring me a prohibited immigrant and sending me back to Bechuanaland. Nonetheless there was some sixth sense that scrupled against the trip. It was reckless. A senseless adventure destined to culminate in disaster. The sixth sense contested with my blind sense of loyalty. Nothing venture, nothing win. I took the plunge.

The ill-fated trip seemed doomed from the start. Police surveillance, which had visibly slackened in the immediate past, intensified after the Lusaka telegram. It might have been due to my own heightened alertness on the eve of my departure. Whatever it was, police and suspected police informers kept a close vigil by me. The morning of my departure, I walked into the bank in Lobatse to draw some cash for my train ticket. The teller picked up my savings book and walked up to the accountant's dais. After sly glances at me and whispered exchanges he returned to serve me. I wondered why the unusual behaviour of the teller. Just the nervousness of a guilty mind? If the bank officials behaved suspiciously I could not trust the station master. So for my train ticket someone had to buy it for me. To reinforce my precautions I organised a car to take me to Ramotswa station. Lobatse station was always teeming with police. My trick was to miss the train deliberately and then drive out leisurely minutes after it had passed and catch it either in Ramotswa or farther beyond. I boarded the train at Ramotswa after a couple of police who had been obviously waylaying our car had flagged us down to ask an irrelevant question. One of the two got to the platform with me and walked about aimlessly until the train pulled out of the station.

Without any doubt the Bechuanaland police were on full *qui vive*, and if they were, as I was certain they were, what to do? Get off at the next station? And how would I explain my change of mind? Could I admit fear? Could I fearlessly admit that I noticed police watchfulness and feared for my safety? To admit fear is a sign of guts. I had none. My salvation lay in the passport. Yes. The worst they could do to it was to stamp 'Prohibited Immigrant' on it and boot me out of their raped country.

I locked myself up in my compartment and went through my luggage item by item to ascertain that there was not even the tiniest scrap of paper bearing an 'undesirable' message, slogan or any other telltale. My suitcase was clean. But in one pocket of my jacket, I found a leaflet calling for solidarity with Bram Fischer who had been arrested on the same day Smith's UDI was declared. I read the leaflet and thought of Bram – pictured him in his comfortable Oaklands suburb home entertaining friends, black and white. I recalled a common argument among ghetto-dwellers about his nationality. Invariably those who learned for the first time that Bram was an Afrikaner queried the 'implausible' disclosure. The reaction tended to suggest that this good man was being maligned by associating himself with the Afrikaners. The prejudice against Afrikaners is incredible. Yet Bram was an Afrikaner, the son of a former Orange Free State chief justice and grandson of the first President of the Afrikaner Republic of the Orange Free State. He was married to Molly Krige, the niece of General J C Smuts, another prominent Afrikaner and twice prime minister of the Union of South Africa.

Bram was a pukka Afrikaner. His personality tended to confuse many, especially the blacks. Generally, Afrikaners were reputed to be crude, hostile, sectarian, arrogant and complex-ridden. In contrast Bram was polished, friendly, sociable, humble and self-confident.

Following his conviction for statutory sabotage and a sentence of life imprisonment many editorials were written about this un-Afrikaans Afrikaner. The one I remember was in one of the Johannesburg dailies. It characterised Bram Fischer as an idealist and a man who, like his colleagues, mistakenly believed a 'revolutionary situation' existed in South Africa.

Whoever wrote the article misinterpreted Bram Fischer. As a Marxist, Bram would have vehemently denied the tag of idealism. The philosophy of Marx is based on materialism. It interprets the world on the undistorted facts of history and philosophy. On the basis of these facts it foresees inevitable change from an exploitative society to a society which will be free of exploitation of man by man. For the anti-Marxists and the non-Marxists such an interpretation and projection of history is idealistic, a pipe dream. Exploitation is divinely ordained, and anybody who says otherwise irrespective of the substance of his theories is Utopian, an idealist of the first order. Bram was not an idealist. As a Marxist he saw further than his denigrators.

That Bram, like his colleagues, believed a revolutionary situation existed was another misinterpretation and distortion of his motivation and outlook. Bram did what he did when he did it, because he was a man of his convictions – he believed attainment of freedom entails sacrifices; his record of struggle and association with the most oppressed sections of the population committed him to a complete identification with their aspirations and sacrifices. In leaving his comfortable home and his prosperous legal practice Bram did not envisage immediate or personal compensation; he was doing his simple duty as a freedom fighter and contributing in his own humble way to the comfort, social equality and racial harmony of posterity. The majority of white South Africans choose to remain part of the problem of the country. A few opt to be part of the solution. Bram was one of the top few. He paid with his life – for the freedom of all South Africans.

On this fateful train journey, I read this call for solidarity with Bram and pictured the material loss he sustained by leaving his comfortable white home, his lovable children and his flourishing practice. Unlike the majority of freedom fighters who had nothing to lose but their chains, he had a lot to lose.

I tore the incriminating leaflet into pieces, dumped the bits into the toilet, flushed it and watched the water do the rest. I resumed my seat with a clear conscience of freedom from telltale evidence.

At Figtree railway station the train stopped for a long time. All the time I sat in my compartment and read an uninteresting novel. Then I heard someone in the corridor asking a relevant question: 'Is there an African in this coach?' 'Yes!' answered one of the white schoolboys who were playing in the corridor. 'Where is he?' 'In there,' replied the same schoolboy. There was a knock at my door. Two faces, one black, one white, peered into my compartment. 'Are you Michael Dingake?' enquired the white face. 'Yes, I am he,' I admitted. Sergeant MacKay then introduced himself and his colleague. They were the British

South African (BSA) police, they informed me, and 'may we search your luggage?' they asked. 'Why?' 'Oh, well you see, our duties entitle us.' 'Go ahead then,' I gesticulated with my palms towards the luggage. No, the duo wanted to do the search outside the train. 'No, that can't happen. I might miss my connection in Bulawayo.' 'Mr Dingake, you know the Lusaka connection is in the evening, besides we are also driving to Bulawayo. We will give you a lift to the station.' I groused futilely.

On the platform the duo became a trio. The search proceeded methodically. Every seam of every garment was gingerly felt, the lining of the suitcase was frisked and all pockets were turned inside out. My small livestock licence from the Botswana Meat Commission was picked up and studied. 'So you deal in small livestock?' 'Yes, I do.' 'What else do you deal in – terrorists?' the rude one interrogated. One, the polite one, intervened and mediated in the verbal skirmish that ensued after the impudently defamatory question. Our drive to Bulawayo was sustained by a make-do conversation on rain. In Southern Africa, whites and blacks, for decades shared very few things in common. One of the few was and still is, the weather.

Bulawayo is not very far from Figtree and before the rain conversation dried up we arrived. Not at the railway station, but at a police station. 'Khulul amanyathelo (Take off your shoes) . . .' a half-dozen police voices were chorusing to me. 'Khulul amanyathelo! Khulul amanyathelo!' The cacophony was deafening and confusing. I had been led by devious ways into a police station. And the moment I was deposited into what at first appeared to be an empty office, my captors beat an apparently well-rehearsed hasty retreat without informing me of my fate. The men who now sang 'Khulul amany-athelo' jarringly, suddenly emerged from under the counters and from nowhere. It was a dramatic turn of events. Inexplicable too. 'Why am I under arrest?' I asked. None of the dramatis personae was prepared to come forth with a denouement. 'Charge me! Charge me! Let me know what I am in here for.'

I was led to the cell protesting. Friday night, Saturday night passed uneventfully. Sunday morning, the Superintendent ('Super') of the police station came round at my request. He was blank when I demanded to know about my arrest. He did not know anything. In spite of his ignorance, which implied that my detention was illegal, he refused to authorise my release. He however gave instructions that I had to be moved to another cell which housed three Zapu activists (one of them Ntuli, deputy minister in the first cabinet of Mugabe, L Gumpo, and Madzimbamoto, who created headlines contesting the emergency regulations of Smith). The four of us did not know why we were detained, but since the other three confessed to being Zapu members, it was clear it was a political detention.

On Monday morning we were called to the police charge office to check our property. Our shoes were restored to us. 'You are free to go home,' we were informed. When we tried to leave through the front door, we were courteously asked to use the back door. The back door of course led into the police station yard and into an open police van. 'Inside!' The policeman's finger pointed into the van. Inside we found our detention warrants. We were detained in terms of the emergency regulations that had been promulgated with Ian Smith's UDI. It had taken the rebel government of Smith four days to come out openly against its opponents and an opponent of its ally. Was it inefficiency, insolent newfound bureaucracy or just an exercise in psychological torture?

From Central Police Station we moved to Grey Street gaol and from there to Khami medium security prison. Khami prison was divided into the maximum security prison, the common-law prisoners' section and the political prisoners' section. The three Zapu men were obviously veterans of the struggle in Zimbabwe. Khami prison was a 'holiday resort' for them. As we came into the prison yard, detainees peeping through the cell windows were already shouting their names in welcome. Nobody shouted my name. I was a stranger in a strange country. Or was I? In the cell someone recognised me. It was Francis Moyo. Francis and I had worked for one firm in Eloff Street, Johannesburg – Thrupps. We had lived together in Sophiatown before I moved to Alexandra. In Alexandra I had become acquainted with his elder brother who was trying a 'dairy business'.

With my three friends from Bulawayo I had been secretive and non-committal in connection with speculation about my arrest. Francis knew about my involvement with the ANC although I did not know about his with Zapu. We expressed fears about my ultimate fate – a victim of the 'unholy alliance'. The reunion was enlightening and stimulating. The following morning from the other cells there were more detainees who knew me or who knew my father in Bobonong or my sister or her family in Gungwe (Rhodesia). Southern Africa is a small region.

Conditions in the political section of Khami medium security prison were easy and tolerable. The same could not be said of the common-law prisoners' section across the fence. On a number of occasions inmates of the political section felt called upon to intervene with the prison authorities when screams or reports of brutalities came to their notice. Though we were often told to mind our own business, in practice representation from the political section audibly reduced the tension in the other section. It was not always that the 'Super' (Superintendent) made concessions to us. Shortly after Christmas almost the entire political section was afflicted with diarrhoea. We traced the disease to our diet of beans. I was among the deputation that saw the 'Super' to complain about the beans. The 'Super' was unco-operative and aggressive. There was nothing wrong with the beans and he did not want any trouble. Further, he reminded one of the delegation of what could happen if we started trouble. The 'Super' was alluding to a previous occasion when he had ordered the warders to open fire on the inmates because they allegedly disobeyed an order to go into their cells. We were not intimidated. We boycotted the beans and continued our representation. Eventually, a fresh supply of beans arrived. The afflictive ration was withdrawn. It was later revealed there had been 'nothing wrong' with the beans. Our tummies were just 'fussy' to a preservative with which the beans had been treated.

The three weeks I spent in Khami medium prison went fast. I read two new books I had not been able to read in South Africa: Nelson Mandela's *No Easy Walk to Freedom*, and Chief Luthuli's *Let My People Go*. Here in Khami medium there were no single cells, only communal cells. Revolutionary songs as well as revolutionary discussions went on continuously, inside and outside the cells. The main debate was of course UDI. What it meant to the Zimbabwean freedom struggle and to the struggle in South Africa and Mozambique and how it would be resolved. There was a lot of optimism about freedom prospects following UDI by Smith. I was given a standing invitation to the imminent Zimbabwean independence. 'Been to the Victoria Falls?' 'Yes I have!' 'The Zimbabwe Ruins?' 'No I haven't.' 'Well, come to our independence celebrations. We'll take you on a tour to these historic ruins!'

I had never been to an independence celebration before. The previous year, I had passed through Zambia a couple of weeks before the country celebrated its independence. I had to miss the event. My 'idealism' was propelling me back to South Africa to expedite the independence of that southern tip of Africa. A big question mark hung over my prospects of celebrating the independence of Botswana, my country of birth. When it came to independence celebrations I seemed to be jinxed. Normally an optimist in general, I was pessimistic at the imminence of Zimbabwean independence and my sampling of it. In the debate that centred on the how and the when of independence in Rhodesia I found myself expressing an unpopular viewpoint and advocating a new phase of struggle in Rhodesia. The British Prime Minister Harold Wilson sporting an oversized entourage, had descended upon Smith's UDI/Rhodesia breathing fire and brimstone within days of the rebellious declaration. He had gone back muttering political imprecations against Smith's regime. Who would not be impressed? I was not. The elation in the South African media, press and radio, implied open connivance by the Pretoria regime. Smith had a strong ally and accomplice in his adventure, on his doorstep. The sanctimonious noises from Harold & Co were but a predictable dramatic show, ironically to expose further the decline of the British Empire. The sun of the British Empire was setting everywhere. Harold Wilson's noises soon became a whimper when he was being urged to act to maintain or salvage that real but intangible British image. No! He was not going to be pushed. One could see the pushing receding after that. But not from Smith's side. Smith had to push to consolidate his UDI. He pushed. Members of the Judiciary who took their allegiance to the previous constitution seriously or could not reconcile their ethical code with the new regime could go, Smith would not lose any sleep over their unmanly qualms. The Governor-General, the representative of the Queen in Rhodesia, was plucked of his feathers, one by one. He was divested of his symbols of power and authority. He looked pathetic trying to uphold the royal image without the symbols of the sceptre and the crown. The British press chided Smith and goaded Wilson to do something to restore the dignity of the Crown and unseat the rebel. Speculation as to whether the British government could take up arms against Smith was of course dismissed as impracticable. The British take up arms against their own kith and kin? What insanity!

The Labour government, in order to save a small part of the face, flew a contingent force of the Highlanders, who were stationed in Swaziland, to Botswana – ostensibly as the vanguard of 'disciplinary force' to be engaged when the situation warranted it. A radio station was installed outside Francistown in Botswana to monitor events inside Rhodesia and beam anti-Smith propaganda into the country. It was grandiose and comical.

My viewpoint was that nothing would come of the whole effort. I was cynical. What made me more so was that the whole anti-Smith media propaganda was concerned with British interests, image and prestige. Not with the interests of the majority of the inhabitants who had long struggled and suffered for their freedom. That was why I maintained two points: that Smith, however much I disagreed with him, had exposed the perfidy of Albion. For years now the British government had wavered on the question of Rhodesia's independence. In my opinion they did so because they could not countenance the prospect of majority rule. Secondly, for real independence to come to Rhodesia, the majority indigenous people had to fight for it. Hard. They had to take up arms to regain their independence. No coloniser/oppressor would ever bow gracefully from the stage of dominance, especially the highly decorated one of Rhodesia.

In Khami there was much to reflect upon. The politics of the region and my own fate. Every day of my stay in Khami convinced me of an international plot – between South Africa and Rhodesia – to consign me to the 'haven' of 'disappeared' persons. I did not want to disappear without trace. I smuggled out two letters. One to my wife and one to the sender of the fateful telegram. Let me disappear, but at least the world should know at what point of my journey I disappeared and why.

A day or two after the new year I was transferred to Khami maximum prison. Things were looking up. I was shunted into an isolation cell and looked after by a grumpy set of warders who grunted, growled

94

and cursed most of the time. The change from medium to maximum was enormous. I missed the warm companionship and the stimulating discussion I enjoyed a few metres away in the medium gaol.

On 5 January 1966 I was transferred from Khami maximum to Grey Street gaol in Bulawayo. The following morning Sergeant MacKay appeared and informed me I was to be deported. For this he drove me to the Immigration Office. While he closeted himself in the office with the immigration officer, I completed some forms in a back room assisted by a black staff member of the immigration department. My name, surname, nationality, country of birth, passport number, date issued and date of expiry, were the main particulars required on the forms I sat and completed in the immigration backroom. My assistant fingerprinted me as well. When I asked why I had to have my fingerprints taken he answered, 'It is the law', full stop. I reserved my cross examination. It took the immigration officer a long time to round off their hush-hush dialogue. When I was finally summoned before the immigration officer, he adjusted his tie, scrutinised my blank face and pronounced last judgment and sentence. Paraphrased, the judgment was, that from the sixth day of January 1966, I, Michael Kitso Dingake, was a prohibited immigrant (PI) in Rhodesia. The sentence, equally paraphrased, was: repatriation. There was a warning: disregard of the order would be penalised by severe imprisonment. 'The officer (Sergeant MacKay) will give you your passport.' The promise was not fulfilled.

Outside the Immigration Office building three plainclothes police, one white and two blacks, sat in a parked car. Before I was handcuffed to the two blacks, one on each wrist, I demanded my passport. 'Don't worry, Mr Dingake, you will get your passport,' I was assured. 'Why must it be postponed?' I wanted to know. 'You'll get it, Dingake. I can't use your passport, can I? It is yours.' We drove along the beautiful wide streets of Bulawayo, but we drove west, then north, then east. Then a signpost: '200 miles to Beitbridge'. Eight eyes turned robot-like and focused on my facial expression. Ensconced between the two of my colour-brothers, I felt innocent and unruffled. Deadpan. Four weeks in Rhodesian prisons had helped my rehearsal for this performance. Sergeant MacKay must have felt let down by his futile dramatics. The anticipated hysteria from me failed to materialise.

We did Bulawayo to Beitbridge in record time. At the Beitbridge police station where I stopped with my black escorts while the two white police rushed to the Immigration Office to clinch the transaction, a drunken black constable abused me and called me 'terrorist'. The white duo returned rubbing their hands in glee. 'Come, Mr Dingake. Let's take a short walk.' We walked to the Rhodesian border Immigration Office. Outside, in front of the office, paced a South African security officer. Inside, standing behind the counter, stood Lieutenant Dirker grinning. Through some small window of a room that looked like a refreshment room peered a black face. There was mutual recognition. Dirker barked a harsh objection when my acquaintance tried to greet me. Except for Lt Dirker and the black Rhodesian, the Immigration Office was empty. It was 12.30 pm. The lunch hour was still ahead. The proceedings were formal and brief. 'Lieutenant,' said MacKay to Dirker, 'here is your man!' 'Dingake,' I was addressed by MacKay after the handover, 'here is your passport.' Lieutenant Dirker snatched the passport from MacKay. 'Give it here.' After the bizarre proceedings there was an exchange of smiles, hearty bye-byes and allround bonhomie. We crossed the Limpopo river into the Transvaal, South Africa. 'Why did you leave Johannesburg? You must have missed it a lot. Eh, Dingake?' Dirker was in his element.

INTERROGATION

'Teen die muur, teen die muur! (Against the wall, against the wall!) . . .' several voices commanded. Kicks and blows accompanied the command. 'Teen die muur! Teen die muur!' Seven security police led by Captain Swanepoel shouted abuse and assaulted me because I refused to make a statement. The assault continued for a long hour in a crammed cell of Compol Building, Pretoria. At one stage, one lieutenant, Van Rensburg, tried live wires while Swanepoel was out. The captain ruled against electric shocks when he came back: 'Nee, donder julle hom net! (No just beat him up!)' Blows rained from all sides. Blows. Abuse. More blows. More abuse. I had read somewhere that the human body could absorb unlimited punishment. I wished the hypothesis, that the human body could absorb unlimited punishment would be confirmed by my own personal experience (though I did not mind death). When sweat was pouring down my face and my hurting body, Captain Van Rensburg walked in and 'pleaded' with his colleagues to allow him to have a chat with me in camera (there were two Van Rensburgs, a lieutenant and a captain, but unrelated – the captain was nicknamed 'Smiler' by his colleagues; he did not smile much but he played a role of a charmer). The plea was granted. 'Smiler' and I transferred into a spacious office where I was offered a cosy sofa. The Captain noticed me eyeing an unbarred window overlooking the street. He moved quickly to shut the window.

'Mike, I do not like what has been happening to you. Those men are brutes. I would like to help you. I don't want you to make an incriminating statement. But if you give me a little information about the ANC, what sort of organisation it is, its aims and objectives, I'll go back to those pigs and tell them, "Leave him alone, he has talked, he has said something. Here"' and he looked at me plaintively.

I was not persuaded. Another security man who had tried in vain to interrogate me shortly after my arrival in Pretoria Local Prison came into the office, studied my woebegone appearance and offered me a cigarette. I declined the offer with tremendous effort. Though I had stopped smoking for some months the craving for cigarettes was upon me in full force at the moment the offer was made.

The intruding Security Branch man studied my dishevelled appearance further and gave me a look that said: 'I told you, you would shit and talk.' I had not done either yet. To the 'intruder' I looked finito, kaput. There was no way I could escape either. Captain 'Smiler' continued to plead with me after the intruder had left the office. 'Well, if you won't co-operate with me, I am sorry for what is going to happen to you. Do you know Captain Swanepoel? He does not joke. I am the only one who can restrain him.' I remained unco-operative in spite of the warning.

'Co-operation' is a basic term in the policies, programmes and ideology of the apartheid government. The government department that administers the woes of the Africans was, until recently, known by the name, the Department of Co-operation and Development. The title is a misnomer. A cynical euphemism. Neither co-operation nor development characterises the department nor is it envisaged in the long term, even allowing the rider that development is along 'own' lines, 'parallel' or separate. There is no development in political, social and economic life for the Africans in South Africa. Disenfranchisement, discrimination and poverty have not been eased since 1910. If anything, the lot of the Africans is worsening with the application of cosmetics meant to daub these ugly features of life in South Africa. 'Deterioration' in place of 'development' would better describe the one element of the government department entrusted with African affairs.

Co-operation should be replaced by 'coercion' to complete the picture of the department. The department should have been the Department of Coercion and Deterioration. In South Africa the Africans are coerced in everything from cradle to grave. They are coerced to regard themselves as inferior and to look upon whites as their superiors; they are coerced to live where they live in the ghettos; to accept bantustans, to imbibe 'Bantu Education', to earn starvation wages in the urban areas or to starve to death in the 'reserves'; they are coerced to form or join organisations that undermine their own interests and promote their oppressors' interests, the moribund Native Representative Councils or modern Community Councils and Black Local Authorities; to dissociate themselves from their representative organisations through bans, banishments, house arrests, intimidation and detentions. In detention they are tortured and coerced to make incriminating statements against themselves and give evidence against their colleagues. It is co-operation. 'Samewerking' in Afrikaans. 'Jy moet saam werk. (You must co-operate)'.

In the Compol building cell I was beaten to make me co-operate. In the spacious office of the same building there was an attempt to hoodwink me with glib talk. It was a softening-up process aimed at coerced co-operation. It felt good to resist while I could. I resisted. Captain 'Smiler' led me out of the office to the 'torture chamber'. After the interval the interrogators were more invigorated. Captain Coetzee, tall, taciturn and sinewy, let loose with a solid punch to the solar plexus. My lights went out. I came to with water dripping all over me. Difficult to guess how long I was out, but my interrogators seemed scared to continue their free for all punch-and-kick game. Instead I was made to stand on a marked spot away from the wall. The contingent of my interrogators was now divided into three teams of two with the seventh man, Captain Swanepoel, acting as supervisor. The three teams worked in relays. It was 19 January 1966.

For 12 days since I arrived from Bulawayo I had been expecting this interrogation to take place. The delay was terrible torture. Ex-detainees had informed me that interrogation took place immediately after arrest. Why was I being tortured by this postponement of torture? It is worse not to know the form the torture is going to take. But worst to know the certainty of torture, yet to be ignorant of the form as well as the time. When is this torture coming? I want to get done with it! Torture, hurry! I was scared, but tried not to be scared by invoking the bravado of Julius Caesar: 'Danger knows full well, that Caesar is more dangerous than he . . .'

Actually my interrogation had started the moment we left the Beitbridge immigration office after the 'handing over'. Lieutenant Dirker had fired the first shots: 'Where is Stocks-and-dice? Are you a member of the South African Communist Party? How many terrorists have you infiltrated into the country?' When I ignored the questions Dirker made threats: 'Ha! you are one of those who say they won't talk. Don't worry you'll talk until we say "Hokaai (enough)".' Dirker tried another line of interrogation: 'Where is Tom Nkobi? Does he still want to take over South Africa? Huh! He can hardly take over a lavatory . . . Dingake, one day we are going to run over the so-called independent states up to Cairo!' The bait failed to work. I listened and kept my peace. At Pietersburg, one of the Northern Transvaal towns, Dirker reminded me that I had attended Secondary School there and that my father had been born in that area. He was right about me. My father had definitely been born in Palapye BP. It was my grandfather he was referring to. I was amazed nevertheless by the extent of their investigations.

Warrant Officer 'Rasie' Erasmus, our driver from Beitbridge, drove past Pretoria Local Prison. It was unexpected. All the way from Beitbridge I believed our destination to be Pretoria Local. It was a welcome turn of events. Pretoria and Johannesburg are not very far from each other in kilometres. In reputation they are poles apart. Pretoria is the administrative capital of South Africa, teeming with civil servants, overwhelmingly Afrikaner. Their attitudes very often reflect the law they administer. Racially prejudiced, harsh, intolerant and brutish. Johannesburg is the industrial and commercial capital of South Africa. Its population is cosmopolitan, more worldly and inclined to a more or less laissez-faire racial attitude. Racial discrimination obviously applies in both cities. It is a fundamental legal concept and practice in South Africa. It is grounded in the constitution, statutes, bye-laws and regulations of the country, the provinces and the councils of all sizes and shapes. All the same, Johannesburg and Pretoria are different. The Afrikaners of the two cities also differ. Pretorians are basically crude. Johannesburgers are a bit sophisticated. The prison warders are different too. In Johannesburg 'smokkel (smuggling)' and other corrupt practices occur between prisoners and warders. It is common knowledge. These practices might have occurred in Pretoria gaols as well. But I had never heard of them. They were probably confined to white warders and white prisoners. Money had no colour in Johannesburg. I was happy I was to be detained in Johannesburg. Things would not be all that bad.

Two young policemen were in the charge office at Marshall Square police station when we arrived. They were both sergeants. Lieutenant Dirker took advantage of their age and rank. He thundered at them and threatened them with dire consequences if 'this man escapes'. He instructed them: 'Don't allow any Bantu constable near him. You must check his luggage yourselves and make a record of everything. Blah blah blah.' As soon as Dirker turned his back, the two warders took me down to the basement to an African police sergeant and delegated their duties to him. I felt good. Johannesburg was different.

I grabbed the opportunity. The most urgent task was to communicate with the outside. To let my wife and relatives know where I was. 'Do me a favour,' I pleaded with the sergeant. 'Where do you live? Orlando? My in-laws are next to you in Diepkloof. Will you let them know I am here? Please! I was kidnapped in Rhodesia . . .' 'I cannot do it, it is dangerous. I might get into trouble . . .' 'No, you won't. My in-laws won't put you into trouble.' The poor man was scared. There was a mixture of fear and sympathy in his voice. I would not take 'no' for an answer. I pressed on with tendentious arguments until he eventually yielded, probably just to shake me off. In the morning, a younger and more understanding constable came on duty. He enthusiastically undertook the dangerous mission. Hardly half an hour after the deal, 'Rasie' Erasmus came to take me away. 'Kom, kom! (Come, come!)' We drove to the prison I dreaded, Pretoria Local.

Chief warder Schnepel came bristling at me when he heard who I was. 'Piet se vriend! Waar kry julle hom? (Piet's friend! Where did you find him?)' I stood petrified as Chief Warder moved towards me in combat readiness. What made him change his mind, I do not know. The imminent assault did not materialise, it petered out in feints and expletives. It was an inauspicious induction to Pretoria Local, nevertheless.

At the time of my arrest Pretoria Local Prison was in the news headlines. Harold Strachan, who had just completed his two year sentence on an explosives charge had exposed the horrible conditions of the gaol in a series of articles written by Benjamin Pogrund and published by the *Rand Daily Mail.* In making the statements about gaol conditions Strachan had contravened the Prisons Act. He was re-detained and charged. Benjamin Pogrund and the *Rand Daily Mail* editor, Lawrence Gandar, were also arraigned for contravention of the Prisons Act.

In spite of the vindictiveness of the law against Strachan and his media collaborators, I expected an improvement in the general prison conditions – they could not remain the same after the copious airing they had received. After registration of my property items, I was taken to cell number four on the first floor. The steel door shut with a bang behind me and left me free to survey my new room. The floor of the cell was polished black. It was spotless and glossy. A heap of blankets, expertly folded, lay in one corner atop two rolled mats, one felt, one sisal. In another corner, a sanitary enamel bucket, and in the opposite corner, on an elevation, a water bucket. These were the standard effects in a South African prison cell. The cell had a small window overlooking the prison yard, where isolated prisoners did their exercises. Since the walls of the cell were so high, the window was virtually inaccessible. To enjoy the rare view of other prisoners exercising down below, I had to stand on my pile of blankets and mats and heave myself up to the window bars, swing there for as long as my arms could hold out and feast on the forbidden vision of fellow prisoners.

The cell was narrow. It reminded me of Gray's elegy: 'Each in his narrow cell for ever laid'. Of course, I was far from dead. When you are locked in a fight for the survival of humanity you are far from dead. The cell was narrow all the same. The width of the cell measured the same as my prostrate figure with my arms stretched over head. I am five feet 10 inches in my flat sandals. The length might have been half a foot longer. It felt claustrophobic. I caught my breath to take in more of my fateful room. The writing was on the wall. Literally: 'My country dead or alive'. The author was anonymous. It could have been one of the many detainees who had preceded me to the cell. On another wall someone had written 'Biza was here'. Biza is a common name in the Johannesburg ghettos. But Biza would not have written that political sentiment, 'My country dead or alive'. The Bizas of Soweto generally do not express their defiance and outlawry in political slogans, they express that in anti-social crime, robbery, mugging and murder. Often the crimes are against their own kind: a typical example of displaced aggression. But the 'Bizas' are quick to appreciate the causal background to their

100

crimes. In gaol I was amazed at the potential awareness of the common-law prisoner to the root of his motivation. 'My country, dead or alive'; 'Biza was here'. I wondered whether Biza had noticed the slogan and what he made of it. When I found some instrument to scratch the cell wall, I would write two: 'ANC leads the struggle' and 'Better to die on your feet than to live on your knees'. Yes. It was a promise. A promise to myself. The message must spread. Even in gaol. In accordance with the ANC song: 'Mayihambe le vangeli . . . Let this gospel spread. Let it encompass the whole world . . .'

The prison bell went at eight o'clock. The chatter and the singing from the communal cells came to an abrupt end. A highpitched voice from the single cells rent the bell-imposed silence, 'Kubi! (It is bad!)' it cried. Gaol is bad. A barbaric institution. Fit to be banished in civilised society. I made my bed and passed my first night in Pretoria Local.

In the morning the wake-up gong sounded at 5.30am. What to do? I had no guide. Do nothing, I thought. Let them, the gaol officers, explain. I lay under the blankets and debated my anticipated behaviour with myself. I was unanimous with myself that one had to get up. So I got up and struggled to fold my blankets the way I found them folded. It was not easy. Blanket folding in gaol is a skill. It matures with time. It depends on one's aptitude. Some never acquired it. My friend George never did on Robben Island, I wonder whether he will have mastered it by his twenty-first year in gaol.

Having folded the blankets my way, I sat on them and waited. The key was thrust into the heavy steel door and the door flung open with practised precision. 'Staan reg! (Attention!)' the opener of the door commanded. Before I could interpret and obey the order according to my inclinations, a retinue of officers paused at my door bewildered by my relaxation on my unskilfully bundled blankets. 'Drie maaltye!' the potbellied officer at the head barked. The procession proceeded along the corridor, preceded by the well-aimed key, wielded by an expert turnkey, and the swiftly opened cell doors.

A short while after inspection a serving prisoner collected my sanitary bucket to empty and wash it. My door was shut and locked. In the evening when the eight o'clock bedtime bell rang I realised that I had been deprived of my meals for the day. Yes, 'drie maaltye' meant three meals. But why? The following morning when the procession approached I was at the door, not to do what I did not know, but to protest against meal deprivation. 'Excuse me, sir!' I tried in vain to intercept the inspection retinue . . . I was ignored. Only later in the day did the young warder give me the charge for the crime I had already been punished for. The charge: I had not stood at attention by the door and I had failed to show my prison card. 'Regulations, please! Prison regulations.' The young warder laughed at me. 'Regulations? Prison regulations? See the chief.' I saw the chief. He referred me to the ANC and the Communist Party. 'Ask them to give

101

you the prison regulations. They sent you to gaol. Not me!!' Pretoria Local was going to be fun and games! At my expense.

My wife's birthday is on 18 January. A week or so before the date I applied for permission to send her a short birthday greeting. 'When is her birthday?' asked the chief warder, interested. '18 January.' 'Put your application in writing to the Commanding Officer.' I did so. Permission granted. I wrote a short birthday message and handed it to the chief.

On 19 January while my wife's birthday was still fresh in my memory, I was taken to Compol building for interrogation. 'Teen die muur, teen die muur.' Punching and kicking by the 'brutes' did not yield any positive results. I refused to talk. Sweet-talk and all the wheedling by 'Smiler' the charmer did not make a better impression. Stubborn resistance was still in me. Coetzee the hardpunching captain half-killed me with his solar-plexus blow. They revived me with water. I still refused to co-operate.

The South African security police, I do not know others, have a repertoire of torture methods. One single method might work with one detainee. It may not work with another. In that case the police resort to variations. South African police are resourceful and adaptable. Sometimes they lose their cool and their judgement. Then the victim of torture dies through temperamental overexertion by the interrogators. I almost did. It would have been a mistake. The interrogators wanted me talking, not dead. Beatings and kicks stopped. I was made to stand in one place. The interrogation shifted decisively to an intellectual level. Each interrogator armed himself with some colleague's statement and fired questions on the basis of information implicating me. Mum was the word. One security officer quickly got bored with reading and interrogating from statements and dossiers. He tried gibes and insults. 'You are fighting with your back against the wall', he quipped while he surveyed me and the wall behind me. 'That's what the ANC, your organisation, is doing, fighting with its back against the wall . . . How many white girls have you fucked? It will be a long long time before you fuck them again.'

The next taunt riled me. I do not know why. It was this: 'You are a very ungrateful Bantu. We admitted you to our schools, gave you employment and all our hospitality, although you are a foreigner . . .' 'Don't call me a foreigner,' I responded with exceptional vehemence. 'My ancestors are of this continent. My grandfather was born in South Africa and my father contributed to the wealth of South Africa by his thankless, but profitable labour in the gold mines. Call your Prime Minister Verwoerd, a foreigner!' That was a *casus belli*. 'Don't you dare call my Prime Minister "Verwoerd". He is not your Bram Fischer. He is Doctor Verwoerd. And "baas" to you. C'mon, say "baas Verwoerd"!' 'Rasie' Erasmus was foaming at the mouth. He had boasted to me he had beaten up Harold Strachan in Port Elizabeth

102

when he was detained for the explosives charge, and broken John Harris' jaw when he interrogated him after the Johannesburg station bomb in 1964. 'Say baas Verwoerd!' he bawled at me. He looked like a possessed monster. 'Say baas Verwoerd!' he continued 'prompting' me. I was terrified. I felt the ugly title word struggle through my vocal cords to be uttered. I tried to swallow it, it rose up the vocal cords inexorably, coaxed by the menacing attitude of Erasmus. Just on the tip of my tongue the scornful word got stuck and remained stuck. I could have given my tongue a kiss if I had had another tongue. Simultaneously Erasmus got out of breath. For he ceased screaming indignities and exhortations.

The sun went down on Wednesday 19 January and left me standing. It rose in the morning of Thursday to find me a faithful sentinel at my post. Thursday night, Friday morning. Friday evening, 21 January, I still stood at one spot. My legs felt like lead. I had not eaten since my breakfast on Wednesday. I had not slept a wink. The barrage of questions continued. I did not talk. The questions were knowledgeable. Captain Swanepoel at one stage had told me: 'We want to know what you have been doing in Bechuanaland. We are not really interested in your activities before you left. Those, we know better than you. We can tell you things you do not know about your organisation inside the country.' Still they asked questions relating to the ANC in the country and made statements about ANC activities in Bechuanaland and farther. It all seemed to be contradictory. In spite of intelligence gaps in their statements, the police seemed to know more than one would have credited them.

When that feeling builds up in the interrogated, then the interrogated is on slippery ground. I knew it. It helped to recharge me for more resistance. Yes, the police knew all right, but they did not know everything. Otherwise why spend so many hours questioning me? No, I was not talking. The spirit was willing. The flesh was weak. Sixty odd sleepless and foodless hours were beginning to take their toll. Fatigue was beginning to assert itself. One small voice said: 'Talk!' One proud one objected: 'No, don't!' The small one persisted: 'Talk! They know everything.' Something inside me caved in. It was as if a fortress wall came crumbling down leaving the defenders exposed to a besieging army. The small voice grew bolder and louder: 'I'll talk!' Captain Coetzee (the same one who floored me for a full count) was almost dozing, and appeared startled. It must have sounded like an impossible dream. His practised eye scanned my expression, the expression of a broken man. His face lit up. He recognised the breakdown. 'Sit down!' he said pointing to a chair. A split minute after taking the chair the proud voice resurged: 'Sell out! Shame on you. Stop it!'

Captain Coetzee was already poised with pen and paper to take down a confession of a 'terrorist'. 'Captain,' I addressed him, 'I have not

103

slept for three nights, you know it. I am not in a position to make a coherent statement now. Won't you allow me to sleep. I can make the statement tomorrow.' Coetzee the experienced interrogator knew that I was getting second wind. 'Staan op! (Stand up!)' he screamed. 'Teen die muur. Teen die muur!' he shouted, his eyes bulging. The second wind was ephemeral, gone in minutes. Without the flesh, the spirit is inanimate. 'Where do I start, Captain?' 'Begin from the beginning. From the time you joined the ANC. Why you joined. Who enrolled you. When you became an office bearer. The whole story up to the day of your arrest.' Coetzee did not hear me sigh. Talking about the legal days of the ANC and the reasons for joining the ANC was my pet subject. I lectured to Coetzee. He took down notes for an hour or so. Coetzee, pleased with the fact that I was talking, allowed me to sleep in the early hours of Saturday morning, 22 January.

After three nights of sleeplessness and non-stop bombardment with imputative questions, sleep had deserted my eyes and my brain. My mind recapitulated all the questions and statements the police had posed and reiterated. To talk is wrong. But what one talks about might mitigate or aggravate the wrong in the talking. My mind was feverish. I had started talking. No real damage had been done so far. I wanted to stop. I knew I could not. The brutes would not let me. I had many wishes. A wish to die. A wish to know how to pray to die. I had forgotten how to pray. I wished I could remember how to pray. I wished the wishes one wishes could come true. I wished my strength of the past three days could return to me. All those wishes seemed extremely wishful. My mind raced on. I could not countenance giving the police all the information they demanded. The alternative was to hedge, prevaricate, evade and lie outright where loopholes presented themselves in the interrogation. It would mean outwitting the police and constructing a consistent story that could cast doubt or neutralise previous statements by comrades and persons unknown. It was not going to be easy but I could try. It was a challenge. Although Captain Swanepoel at some stage branded me a liar, a liar who could not even lie properly, I was reasonably satisfied with my performance in the end.

Police methods of interrogation in any case are a genesis of liars and lies. For instance I found that the police had tortured some comrades to lie about me. In turn I was tortured to lie to corroborate the tortured lies. That is what happens in Compol building corridors and other chambers of torture in South Africa. If one answers, I do not know, the police retort, you know, I don't know, you persist. You lie. You know, they insist. Threats and torture follow. In the end to save your skin you agree. Yes, I know; although you do not know.

Swanepoel was not satisfied with the authenticity of my statement on Saturday 22 January 1966. He nevertheless gave instructions that I could be taken back to Pretoria Local Prison. Compared with Compol building, Pretoria Local was relative freedom. A friendly cleaner,

104

obviously with the collaboration of some sympathetic warder who remained in the background, smuggled newspapers to me. I read about the coup in Nigeria and the flight of Ben Turok, who had recently completed a three-year sentence under the Explosives Act, in a hired vehicle to Bechuanaland, and I read about other things that depicted the consistent piquancy of social life. I read all these things and wondered what turn my interrogation would take when it resumed. For I had a hunch that the sordid business was not over. Four days in the company of the Sabotage squad, for that was the designation of Swanepoel & Co, impressed upon me that they do not do things in half measures.

On Monday 24 January Warrant Officer Erasmus fetched me from Pretoria Local back to Compol building. I sensed trouble. Big trouble. And I shuddered a bit. An augmented group of interrogators sat at a round table waiting for me. Captain Swanepoel let loose a barrage of shrill accusations and abuses as I approached the round table with my escort: 'Your statement was a tissue of lies! A tissue of lies! I want another statement from you, now and here! I don't care if you kill him!' he announced viciously to the squad. I do not know where I got the guts from but I shouted back: 'Yes you can kill me, I don't care . . .!' Swanepoel then appeared to mellow suddenly: 'Nee, Dingake, ons sal you nie dood maak nie. Ons soek informasie. Informasie. (No, Dingake, we won't kill you. We want information. Information . . .)' he concluded with heavy emphasis.

Swanepoel was interrupted by a member of the squad I had not noticed during the altercation but one whom I recognised immediately. 'Captain, let me ask him a few questions,' he had said. This was my Lobatse 'shadow'. The man who lingered around Lobatse pubs and parked his car outside Lobatse Post Office daily, the man who to all intents and purposes bore the stamp of an accredited representative of SA security police in Bechuanaland. The questions the man proceeded to ask exposed the man's close connections with the Bechuanaland police and the often false deductions police make from observing movements and associations of their quarries.

The security officers of Bechuanaland Protectorate force saw me meeting a local resident arriving on a midnight mail train from Johannesburg. Subsequently they must have reported the event to my 'shadow' and he or they, together, concluded that the midnight passenger was my ANC courier between Johannesburg and Lobatse. I exploded the spying conjectures of the police. Next. Unknown agents and/or informers deduced from my occasion visits to Molapo-wa-bojang area (near Kanye) that I was hiding some trained guerrillas there. I ridiculed the deduction but the man stuck to his imaginary guns. It was a deadlock. Coded letters from the ANC office in Lusaka were a different kettle of fish. These were decoded by the police, because we had continued to use the same book we used in Johannesburg on the assumption that the postal services in

105

Bechuanaland were free from interference from the Security Branch in South Africa. It was amateurish in the extreme. We learn the hard way. I learned the painful way. Fortunately the messages never conveyed really sensitive and confidential matters. They dealt with purely routine organisational matters. These however established my undeniable link with the external mission of the ANC and my statement had to be amended to take account of this fact.

My 'shadow's' interrogation also revealed the connections the South African Security Branch had with the banks in Bechuanaland. The theory of the confidentiality of client's business with the banking institutions was totally shattered. The small savings accounts I had with both the Standard and Barclays branches in Lobatse were a syllabus of the South African security police college. So I had to answer questions on all the deposits and withdrawals. South African security police are cute and resourceful.

The statement that emerged after the encounter with my 'shadow' was accepted. With reservations. The reservations were largely because the police suspected strongly that there were trained guerrillas who were poised to enter South Africa and that I was the main link with them. I would not budge on my denial. The police refused to budge on their allegation too. A deadlock ensued. The deadlock led to my second round of interrogation and severe torture in 1967. About that later.

For the time being the grilling I had been subjected to was suspended on the evening of 24 January 1966. I was shuttled back to Local prison.

The rusty half-washed aluminium dishes that had served prisoners' food before Harold Strachan's bold exposure of prison conditions, had given way to shiny, new aluminium dishes. The food however had not improved appreciably. It remained preponderantly starchy, tasteless and often half-cooked. The dilemma of an isolated detainee: he can complain but substantial action cannot be undertaken to seek redress. Nonetheless detainees in isolation being the most aggrieved section of the prison population complain the most. About their isolated status, the inadequate exercise periods and other nagging prison pin-pricks. I complained about all those, including the quality and preparation of food. I went further and suggested that since I was an unconvicted prisoner I should be allowed to buy my own food as much as I could afford. I put the complaint-cum-request in writing as I was asked to do after outlining it verbally.

Gaol requests and complaints, in the nature of gaol conditions, often go unanswered or they are arbitrarily rejected. In my case the response was positive and prompt. I was shifted from my cell to another section of the prison close to the white section. My diet also began to approximate to the section I was now neighbouring. The transformation was remarkable. Strangely enough, the concession

106

made me feel suspicious and compromised. I would have been happier with permission to supplement my prison diet with extra purchases at my own expense. To be favoured above others in prison was a source of suspicious alarm. I smuggled a note to Siegfried Bhengu a fellow comrade and apprised him of the new turn of events. 'Eat the good food,' replied Siegfried, 'you need it. And stick to your principles.' I was happy. Siegfried was a former warder in Pretoria Local prison. During all that time he was a member of the ANC and had stuck to his principles by identifying himself clandestinely with the State of Emergency detainees in 1960, by doing appropriate favours for them. His fifth columnist tendencies had eventually been discovered. He was booted out of the prison service. He volunteered for MK training. After completing his military training in Morocco, Algeria and Egypt he came back in 1964. The law caught up with him in 1965 and he was then serving a recently imposed ten-year sentence. I was happy with his advice because it coincided with my original reaction and if anybody knew about the manipulations, manoeuvres and counter-responses in the maze and intrigue of the prison labyrinth, Siegfried was the one. I ate the good food with a clear conscience and a ravenous appetite and waited for developments.

BAITED

The first time I was arrested was for a pass offence. I spent three days and three nights in Jeppe Police Station. That was the incident where a police constable had asked for my name after I had shown him my pass, and I was cheeky enough to ask whether he could read or not.

Jeppe Police Station is built next to the rail line. The noise and clatter of trains speeding past is interminable. It makes sleep impossible unless one has been long enough at the police station to get used to it. The Friday of my apprehension for an alleged pass offence was extraordinarily noisy. The clatter of the train wheels outside vied with the abusive shouts of the police in the cells. Many inmates were dragged from shebeens where they were drinking prohibited white liquor and other illicit concoctions. They were shouted at and thrown into the crowded cells. Some fell asleep instantly on the spot they hit the floor, and started snoring. Others, shaken by the mighty heave of the police, started retching full throatedly on some of us who were already lying down when they were brought in. The pattern remained unchanged until the early hours of the Saturday morning. Police were very active. They rattled their keys in the cell door, pulled the door open, propelled a few bodies in, under an abusive barrage, banged the door shut and went back on another raid to repeat the whole process. The experience was a good induction for a future jailbird. Life in jail is a catalogue of discomfort. It calls for tremendous self-discipline.

Almost 20 years later, I revisited Jeppe Police Station. Three or four days before my transfer from Pretoria Local Prison to Jeppe, I had been shifted from one wing of the prison to another. The motive behind the transfer was unclear to me. It seemed to be for the 'better' for it was synchronised with a change of diet. Bread and butter, breakfast cereals with milk and white coffee for breakfast; meat, vegetables, bread and tea for lunch; supper was just as substantial and sumptuous. It aroused lots of speculation and suspicion. After a few days in this new hotel apartment, I was called to the reception office, handed my property bag and given the book to book out.

Outside a VW Beetle welcomed me to its back seat. Two burly escorts drove me to Grays, security police headquarters in Johannesburg. Lieutenant Dirker was waiting for me in one office on the fifth floor of Grays. 'Dingake, I have brought you here to talk business with you. Don't give me your answer now. No, no. Think about it carefully. You will be kept in Jeppe Police Station. You see, Dingake, here are your dossiers.' He shoved me two. 'See how fat they are! Look at this one. It is Bram Fischer's. Do you know why it is so thin, although he has been active in the Communist Party long before you dreamt of joining the ANC? Let me tell you.' He edged towards me conspiratorially. 'Bram and other white communists use you blacks as their tools. They keep in the background and push you, their instruments, forward. We, the police, have difficulty in knowing what they are doing because they are sheltering behind you. But we can always see what (you) their tools are doing. Thus your dossiers grow thicker and thicker while theirs remain thin. What I want you to think about is: give evidence against Bram, and you will be a free man.' 'You are wasting your time and your breath, Lt Dirker . . .' 'Come, come. I don't want your answer now. We'll talk at Jeppe Police Station on Monday,' Lt Dirker interrupted me, fidgeting with a mass of dossiers in front of him. It was Friday, 11 February 1966. My birthday.

When we arrived at the police station, Lt Dirker moved importantly. He talked down to the station commander, a lieutenant like himself. He recited a welter of instructions to the station commander. 'Die man is gevaarlik (This man is dangerous).' He must be kept by himself in a secure cell. I must inspect the cell before I go. He must be checked at regular intervals, day and night. He must not be given any newspaper or reading material. No Bantu police must have any access to him. Although he has money in his property bag, he must not be allowed to buy anything. As far as food is concerned, give him goeie kos (good food).' The station commander was not sure about 'goeie kos' and he stutteringly solicited for some definition: 'Watter soort (What kind) . . . Lieutenant?' 'Good food, good food. The same food you eat. Give him what he wants if he has special preference.' The station commander understood and nodded enthusiastically to impress that he was ready and willing to obey for 'die land en volk (country and nation)'.

The cell was spacious. Twenty or more detainees could be

accommodated in it. This time it was mine alone, in seclusion. It stood detached from other cells. Hope for contact with other prisoners died the moment I walked into it. I was shown a heap of blankets in one corner of the cell. They were filthy and stuffy. I protested and got three new ones over and above the bedding filth. Supper was delicious. Bacon, macaroni, bread, cheese, butter and dessert aplenty. It was a fete. I had the right to be entertained. February 11! In the morning the police sergeant assigned to my cell carried my sanitary bucket out of the cell. With his own white hands! I gaped in disbelief. The man was following the instructions strictly. No 'Bantu' near him!

However, degrading military instructions run the risk of being disobeyed or circumvented. The following morning the white sergeant smuggled a black constable into my cell to remove the bucket. I can imagine that it was one event the sergeant had to invoke a defensive mechanism of repression against. It was good to speculate on the revulsion he felt. The utter degradation of serving a 'Bantu' in that capacity! It was a pity, I mused inwardly, the unfortunate sergeant could not compare his 'degradation' with the daily humiliations of the blacks under the laws of the government.

The trains still rattled past the police station. However, I could not blame them for my deprivation of sleep at night. The police had instructions to check on me regularly, presumably to ensure that any escape attempts would be frustrated, or that any suicide attempt should not succeed. Bang! bang! on the door: 'Dingake, are you all right?' Or the door would be flung open and banged shut just as I was beginning to doze off. Sleep was impossible. I protested. 'Dingake, it is an order'; and the disturbing checks continued without let or hindrance. The security of the country was at stake. There was no compromise in that respect.

One late morning a magistrate came to see me in my cell. He stood before me, arms akimbo, scowling and apparently disgusted by the distastefulness of the nature of his duties: listening to complaints from 'Bantu terrorists'. He did not greet me. I took my cue from him and we stood eyeing each other with mutual hostility. After some time he opened his mouth: 'Ja, is jy reg?'. Thinking that I had a language problem he switched to English. 'Are you all right?' I was not interested in communicating with a would-be judicial officer whose whole attitude reeked of racial arrogance and prejudice. I continued to look at him dumbly. At last he got the message. With one last malevolent look at me he turned and withdrew from my cell. I am still curious to know what he reported.

Under South African laws, detainees face a formidable predicament. Technically the law under which I was detained, the '180-day clause', provided some safeguards for the detainees. Under this legislation, magistrates were entrusted with the duty of visiting

109

detainees, ostensibly to note their complaints against any illegal treatment in detention. But the experience of many detainees was that laying any complaint before the majority of the magistrates was to expose oneself to further assaults from the security police. Moreover their open hostility against detainees was usually intimidating and discouraging. A detainee needed two things: guts, to report in such an atmosphere, and extreme optimism to expect the slightest good to come out of a complaint to a visiting magistrate. Guts was not my problem on this particular occasion, but I was absolutely diffident about the outcome of any interview with this formidable officer.

The only relief from the pervasive atmosphere of isolation here was the gambling noises of the station police over the weekends. My cell, judging by the goings-on, was apparently attached to some shed or structure to which the black police had access. Every Friday, sometimes Saturday too, in the evening, off-duty black police could be heard throwing the dice. Only the cell wall separated me from this gambling fraternity. The incantations uttered with every throw brought back the memories of my gambling days: 'Six-five; I do. Five rands, I do. Pop. Five-two . . .' Typical of gamblers, arguments rose, threats and counter-threats were bandied around but the dice throwing went on. Sooner or later one of the gamblers would be heard saying: 'Manne/Gentlemen, Jockey the winning horse. Who says I do . . .' then I knew the poor guy had lost. I always looked forward to Fridays for this most welcome diversion. It was 15 years since I had stopped throwing dice and I had never dreamt the gambling noise could be so entertaining and relieving.

Monday, 14 February 1966 arrived. Lt Dirker also arrived as per appointment. I had used the weekend to plan my strategy and tactics. My mind was of course made up. To give evidence against any of my colleagues was unthinkable. I tried to reflect why the security police took it upon themselves to adopt this tactic with me. The interrogation experience, I thought, would have placed me beyond the potential pale. Later I realised the Afrikaner police had embraced the hard-nosed philosophy of 'not to take "no" for an answer'. My tactics were not to antagonise Lt Dirker immediately by refusing to discuss the matter with him, which was my reflex attitude when he broached the offer. Secondly, I decided to use the obvious bargaining position I enjoyed to extract some essential privileges. The strategy was an argued build-up to a final rejection of the despicable offer.

'Lt Dirker, before we get on to your business, let us clear a few personal matters: one, I have been denied toilet soap, allegedly on your instructions. I am stinking, I need a wash, now. Two, I am asking for permission to write to my wife. She has not heard from me since my arrest, and it must be killing her. Three, I would like one of my sisters-in-law to be allowed to come and collect my washing to wash, there are no laundry facilities here. Four, I need some reading material', I opened the dialogue. Requests one, two and three granted. Request four, disapproved . . . Haggling took us no further.

After the refreshing shower, Lt Dirker and I sat down to the business in hand. 'Dingake, we want you to give evidence in Bram's case as I indicated to you. Have you thought of the matter?' 'Lieutenant, you know my answer already. I have not changed. But just for the sake of argument and interest, have you read the statement your colleagues extracted from me through methods of torture?' 'Yes I have.' 'Well if you have, then you know there is no word, phrase or sentence implicating Bram directly or indirectly in the statement. This, in spite of the fact that your interrogating colleagues desperately wanted me to agree under duress that I worked with Bram in Johannesburg and corresponded with him from Bechuanaland. I flatly refused to make any such false declaration. Now, how do I give evidence against someone I had no connection with at all?' 'Oh, we can talk about that. If you agree in principle, the prosecutor will discuss everything with you . . .' 'Does it mean that he will advise or persuade me to accuse Bram falsely?' 'No, Dingake, that is not what I mean . . .' and he mumbled inaudibly. 'Then what do you mean, Lieutenant? It is difficult to find a different interpretation to what you have just stated.' Lt Dirker was in a jam. He sputtered, hedged and diverged from the point.

Around this period the white Nationalist government and their agents had not shaken off the hangover of their anti-semitism of the thirties and forties. They had a negative attitude towards the South African Jews. They suspected them of all real as well as imaginary subversive activities against the South African state, begrudged them their business successes and decried them as moneymongers come to rob South Africa of its wealth. Times change. Today, Jews are wooed into the party of Afrikanerdom. The apartheid regime in South Africa and the Israeli regime in the Middle East are thick as thieves. At Jeppe Police Station, February 1966, the revolution in the new-fangled bilateral relations was not yet. 'You are being misled by Jewish communists. They are pulling you by the nose. Such an intelligent young man! Can't you realise you are a stooge of white communists. Jews! The Rusty Bernsteins, the Ben Turoks, the Joe Slovos. Why must you allow them to meddle in your organisations. They hoodwink you, and call you comrade, comrade. Do they mean it? Ha! It's only eyewash!' He snorted contemptuously. 'You have been a fulltime functionary of the ANC. How much did you get? R70. What about Mike Harmel who did the same job for the party? Six times more than you. Did you know that? Call that comradeship and equality!' He snorted again. I was tempted to tell him: 'Don't sell that cheap propaganda to me. And go to hell.'

The reaction might have terminated the timekilling, albeit circular, conversation. In detention, especially under solitary confinement,

111

you learn to talk to yourself, to the walls, to the floor, to the blankets, the pisspot, the bugs and any object tangible or in sight. Talking to someone even the likes of Lt Dirker, is a social bonanza not to be lightly cast aside. Dirker was playing the role of a dubious social companion unwittingly. My role was to make the social companionship last as long as possible. The social nature of humans can be an embarrassment at times. It can associate the most unlikely bedfellows.

I took up the conversation: 'Lt Dirker, I see you disapprove that I should be a stooge of communists and Jews. Well and good. But why do you want me to be your stooge, a stooge of the Boers. Why? Anyway, I have no intention of being anybody's stooge. It is good enough I am my own 'stooge' and hopefully a 'stooge' of my own people's aspirations. I won't be any oppressor's mindless puppet. No, Sir.'

Lieutenant Dirker slightly taken aback replied in stock phrases: 'independence in Bantu Homelands, separate development was the answer, white communists and Russian imperialists were the enemies, blah blah blah'. Our discussion was becoming deadlocked in rival camp propaganda and cliches. Lt Dirker was not deterred however, he was going to come back again. 'Dingake, think about my offer. Think about it seriously . . .' With that pep talk, he left me, to return at some later day. I could look forward to another day of mixed blessings. Sterile discussion. Dubious companionship and a relief from unmitigated boredom. Two days after our 'business' talk with Lt Dirker, the police sergeant in charge asked me to hand over my dirty washing as my sister-in-law had come to collect it. It implied I was not to see her. 'No,' I said. 'I want to see her. I cannot just hand over my clothes to someone I don't see. How shall I know it was my sister?' His instructions were that I must not see her. I questioned the rationale of the instructions. 'Dingake, a command is a command', was the firm reply. We haggled and finally reached a compromise. Helen, my sister-in-law, was to stand on an elevation outside the cell yard, from where I could be able to identify her. Then, after satisfying myself that it was my sister-in-law I could hand over the washing. 'Hello,' she cried in her melodious voice, nostalgically reminding me of my wife's. 'Hello,' I echoed back, waving and absolutely thrilled to see her. The police sergeant intervened. No. We were not to talk and he planted himself in front of me to obscure my forbidden vision. Try as I did to keep my focus on the object of admiration outside, the vigilant sergeant was unrelenting. I gave up the futile game and collected the washing from the cell. 'Bye bye,' she called; 'Love to my wife,' I called back.

Helen turned and receded into the dreamlike bustle of social life. I slunk into the vacuum of my cell and its dehumanising solitude. The sweetness of the brief, extorted visit mingled with the bitterness of the uncongenial present and the vagueness of the blurred future.

Family, friends and acquaintances. Were all of them to remain forfeit and inaccessible as long as I rejected the offer! I burst into revolutionary song: 'Asikhathali noma siya botshwa, sizimisel' inkululeko (We care not whether we are arrested, we are determined to be free). Unzima lomthwalo (This burden is heavy) . . .' I felt better.

Three or four days later I was pacing my cell and trying to keep a mental score of trains rattling by. I lost count as my mind veered into the coaches of the Soweto trains and the crowded platforms at the railway stations, especially Johannesburg. I was thinking these thoughts when I was distracted by a female voice outside my cell yard. The cell yard gate opened and several male voices mingled with the female voice in the yard. When the cell door opened I was curious. Who could be the lady visitor? Captain 'Smiler' Van Rensburg and another Special Branch man walked in. Smiler the 'softener' was playing an aggressive role on this occasion. 'You used House Number 1612 Naledi as your hideout,' he accused me crossly. 'Govan Mbeki also used the same place. You communists are unscrupulous. You don't care whether innocent people get into trouble by involving them in your shit. Now the poor woman is going to suffer . . .' He gave me a reproachful look. I was not baited. My immediate interest was the female voice outside. I heard Smiler's invective. It sounded gibberish. My mind was outside.

Eventually, Smiler and companion retreated into the yard. A white lady walked in with the police sergeant. 'I am Olga Mann,' she introduced herself simply. Olga Mann. Yes, I remembered Olga Mann from the press. The first Johannesburg woman prosecutor. Now the first Johannesburg woman magistrate. I remembered her two 'firsts' very well and I told her. She bore no resemblance in manners to the previous visiting magistrate. A real sweet contrast. She appeared genuinely interested in my welfare. She encouraged me to air my complaints and suggested certain requests. 'Why don't you ask for a bed? You can't be comfortable on this floor.' 'A bed? Can I get one?' 'Why not? Bartholomew Hlapane has got one. I have just been to see him in Langlaagte.' Ah, I thought, that's where Smiler got the information about 1612 Naledi. Maybe Olga Mann did not know what I knew, that Bartholomew had sold his soul to the political devil. He had already agreed to go down in history as a traitor to the South African liberation struggle. His seducers were honour bound to reward him with small comforts while he was being held in protective custody prior to parading him as living evidence of their catalogue of successes against 'terrorism'.

Anyway, it was not my duty to enlighten Olga Mann on what Hlapane was, nor would it be tactful to dampen her enthusiastic goodwill by declining to make the request. Who knows, the security police might consider it as an additional inducement to clinch the witness deal. I nodded to the suggestion. Olga reduced the request to writing and was ready to hear another request or complaint. We

113

consulted on a number of negotiable privileges, with her the more optimistic. 'How do you while away time? Ask for a pack of cards!' 'Cards? All right.' 'Do they allow you exercises?' 'Yes they do.' 'What about your food?' 'Food is the one thing I cannot complain about.'

The one serious complaint-cum-request I made independently concerned reading material. Since my detention, I had not been allowed anything to read. Not even the Holy Bible. When I pleaded with Schnepel in Pretoria Local Prison to allow me to read the Bible, at least, he was very sarcastic. 'I don't want you to be expelled from the Communist Party,' he answered. In Pretoria Local Prison, however, isolation was not half as severe as at Jeppe. Although kept alone in a cell, one heard other prisoners all the time. In the evenings there was regular singing from awaiting-trial prisoners. Some sympathetic cleaners smuggled newspapers into one's cell and isolation was not so complete as at Jeppe.

Olga Mann thought the privation was outrageous. 'Not even the Bible!' Oh no, she was going to take it up very strongly. The interview lifted my spirits. One could not be over-optimistic. But it made a difference to converse with a judicial officer who was not grumpy and openly biased.

Lieutenant Dirker came back to continue where he left off. 'Dingake, you have got a wife and a daughter. Who will look after them when you are in gaol? Do you think the ANC will look after them? Forget it. They have already forgotten you. Your family is already suffering. What for? Just because you want to protect a white communist?' and he snorted his characteristic snort. On this occasion my mood was a bit abrasive. The dialogue was cut short. When we parted company with Dirker I was convinced it was the last I had seen of him, in the same role. I was mistaken. Like a yo-yo he came bouncing back. Boers are a tenacious tribe.

Early one morning, shortly after my cool social encounter with Dirker, I was summoned to the Station Commander's office. In the corridor I met Olga Mann. Her leg was in plaster and she informed me she had been involved in a car accident. It was hard to repress a feeling of grief over her mishap. She was still as good natured as on the first day I met her. On this day, however, her visit coincided with that of the security police and, needless to say, the security police took precedence over any other law agency. Before she could report on what had transpired in connection with her representations from the past visit, I was shown the Station Commander's office where I found Captain Swanepoel and Lt Dirker. My spirits slumped. Captain Swanepoel is not the right person to behold even when he is all smiles and trying to look human as he was doing at that moment. His whole physical exterior betrays his ugly, savage and unscrupulous interior. Gruff, grating voice, squat figure, pock-marked face, freckled face and crewcut hair identified him as a ruthless no-nonsense

114

policeman. He was reputed to have been responsible for a number of deaths in detention. I remembered his arrogance at Babla Salojee's inquest. Babla was alleged to have jumped through one of the seventh-floor windows of the Grays. When Swanepoel was cross-examined on the detention law at the inquest, he shouted at Dr Lowen: 'I won't allow any propaganda against my government.' Dr Lowen was the counsel for the family of the deceased.

We drove to the Grays. The Captain and his lieutenant were in a jovial mood. It was irritating. As we drove down Commissioner Street, Swanepoel in a rare expansive mood drew my attention to a newspaper poster announcing heavy rains in Bechuanaland. 'Look how much rain the Batswana are having this year. There is going to be a good harvest out there. You could share the year's prosperity with your people. By the way, how old is your daughter? Three months? You must think of her.' Obviously the battle for my allegiance was intensifying. My family instincts were to be the new weapons. I was arrested two weeks after my daughter's birth and I had looked forward to bringing her up and watching her stage-by-stage growth and development. Already I had a diary in which I was going to make meticulous daily entries of her young history. It was going to be the most annotated historical sketch. Swanepoel was reminding me of my aborted doting plans. He was responsible for the checkmate. It was too late to get out of it. It was no longer check. It was mate.

Captain Swanepoel's office was choc-a-bloc with Security Branch officers. A sea of beefy pink faces encircled me. I tried not to be overawed by this intimidating arrangement. Those in front of me and on the sides stared at me unwinking. Behind me there were whispers, probably about my untenable fate. The Captain, directly in front of me on the other side of the counter, flanked by Lt Dirker and another lieutenant, started the day's proceedings without beating about the bush: 'Dingake, I want you to give evidence for the State in Bram's case. You can ask for any price. Ask anybody, I have never gone back on my word. What I promise I fulfil. Want to go into business, any type, any size, any place in South Africa, you have it. Money is not our problem. Should you prefer to return to Bechuanaland and start a business or a political party, we are ready to support you. Bechuanaland needs a party that can work in harmony with the Republic of South Africa. What can Bechuanaland do without South Africa? Absolutely nothing. But Seretse is a communist and a fool. His statements against our policies won't get him anywhere. You can't bite the hand that feeds you . . .' I could not suppress a smile on learning of Seretse Khama's new ideology. Swanepoel probably mistook my smile as approbation of his remarks, for he dramatically followed up with what he considered a *coup de grace*. 'Have you read this?' he asked me as he handed me the Johannesburg *Star* of the previous day. 'Read it,' he urged me.

It was Bartholomew Hlapane's evidence against Bram Fischer. I read it. All around me there was eager anticipation as I read the paper silently. I was not shocked by what I read. I had ample independent clues about Hlapane's reliability. I gave the paper back to Captain Swanepoel and shook my head. 'Let Bartholomew Hlapane betray the struggle. I refuse to be a traitor to my people.' 'I am not asking you to give evidence against any Bantu and the ANC. Our fight is against white communists and Russian imperialism. That, we shall not tolerate!' His eyes expressed an intractable and vicious determination as he spat out the last words. He continued: 'You know, Dingake. We were fools in the Rivonia trial. We should have asked all the Bantu, including Mandela and Sisulu to give evidence against the whites – James Kantor, Rusty Bernstein, Bob Hepple and Denis Goldberg . . .' He elaborated to answer my incredulous facial reaction. 'Yes, if I had my way I would have offered them the opportunity to save themselves from life imprisonment.' The preposterousness of the idea! Swanepoel's statement was a shameless effrontery not only to my intelligence and political principles but a reflection of the Afrikaners' (and most South African whites') contemptuous disregard of the blacks' political sentiments. 'Boy', 'girl', they called every adult African and believed that every black person was indeed an infant incapable of translating the reality around him/her. For this reason, whenever a black person raised his voice against injustice, he was being incited by liberals and communists. The task of the Afrikaners was to wean away the Bantu from the liberals and communists by offering them the Bantu Homelands, bribing those who were misled to betray the struggle, and sending the dyed-in-the-wool agitators to long terms of imprisonment if torture methods failed to dispose of them.

I hate oppression. But I hate more that my resistance and commitment against oppression should be treated as a joke. I let Swanepoel know it. 'Oh, you want to be a martyr. Well, if you want to face the music, it's your choice . . . You will not get anything less than 20 years. You are a fool. Maybe you are afraid the ANC will eliminate you. They have never killed anybody. You know it, and we mean to smash the ANC. It will never rise again when we have finished with it.' 'Good luck!' I replied with careless sarcasm. By this time Swanepoel's earlier effusive mood had given way to a violent temper. He shouted and threatened the direst consequences at my foolhardiness.

The young officer who drove me back to Jeppe Police Station berated me for shortsightedness and ingratitude. 'The ANC is finished,' he reiterated. 'No future for it. You are going to rot and die in jail,' he said venomously. 'The Captain was prepared to give you the moon and do you think you are too good for the moon? What exactly do you want? You'll die on Robben Island. They are not going to play with you there . . .' My escort sounded very offended. It was a typical

116

reaction of a Boer. Contradiction is not his popular custom. It is worse if it comes from a Bantu. A Bantu is not supposed to know the word 'nee (no)'. He must learn to say 'ja (yes)'. Ja baas, ja oubaas, ja kleinbaas, ja missus, ja klein missus. 'Nee' is verboten for the Bantu. It is an offence. Afrikaners in particular and whites generally know what is good for the Bantu. When a Bantu is told 'jump', 'sit', he must sit, 'sing', he must sing, 'say baas', he/she must say 'baas'.

The injustices the blacks endured – discrimination everywhere, disenfranchisement, inferior education, landlessness (in spite of the fact that Africans constitute more than 70 per cent of the population they are legally entitled to less than 13 per cent of the land under the Land Act of 1913), influx control applied through the degrading pass laws and enforced by a racist police force, inadequate and poor housing, lack of amenities in segregated residential areas, poor wages, banning of black organisations and their leaders, arbitrary arrests and long terms of imprisonment for those who challenged the apartheid regime and many more – were a figment of the imagination of misled Bantu, misled by liberals and communists.

All these grievances I outlined to the young officer who seemed to believe his Captain was trying to do me a big favour. To the question 'What exactly do you want?' I told him I wanted a South Africa that is administered within the framework of the Freedom Charter. 'Agh, man, don't tell me about the Freedom Charter. It is a communist document. And like all communist documents theoretically it sounds the ideal thing, but in practice it is unattainable. If the society envisaged by communists were practicable, I would be a communist. Everybody would be a communist. But it's all bullshit . . . Look what goes on between Russia and China. At each other's throat all the time . . . Were you to take over you would oppress the whites, fight among yourselves and forget your big talk about equality and human brotherhood.' We arrived at Jeppe Police Station still arguing.

Alone in my cell I reviewed the day's events. It was good, it was over, I thought, from the beginning I was never in doubt about the final outcome. I knew and felt I could never play the role the police wanted me to play. I was convinced Swanepoel and company would not have attempted to recruit me for their vile plans if they understood my strong anti-apartheid stand and my resentment to the daily humiliation I was subjected to as a black man. But the police did not understand. Some people change their views. They denounce principles they might have held sacred in life. They recast their personalities. What influences such behaviour is not easy to define. Many unknown factors might be responsible. I did not know. The police did not know. Both sides were engaged in an experiment. At the end of it I was happy that the experiment proved what I needed to prove, that compromise with oppression was not possible from my point of view. Torture and bribes can only induce the half-hearted, the revolutionary charlatans – those who play at revolution.

The question, nevertheless, remains intriguing: what makes a man change heart under certain circumstances? I speculated on this with regard to three erstwhile comrades: Bopela, Beyleveld and Hlapane.

Bopela was not tortured from what he personally told me. He was merely threatened with a mild form of torture: carrying a telephone directory above his head with his arms raised. He promised full co-operation and did so, to the extent of lying strictly according to police instructions. He was the only man I knew who gave evidence against himself. He received 10 years for training in the USSR and People's Republic of China. He was released after serving half his sentence. What happened to Bopela?

Piet Beyleveld was an ex-member of the Springbok Legion, a veteran of the 1939-45 war. Before his detention, he often conjectured on the staying power of newly detained comrades. 'M is detained. Do you think he won't break and start spilling the beans?' he asked me one day. When I replied that it was difficult to say, he made it known he did not trust Comrade M. 'I have never been M's fan,' he declared. He sounded like a solid rock. I believed he was as good and strong as he sounded. Piet's turn came. He sang like a canary and gave evidence in a number of cases including mine. What happened to Piet?

Hlapane was a hardworking activist. He was always on the go. None could doubt that he earned every cent of his functionary duties. He held top executive positions in both the SACP and the ANC. He was in the forefront of those who, in the very early days of violent methods of struggle, advocated elimination of sell-outs. He was to die a death of a sell-out. What happened to him? Well, I was happy I had survived and overcome both the stick and the carrot of the police. I was ready to join the army in the frontline. Robben Island was now scheduled as my next station. It was not my choice. Had I had viable alternatives I would not have chosen this option.

The present generation of Boers, like their fathers before them are a tenacious lot. Lt Dirker was typical. After the Grays' fiasco I was overconfident that none of the posse that had attended the event would still try to resume the wooing. I was mistaken. Dirker bounced back grinning, and persuasive: 'Dingake, haven't you changed your mind yet?' The man was a comic. My guffaw was spontaneous. Dirker understood. Every day after Dirker's last visit I chafed at the delay by the police. I was ready to be charged, tried and sentenced to a term of imprisonment on Robben Island. There was no hope of escaping the wrath I had invited. I was ready to face the music.

Nebulous pictures of the notorious island were beginning to crystallise on the mental horizon. The 'longing' to join the long incarcerated comrades now became a deliberate psychological effort. My relative freedom was past. It was no use wishing otherwise. I had crossed the Rubicon.

The police sergeant escorted me to the showers in the next block of cells. Outside my cell yard I spotted part of a newspaper hugging the wall. It appeared to have been blown there by the wind. With the agility, timing and derring-do of a prisoner I swept the vagrant newspaper under my shirt under the nose of the sergeant. My shower was to say the least perfunctory that day. Since I had arrived in Jeppe Police Station I had never caught a glimpse of a newspaper. I was in a hurry to peep through this tiny window into the world outside.

Back in the cell, in the privacy of a locked steel door, I spread the newsy loot before me. Kwame Nkrumah, the Osagyefo, had been couped.

Despite the severe setback in Ghana, the independence struggle was still on and gaining momentum. All the same a setback was a setback; one cannot run away from that fact. It was bad news. Bad news in gaol is bad. Bad squared. Police and prison warders know it. Therefore to them bad news is good, good news is bad. Prisoners must be sheltered against good news, it is bad for their morale. Bad news is right. Good for morale. Easy access to the coup news was suspicious. Did I really outmanoeuvre the normally vigilant sergeant in swiping the paper or did he conveniently turn a blind eye? The fight is multi-fronted. This was a psychological front.

18 March 1966. It is after lunch. I am relaxing after a menu of pork chops, fried potatoes and other mouthwatering goodies. Actually I am at the point of dozing off to allow the digestive system to discharge its functions unperturbed. Just at that moment there was a jingle of keys and the cell door opened to welcome two Security Branch officers accompanied by the police sergeant. One officer is Captain Broodryk, the other man is 'Tiny' Pretorius, a seven-footer hulk, contrary to his name. 'Tiny', to demonstrate his physical prowess, grabbed me by my belt and half-walked, half-pushed me, as we walked out of the cell. Attempts to resist the man's physical dictates made me move in a crablike fashion – forwards and sideways. The distance between my cell and the charge office, where I was being dragged to, was a mere 50 metres. It felt like the Chinese long march.

In the charge office I was fingerprinted and formally charged with statutory sabotage and other related counts. The charge sheet covered the period 1962 to 1965. From that moment I became an awaiting-trial prisoner. I was no longer a 180-day detainee, living under a cloud of complete uncertainty, a helpless client of the whims of the security police. I could now have access to a lawyer and perhaps to my family. True, the security police could still make it difficult for me to enjoy the rights I was entitled to under the law, but they would be acting unlawfully. Under the detention law there was nothing unlawful about holding me incommunicado. Even the torture they so lavishly administered in interrogation was not against the law, strictly speaking. The intention of the legislator was clear: suspects were to be coerced to 'co-operate' with the police.

As I stepped out of the charge office my eyes caught a newspaper poster I knew was not there when we had come in. The poster had been so strategically placed I could not have missed it. Certainly not with my searchlight focus on newsy exhibits. There it was, making a demoralising announcement: 'Defence and Aid Fund Banned'. The Defence and Aid Fund was originally founded by Rev Canon Collins in 1956 to assist in the defence of the 156 treason trialists. It continued its good work following the ignominious collapse of the State case after six years. People charged for political offences were always assured of some legal defence through the efforts of the Fund. More importantly, the dependants of the detainees could look forward to some limited maintenance from the Defence and Aid Fund. The government authorities had never liked its audacity. To provide help and defence counsel for people accused of political offences was tantamount to subversion in the eyes of the government.

Defence and Aid Fund functionaries became targets of sniping police meanness. They were shadowed by the Security Branch, their names and other particulars taken, and were generally harassed. Some were banned. Canon Collins, the spirit behind the organisation, was stigmatised as a Moscow agent. It was obvious that the organisation operated on borrowed time. The ban did not shock nor dismay me. What intrigued me was the timing of the ban. It was difficult to imagine that the banning of DAF and my formal charge were a mere coincidence. I grieved for a host of freedom fighters who were still to be arraigned without a hope of fair representation. Personally, the ban boosted my ego beyond words. I felt honoured by the ban. It meant I was an important figure to be selected for this great honour.

Actually I had never regarded myself as of any weight in the struggle. My role in the struggle was, I felt, expressive rather than influential. But here were the police making me a heavy of heavies. I know they did not look at it that way. They were just mean, vindictive and vengeful. By refusing to testify against Bram Fischer I had invited the wrath of their spitefulness. I had to be taught a lesson regardless of the side effects of such a lesson.

That night my supper was hard mealie pap in a rusty dish. Goodbye, macaroni, goodbye, pork chops, goodbye, custard and jelly, and goodbye chinaware plates! The mealie pap was dry and coarse. It looked quite inedible. How have the mighty fallen! A welcome change tonight was that two black constables brought the food into my cell unescorted. Before, according to what they told me, they used to carry the food from the kitchen up to the cell yard gate. From there the white sergeant took over. Blacks could not be trusted to keep their mouths shut about black detainees. They might let the cat out of the bag, when the letter and the spirit of the detention law required

120

utmost secrecy of place of detention of a detainee. This night the cloud of secrecy was lifted and the two constables brought in my food. They looked crestfallen and shamefaced as if they were the cause of my diet change. They apologised for serving me dry mealie pap. 'Why has your diet changed, Mr Dingake? You have been getting such good food . . . ?' I briefed them on why I had been spoiled with such nice food. Between themselves they raised a few cents to buy me milk and fish and chips. It was wonderful. That material and moral support will live with me to the grave.

After my fish and chips and milk supper I lay on my prison blankets, thinking. Thinking of my family, relatives, friends, comrades in gaol, in exile and inside the country. We were all sharing a common ideal. A free South Africa, catering for the interests of all its inhabitants regardless of their colour or creed. In the various places where each of us was, our link was the common suffering induced by the yearning for a free South Africa and the conviction that that day would come. I felt relieved, particularly when I remembered that virtually all mankind beyond the borders of South Africa supported the liberation struggle. I lay thinking for a long time.

My head started throbbing. 'Headache tablets, please,' I begged the police who came on inspections. They ignored me. The pain was excruciating. Every time a group came on inspection I asked for headache tablets and every time I was disregarded. The headache vanished on its own in the early hours of the morning. Since then I seem to be immunised from headaches. The callous police apparently did me a favour.

Within 48 hours after my charge I was taken to court for a formal remand. The young constable who drove me to the Johannesburg Magistrates' Court bungled instructions. He had been instructed to collect me from court after the remand and take me to Marshall Square Police Station where I was to stay until my next appearance in court. Instead he left me to my own devices and after the brief court appearance I found myself mingling freely with other prisoners. Strangely enough the security police also forgot about me after they had charged me. For two weeks I was on the loose with non-political prisoners. In 'Number Four' it was uhuru.

ON TRIAL

Prisons are prisons. They are the same. Everywhere. All of them. Just prisons. The proponents of the prison system allege that prisons are for rehabilitation of social miscreants. Rubbish! They are seedbeds for social miscreants. Engines of deviant behaviour. Prisons are a disgrace to society. Human society will never be civilised until it rids itself of this scandalous institution in its present form. Never. Prisons denature, dehumanise, depersonalise, decivilise and de-everything their victims.

In South Africa, they are the same as everywhere and worse than

121

anywhere else. Yet South African prisons are not the same. In South Africa, there are prisons and prisons. Prisons for whites, prisons for blacks, prisons for white males, prisons for black males, prisons for white females, prisons for black females, prisons for common-law offenders, prisons for political prisoners, medium prisons, maximum prisons, ultra-maximum prisons. South Africa has many prisons. The whole of South Africa is a prison. One huge prison compartmentalised into sub-prisons. Sometimes these prisons exist side by side, fence to fence or wall to wall, but they remain the same and not the same. Prisons and prisons and prisons. There are many other prisons in South Africa intangible and invisible. But they are there. They imprison the whole population.

The whites in South Africa live in a variety of prisons. The majority of them live in the Maximum Prison of Fear. They fear the blacks. They fear their overwhelming numbers. They fear their colour. They fear the sullenness of these blacks. They fear their unredressed grievances that erupt now and then in riots, bombs, stone-throwing, strikes, stay-at-home demonstrations and prayer meetings.

The whites also live in the Ultra-Maximum Prison of Prejudice. They despise the blacks, hate them and ridicule their blackness. All demands by blacks are viewed with contempt, let alone indifference. Blacks are non-humans or sub-humans – whichever is the baser; they are doormats to their luxury homes and offices of power; they clean their soiled feet on them, trample them under, to step into their luxurious citadels.

Some whites are prisoners of their conflicting consciences. Their consciences tell them what they do to blacks in the name of Christian civilization is wrong. Yet they stay put, watching the suffering of their fellow human beings. In their conscience straitjacket they cannot raise their arms to strike a blow for their vaunted Christianity.

Others live in the Central Prison of Greed. South Africa is a wealthy country, made wealthier by the sweat of black faces and the blisters of black palms. South Africa is a natural basket of cornucopia. Yet white South Africans are fettered by their infinite greed. They are determined to amass all the country's wealth for themselves, to deny the blacks any of this wealth except the crumbs from their tables. They condemn blacks to a Lazarusian prison.

Blacks are familiar with all prisons in South Africa. The physical and the psychological. Blacks live in ghettos called townships, formerly 'locations'. These serve as quarantines – social, cultural, economic and political quarantines. The privileges of whites must not be allowed to rub off on the unprivileged blacks, nor should the blacks be allowed to spread their infectious poverty, disease, and crime to the whites. Therefore physical contact should be restricted. Blacks must be quarantined and imprisoned in their ghetto prisons. After 11 pm, blacks must lock themselves up in their ghettos, otherwise the law, the law of the fear-imprisoned whites, states they

122

are liable to further imprisonment in the official prison – No. 4, Pretoria Local, Roeland St Gaol, Fort Glamorgan, etc.

Blacks are always in one prison or other. They cannot escape imprisonment for one moment. Blacks also know the prison of fear. They fear the whites. They fear their terrorist laws, the laws that terrorise them, brutalise them and turn them either into common-law criminals, political rebels or cringers and fatalists.

No. 4 was one among the many South African prisons.

No. 4 or the Johannesburg Fort as it was officially known was like any South African prison and unlike any other. It derived its name, the Fort, from its origins. It started as a Boer fortress against British colonialists during one of those hostilities in the dark pages of colonial rivalry. When hostilities ceased and peace was restored, the Fort became superfluous. A white elephant. The divided, disarmed and disenchanted Africans could be beaten back without garrison fortifications. A white laager would do.

Peace conditions are notorious for engendering booms. All kinds of booms. Technology booms, economic booms, influx booms, baby booms and all imaginable booms. In Johannesburg at the turn of the century, after the cessation of hostilities, these booms interacted negatively and positively, not to produce a hybrid boom but a thoroughbred of booms: anti-social crime. This one more than any other was considered scandalous. It had to be arrested, garaged and confined to barracks. Where else but in the underworldly tunnels of the burgeoning town. The Johannesburg Fort was an ideal cupboard to hide the skeletons, the scars and the abortions of Johannesburg the golden city.

No. 4 is no more. Its population was moved to a new prison near Soweto in 1981. All blacks are criminals, the interned and the uninterned. They must reside together, side by side. How else can one interpret the move? During its days in the centre of the metropolis it was a graduation school where the syllabus covered the entire spectrum of social crime and graduands were 'awarded' degrees at all levels of perversion. In Johannesburg townships, if one had not been to the Fort one was a 'moegoe, a barie, a Czao (a mug)'. I had been to No. 4 twice. Once for a tax offence. Another time for a pass offence. Technically I belonged to the 'clevers/smart alecs'.

Both times I came out of No. 4 convinced that it was one of the most productive crime factories in SA; more than other crime factories of its class perhaps it excelled in the quality of its products. 'Clevers' in Johannesburg committed deliberate crimes to enable them to go back to No. 4 to practise their professional careers in the lecture rooms, the surgeries, the drawing rooms and the technikons of their various departments.

'Saint' was my acquaintance long before I got locked up in No. 4 for a pass offence. To all appearances and tendencies, Saint was saintly, in keeping with his name. He was always clean and smartly dressed. He was never short of cash and I believe some of his friends and acquaintances are still indebted to him in cash from his generosity of those days. We knew however that he had a tendency to disappear for short intervals and would come back to report that he had been to the Fort. He always came back richer, healthier looking and more sociable. He was never secretive about making money in No. 4, only about how he made it.

In the reception office of the Fort, the first time I went to No. 4, I found Saint with his colleagues, African convicts and a white warder, doing roaring business, fleecing and initiating the uninitiated. The *modus operandi* was to harass, intimidate and assault newly arrived prisoners while they registered certain of their property items — money, watches and belts. After a few smacks, pushes, kicks and abuses for no rhyme or reason, the bumpkins were dazed, confused and game for the pot. Benumbed they never even heard nor answered the vital question: 'Ushiye malini? (How much money did you submit?)' As a result the reception clerks, Saint among them, filled in wrong amounts or left blanks against prisoners' names and pocketed the difference. The loss would never be recovered by the expropriated!

Except for my 'Hicock' belt, my cash and watch were safe and I was treated with respect, thanks to the acquaintance of Saint. He was actually annoyed that my belt had been irretrievably lost. He promised to get me a better one. That he did not do so was not due to inability on his part, probably it was a question of out of sight, out of mind. My stay had been short. Just a weekend — Friday, Saturday and Sunday.

During that weekend I witnessed some of the most callous bullying of prisoners by fellow prisoners in the communal cells. Hardened prisoners, for sheer sport, bullied, terrorised and assaulted newcomers to prison. Most of these newcomers were generally in for pass offences, liquor law infringements (eg possession of wine, beer or a brandy bottle), tresspass or curfew offences. Many of the newcomers cringed and allowed themselves to be punchbags. Others refused to be bullied and fought back, only to be ganged up against by the bullies and beaten up mercilessly. When the ganging up against the cheeky ones took place, an impromptu choir would be organised to sing some tune. Harmony or discord in the music did not matter, what mattered was the noise to drown the heartrending cries of the victims of the assault. I escaped the assaults, not through Saint's intercession but thanks to other 'clevers' who knew me in Sophiatown or Alexandra.

My heart pained to see fellow Africans reduced to this state of sub-human intercourse. Law-abiding citizens in No. 4 underwent a traumatic experience. After release they could not be the same again. Some might feel it is better to hang for a sheep than for a lamb and go for serious anti-social crime, others might become demoralised and begin to perceive life with jaundiced eyes, as nothing but a vale of tears. Both attitudes presuppose social degeneration.

Besides the bullying of the 'baries/mugs' by the 'clevers/smart alecs', gang warfare raged in No. 4 as a matter of course. Serious injuries were sustained and occasional deaths resulted from the senseless warfare in the cells of No. 4. Usually, gang members avoided cells of a rival gang; but sometimes it was possible for a rival gang member to stray into a wrong cell and then wanton savagery would come into its own.

No. 4 was not only an arena of mayhem and robbery, it impressed me as a convenient centre for the organised planning of future crimes. Here the vagrants exchanged tips about potential targets for stick-up raids and other anti-social mischiefs, analysed their blunders in the previous forays and planned anew for future opportunities. No. 4 was a godsend for hardened lawbreakers and a welcome school for aspirant candidates for outlawry.

Those were my broad impressions on my first two visits to No. 4 for petty offence. Now here I was in a dim-lit No. 4 cell crowded with fellow awaiting-trial prisoners who had appeared in court that day and were remanded in custody. It felt good to be among so many people after almost 12 weeks of isolation. I knew it was a matter of time before I would recognise an old acquaintance, maybe a former friend, in the cell crowd. That would be super. Since we had arrived very late from the Magistrates' Courts, we had not gone through the reception office routine and I had missed the practical reminder of the induction to No. 4 – preplanned harassment that conditioned the uninitiated to the 'kill' by the reception clerks. Perhaps I wanted to believe that No. 4 had changed from its old ways.

My delusion was shortlived. A couple of bullies were at work already in the dim-lit transit cell. Those who had grabbed a few decent blankets on entering the cell were being deprived of them and their noses bloodied for their forwardness. My blankets were among the slightly decent ones so I watched the bullies' bloody path with concern. Should I submit and surrender to the bullying of the couple? Submissiveness does not come easily to me. Not to bullies of any hue in any case. If they touched me, I was going to be hurt. No. 4 bullies do not take kindly to resistance if they can overcome it. I was resigned to any hurt inflicted in a just struggle.

As I stood focusing on the bullies and meditating my reaction to their likely behaviour, someone next to me spoke to me: 'Ek sê broer, is jy nie ou bra Joe Moagi? (I say brother, are you not brother Joe Moagi?)' 'Yes, I am,' I replied. Moagi was my underground pseudonym when I was on the run. My acquaintance had belonged to a study group I occasionally gave a talk to. As soon as he had introduced me to two of his friends I drew their attention to the

125

rampage of the cell bullies and suggested we teach them a lesson if they tried their mischief on any of us. The odds were against them: four to two. The bullies did not overhear us, but they ended up on the opposite side of the cell in some rare telepathic response.

'Why are you here?' I asked Benny. He did not have to ask me. He sensed the source of trouble, he said. As for himself: 'The police allege we killed a white policeman.' The full story was that two drunken police in mufti were observed harassing the law-abiding citizens of Alexandra on a late Sunday afternoon along 14th Avenue, by demanding passes and permits. Benny's group approached the drunken cops: 'Hey, brothers, stop harassing your own brothers. And you are drunk!' Benny and Co then went their way but the township residents were incensed by the unrepentant behaviour of the cops and incited by the fleeting intervention of Benny and Co. A mob encircled the cops, grilled and threatened them. One cop panicked and bolted. He was battered to death. The second one escaped by the skin of his teeth. He reported the hair-raising incident at Wynberg police station and after a few days the 'inciters' were rounded up and charged with murder. The passes, I thought, would remain a single major source of friction between the Africans and the law – a source of tragic and miserable circumstances.

The cell we transferred to the following morning was big. It accommodated more than a hundred prisoners. The four of us had clubbed together since the previous night. It was necessary in the chill and overawing atmosphere that prevailed in the big cell.

A bunch of bullies occupied the centre stage in the cell. Their clean, new blankets and mats were piled right in the middle of the cell. There they relaxed, smoked their dagga cigarettes and kept other cell mates under mischievous surveillance. The rest of the blankets and mats were piled in a corner against the wall. Lice and bugs crawled all over these bundles, stacked against the wall. Just the distant sight of these lousy parasites made one's body uncomfortably creepy. At night the main preoccupation of inmates was an attempt to eliminate these insects. Their reproductive capacity exceeded their mortality rate and the task of elimination was never fulfilled.

The cell big guns in their central position seemed an island unto themselves unplagued by the bugs and the lice. They enjoyed two advantages: good relations with the warders and subservient relations with the majority of the inmates. As the self-appointed spokesmen of the cell they were the ones who asked for extra blankets when the need arose and if the extras were new then their distribution was confined to the big guns alone. The isolation of the new blankets from the lice-infested general pool kept the big guns relatively free from the insects. On occasions when the bugs and lice tended to make a mockery of the quarantine then the army of cowering inmates was mobilised against them. They fell down on their knees and crushed the parasites with their thumbnails.

126

Cell administration was in the hands of the bullies. Every morning they selected cell cleaners and subjected them to indiscriminate assaults while they washed the cell. Water was thrown on the floor, and cleaners, each armed with a piece of rag, stood in a row at one end of the long cell and awaited the order from the cleaning 'supervisor'. The shout 'scooter!' would be the signal for the day's cleaners to start their cleaning race. On their fours, and the span would be on their speedy cleaning routine pushing the water hard and fast; at the same time ensuring that one did not fall behind others. Those who fell behind received beatings, kicks and the word 'scooter' accompanied every assault. Some collapsed along the way from fatigue and were not spared the customary spurs. 'Scooter! scooter!' the supervisors shouted and trampled on the prostrate. Those not involved for the day huddled on the sidelines and exchanged timorous glances. Tomorrow may be anybody's turn. It was dreadful. Indiscriminate assaults were not limited to the cleaning period only, they spread evenly throughout the day. Excuses for assaults, and bully sport were never wanting. A side glance at a bully, an uncontrollable cough, an innocent cheery laugh might be cause for an inquisition and subsequent punishment. Bullies' moods are capricious and unpredictable.

In the course of the day the four of us accumulated more old acquaintances, mainly from Alexandra township. We had sized up the situation and decided we wouldn't allow the big shots to interfere with us in any way. We would resist and defend ourselves. Our attitude was correct, but it might lead to inter-township gang warfare which was not desirable. Moreover, assuming we stood our ground and the big shots respected us on that ground, what would happen to the rest of the inmates who could not master a cohesive defence? Our stand seemed selfish and not in keeping with sound political principles. We did need a self-interested short-term approach as well as a disinterested long-term one.

Every evening prisoners were checked – counted to ensure that no escapes occurred during the day. Before the warders came in to count, it was the big shots' self-assumed duty to see that the inmates fell in line to facilitate the counting procedure. The prisoners fell in line and squatted on their haunches and awaited the warders. The big shots only fell in their own line when the warders entered the cell. The previous evening I had not liked the idea of waiting on my haunches for the warders, so I decided not to fall in, in a hurry. I felt also that the big shots would have enough sense to realise I was not a 'moegoe (mug)' to be given standard treatment. I hung back and ignored the fall-in orders. It took guts. Surprisingly the big boys seemed to ignore my 'challenge'. After a while I walked slowly to join the rear of the squatters. Before I got to the back of the line one of the big shots called me: 'Ek sê broer hoor hier . . . (I say, brother, listen here . . .)' My eyes searched the squatting line to see whether my club saw what was about to happen to me. I hesitated before I walked back to where the big guns were sitting. No doubt, the fat was in the fire. I was going to pay for my indiscipline. Why did I provoke the scene? And it was going to be ugly, for though I felt scared, I was determined not to be a passive participant in the game about to be played at my expense. I kept casting my glance at the squatting rows to see whether my friends were raising their eyebrows at the unfolding event. With my vision impaired by rising anxiety I could not even locate any of them in the lines. They seemed to have been submerged by the prevalent mood of the cell – resignation to bullying.

Now I stood eyeball to eyeball with my summoner. He delighted in keeping me in brief suspense. 'Ken jy my? (Do you recognise me?)' he asked at last. I did not, but the question was an invitation to look harder at the guy. I studied the unscarred, kind, handsome face and wondered why he was mixing with the rough-hewn gang, warfare-scarred characters like Manyiks, the prominent 'Scooter squad' driver. No, I could not place the guy. I might have met him anywhere in Soweto or in the local trains, and we might have argued about football teams, Orlando Pirates/the buccaneers – versus Moroka Swallows/the birds, or politics, or played a game of rummy together in the train, to shorten the long train journey to or from work. Otherwise he was a complete stranger to me. He, on the other hand, knew me very well. He knew my former place of employment, he had been there to see me, sent by my ANC Comrade P. He had also met me in the company of D, another member of the ANC.

After the count check, Mighty introduced me to his friends, the hard hitting Manyiks and the others. We sat down on their new-smelling blankets and a container of hard boiled eggs was placed before us. I was allowed an extra three for my three friends. It was the turn of the tide in our oppressive cell.

These apparently incorrigible criminals were very ordinary human beings playing brutes in a brutal environment. From the moment one of them recognised me as an ANC member and the subsequent talk I had with them about our obligations to each other as an oppressed group, our cell was transformed into a new cell, where peace and sensible social intercourse became the order of things. Our cell soon became a haven for a flood of 'refugees' from adjacent cells where persecution of prisoner by prisoner was still top of the agenda. It became so overcrowded that one of my 'converts' turned to me one night: 'Jy sien bra Mike (You see bra Mike) . . . that's what comes of being nice to these moegoes (mugs). Now we will soon be sleeping on top of each other!' He was quite serious and suggested I should let them reinstate the jungle methods. No, I told him: 'Let us exercise patience. Ons is almal broers! (We are all brothers!)' 'Jy, bra Mike, jy is too much van 'n kristen (You, bra Mike, you are too much of a Christian)' he grumbled. The principle of harmonious relations was

128

further entrenched and consolidated by a series of talks I gave on the ANC, its aims and objectives.

African political grievances in South Africa are basic to all the other grievances, cultural, social and economic. Reactions to my talks varied from incredulous silence to cynical disbelief, from intelligent questions to jubilant applause. The cynics were the most lively and interesting: they supported the aims and objectives of the ANC, they explained, but they did not agree with its methods of 'non-violence'. 'Ons soek twas bra Mike, dis lank wat julle praat, (We want guns, bra Mike; you have been talking too long'), they argued even when I informed them MK was training cadres in military art outside the country. To some of my audience, training outside the country was a waste of time. As far as they were concerned they could handle a gun and they needed no training except possession of guns and an order to shoot the 'lanies' (whites). In spite of the thread of frustration and impatience that ran through the arguments and questions, the perception of the source of social injustice and the spirit to fight against it was evident and inspiring.

After the many weeks I had spent in isolation it was delightful to be among the masses. The section warders kept a very low profile. 'Two-boy', the seven-footer white sergeant featured mainly as supervisor of the prisoners' visits, where he harassed and pretended to harass the visited prisoners while he received bribes and allowed unauthorised articles into the cells—money, dagga, and other contraband of prison. 'Two-boy's' business was smokkel (smuggling). He disguised it very well by his simulated stand-offish manners. When one got to know him better he was the darling of the 'sharp' prisoners. His colleague and right-hand assistant was Sergeant Mhlongo who was just as corrupt, guileful and nice. I presented Mhlongo with an expensive pen because he was the one warder who knew I was in the wrong section and I wanted him to keep that knowledge to himself. He did, thanks to my expensive pen. In fairness to him I must say he looked after me very well on meat days with a meatful plate. Other black warders swore they knew why I was in. Theirs was an erroneous hunch, based on the quality of my clothes, especially my American shoes. They believed that I specialised in bank hold-ups and referred to me, with a wink and a knowing smile, as tycoon. Had they known that on my third day in No. 4 I had to sign the Power of Attorney to enable my wife to withdraw the last R20 from my Barclays Bank account for her monthly rent, they would have been shocked by their wide guesses.

During the day we mixed with inmates from cells next to ours. That was how the word spread that our cell, apart from the bugs and the lice, was the nearest thing to five star accommodation. We attempted to influence the big guns in the neighbouring cells to emulate our example but, in spite of some assurances, the influence never rubbed off if we judged by the steady influx into our cell.

Besides political discussions, I found myself acting as adviser to many inmates on various issues. Those who could not read and write came to me for assistance. Although I speak both Xhosa and Zulu, at the time I could not write these languages very well; nonetheless the letters were dictated and written. Now and then I had to advise on the contents of the letters, because inmates seemed to have a remarkable inclination to tell all, in their letters, to families. The prison authorities had little bother intercepting this correspondence and passing it to the police to use as evidence in court. Poor people.

The most pathetic aspect of the African prisoner's fate is ignorance of the law as well as court procedure. The 'clevers' were exceptions of course. Since the crimes they committed were generally premeditated and planned, 'clevers' often displayed impressive court craft when they appeared before judicial officers. They knew how to exploit the loopholes of the law and how to cast doubts on hearsay evidence. Boy M, a veteran of many court cases, told me a story of how his accomplice was acquitted after challenging the prosecution on 'the irregularities of the identification parade'. I asked Boy M what the standard of education of his friend was. With his characteristic sense of humour, Boy M answered me: 'He ran away from school at playtime.'

For the majority of the prisoners in No. 4 the internationally acclaimed impartiality of South African courts could not be substantiated. How can the impartiality of law courts be objectively evaluated when they administer racial laws or administer the common law to distinct social groups, with disparate cultural backgrounds and enjoying lopsided incomes?

South African whites are not the same as blacks except for their privileged skins. Some of them have distinguished themselves by identifying, against all odds with the struggle of the oppressed. The numbers however are negligible and few and far between. The majority of the whites, thanks to the laws that uphold and enforce segregation in all walks of life, and policy makers who preach and practise racial inequality and race privilege, from dawn to dawn, are patently ignorant of the humanity of the black man, utterly contemptuous of his dignity and consistently prejudiced against black interests. South African judicial officers are an inbred part of the system they help to administer; their impartiality or the allusion to it begs the question—a very complex question.

The second point that militates against the avowed impartiality of South African courts is the cultural and educational background of the people afflicted by the law. The maxim, ignorance of the law is no excuse, is a cultural concept that ignores the cultural background of other groups in an unjust heterogeneous society. Ignorance of the law is a factor of social opportunities. Those who are ignorant of the law when they have the opportunity not to be, cannot complain when the maxim is applied to them. To apply the precept to those without the necessary opportunities is partial and unjust. Unequal opportunities, particularly in education, undermines the impartiality of the South African courts of law towards blacks. The third point against impartiality in favour of blacks is the low incomes accruing to them. Legal defence is a luxury many blacks cannot afford; yet this is the group that needs it most. A black appearing in a court of law is always pitted against an unsympathetic prosecutor who is well read in law, and before a magistrate or judge who passes judgment on the basis of learned argument on abstruse statutes and stereotype rules of procedure. Against that formidable army of judicial process, an undefended black person has a very slim chance of going scot-free in any prosecution.

The disadvantages outlined above are common knowledge to all students of African affairs in South Africa. But nowhere are they so glaring and loathsome as in a No. 4 cell, when you watch and listen to the pathos of ignorance, bewilderment and helplessness of the inmates. The victims of the pass laws, more than any others, arouse the strongest emotions; precisely because in a normal society they are essentially the lawabiding core. They do their best to operate within the law by applying for documents that qualify them for good citizenship, yet these same laws disqualify them, the majority, from these noble social ideals. In the cells you could pick them out at a mile – dumb, dazed and sheepish in their look.

After two weeks on the loose in No. 4 I had to appear in court for formal remand before summary trial. In court I found my sister, Helen, waiting with my attorney, Ruth Hayman, and the British Consul in Johannesburg. It was very heartening. The ban on the Defence and Aid Fund apparently was not meant for me, or I was immune from such petty vindictiveness. Before my turn came to appear before the court I had a reasonable time with the consul, briefing him on my illegal arrest. With my lawyer I raised the passport issue as the most urgent. She was enthusiastic and raring to go on the matter. It was to cost her her freedom and a journey into exile. The moment she approached the police she was mysteriously banned and house-arrested, besides other petty harassments she was subjected to. The passport itself never surfaced. If it was capable of bringing such swift retribution to law agents then I might as well spare the next potential victim the nasty experience.

In court I was joined with Issy Heymann as co-accused. He was already serving 12 months for refusing to give evidence in Mxolisi Jackson Fuzile's case. From court I was taken to the Grays, the Security Branch headquarters in Johannesburg. The game was up. I was back in the hands of the security police. Captain Broodryk accompanied me to my cell in No. 4 to collect my personal effects. Word went round like wildfire in the cell about my transfer to

131

Pretoria. Pandemonium broke loose as every cell mate rushed to the section corridor to bid me farewell. Amid cries of bra Mike, bra Mike, the security police whisked me away. Broodryk could not get over the farewell scene. He asked 'Two-boy' how I had come to be in a communal cell. 'Two-boy' did not know. A serious security lapse had been to my benefit. I will carry the memory of the honour of a time well spent among the wretched of South Africa's dungeons.

In Pretoria Captain Broodryk appeared to be in his element. He bustled around and busied himself with some files – probably mine – and whistled a tune of contentment. 'Do you want us to organise you a lawyer or will you organise one for yourself?' he asked with tongue in cheek and an air of achievement. He was not aware I had a lawyer because he had not been to court. Broodryk could not hide his strong displeasure at the turn of events. 'Who is your lawyer?' he demanded. In the context of the extremely hostile reaction, I dared not reveal any names, Broodryk might commit murder. He was looking berserk for no apparent reason. So my answer had to be roundabout, omissive and plausible. 'My wife,' I said, 'has sent a message to say she has engaged a lawyer for me.' The answer appeared to subdue the captain a bit. In time of course, he would know who the audacious lawyer was, because she would be raising the question of my passport with them. It was dangerous for a known liberal to defend a 'terrorist' when the ban of the Defence and Aid Fund was ostensibly aimed at thwarting that very fellow-travellership.

Ruth Hayman bore the full wrath of the political avengers. However, she had already briefed George Bizos, SC, to represent me in the Pretoria Supreme Court. When George Bizos came to consult me I had already read about Ruth's harassment and house arrest in smuggled newspapers. Pretoria Local was good in that respect.

The first day in court was taken up by the question of my illegal arrest which I raised personally and which was dismissed because the police lied that I was arrested at Beitbridge on the side of South Africa. The disappearance of my passport in the hands of the police was overlooked and not investigated by the court, even when the British Consulate submitted an affidavit which confirmed my Bechuanaland citizenship and the fact that I was carrying a Bechuanaland passport issued at Palapye in 1964. It is true that Justice Viljoen did refer the matter to the Attorney General's office for his decision, but the moment the AG ruled that I had to be tried in spite of the international implications of the case, the good judge went ahead full steam. I refused to plead to the charges on the basis that my arrest was illegal and the Pretoria court had no jurisdiction to try me.

Five non-police witnesses, among them Bartholomew Hlapane and Piet Beyleveld, gave evidence against Issy and myself. My sister-in-law Chloe and Mrs Violet Weinberg, both of whom had been in

132

detention for six months, were subpoenaed to give evidence against us, in terms of the 180-day clause of the General Law Amendment Act. Both of them refused in spite of the danger of being sent to jail for it.

Issy and I were impressed by this stand by the two women; in contrast to the men who were extending themselves in a bid to outclass each other in serving the interests of an unrepresentative government, the women stood their ground and refused to co-operate with the police against their principles. They exploded the myth of the weaker sex beyond any doubt. Chloe was acquitted. Mrs Weinberg was sentenced – to a lenient three months. Thanks to their able defence counsel – it wasn't any worse.

On 6 May 1966 judgment and sentence were passed. Issy received five years, which he would serve in one of the Pretoria prisons. Mine was 15 years which I would serve on Robben Island where the black political activists served their time. From history, I remembered that Robben Island used to be a leper colony. It is an irony of history that the true moral lepers have been able with such impunity to send the non-lepers to a place equated with leprous infection.

Issy and I drove away from court in the same car but already we travelled to our prison sentences in different styles. Issy sat in front, his limbs unfettered. I sat in the back seat, my hands manacled to my back. It was not painful to go into a car like that. Just awkward and mortifying if one was sensitive. Maybe silly if one was new to the whims of the advocates of baaskap. Otherwise humdrum and typical of beautiful South Africa. Back in Pretoria Local to start my 15-year term, one of my casual awaiting-trial prisoners friends, whom I sometimes met during exercise periods, wanted to know my sentence. When I said 15 years, he emitted a little cry of horror. 'Why, bra Mike? Why? What have you done?' he queried with genuine shock. Trying to explain to him that actively demanding equal rights in South Africa was a serious offence, did not make any sense to him. 'Nee, nee, bra Mike . . .' he moaned uncontrollably.

The security police in South Africa are never done with a political detainee even after conviction and sentence. Victory for them is not a once-for-all event, it is rather a process. A statement from a detainee is a win for them but it is not considered real victory if the detainee does not surrender the principles he stood for before confession. Unless he becomes a turncoat by giving evidence against his erstwhile colleague(s) he is still suspect. A court conviction is another battle won and a cause for celebration but it is still not the ultimate with the security men. They continue to watch and nag one, regardless of how strongly one parades one's iron determination.

Shortly before my conviction a prisoner, Raymond Mnyanda, insinuated himself into my lonely company. He was apparently an educated man. Raymond was back from Robben Island where he had

133

served part of his five-year sentence. He was now in Pretoria Local pending his release date. Between Robben Island and Pretoria he had tarried at two prisons: East London and Leeuwkop. At both prisons he had mixed with political prisoners as he had done on Robben Island. He was keen to share a cell with me, he told me. After sentence I had to apply to the Prisons Security Chief, Colonel Aucamp, for permission to be taken out of isolation – it was illegal for a convicted prisoner to be kept in isolation. All this came out of notes we smuggled to each other. Being the newcomer in gaol I was entitled to fish for inside information as much as possible. Robben Island, how was it? Do prisoners know what is going on outside? How and where do they get the information? Do prisoners work hard there? Are they beaten up and tortured? How is Mandela? How is Sisulu? Did you meet them? Are they segregated or living with other prisoners? What is the food like? What are the chances of escape there?

Raymond answered my questions satisfactorily. Though I was suspicious of his unrestrained friendliness, it was clear he was from Robben Island. The story of his arrest however did not stick together. It sounded like a well-rehearsed fabrication that did not reckon with my political background. Raymond was a member of the Progressive Party. He was a journalist by profession. He left the country without a passport to cover the Pafmecsa (Pan African Freedom Movement of East, Central and Southern Africa) Conference in 1961. He was picked up on his return from East Africa where the Conference took place. Five years! That was his story. I could not remember a single black member of the white Progressive Party. I had not read the constitution it probably had. I read all the English language newspapers, dailies and weeklies; the name Raymond Mnyanda was unfamiliar in their columns. The date of the Pafmecsa conference he referred to was a figment of his imagination. Finally, in 1961 leaving the country without a passport was not such a punishable offence as Raymond wanted to make me believe. He had to be watched.

When I acceded to his suggestion to apply for permission to share a cell with him I had already worked out the strategy and tactics of our cell-mateship. According to prison regulations two is the only number that is not permissible in one cell. It might encourage sodomy. When Aucamp granted permission he had to abide by the regulation. The third man who joined us was an ex-Msomi gang member who was doing 15 years for armed robbery. He claimed to know me from Alexandra. I did not remember him although from his conversation he had no doubt been a member of the gang.

Raymond worked hard but in vain to suck information that had eluded the police. I thoroughly enjoyed watching his frustration when his repertoire of wiles came to naught. During the day Raymond worked in the white prisoners' section, where part of his job, according to him, was to wheel around one of the white prisoners, Finkelstein, a paraplegic. He brought daily 'greetings' from

134

all of them, mainly Bram. And every night he was tireless in exhorting me to drop Bram a note. I had to be flexible with my excuses for not writing – laziness. Lack of interesting news to report; distrust of ex-Msomi. Tomorrow. Tomorrow. I'll write. The warders might search you, you know! Raymond persisted. I resisted.

As time went on, Raymond and Aucamp resorted to theatrics. Raymond might start by asking for some permission or other. Aucamp's 'disapproval' would arouse Raymond's 'revolutionary' indignation. Revolutionary slogans would come thick and fast from Raymond, and from Aucamp the attitude would be granite and the language uncouth and uncompromising. After the departure of the Colonel, Raymond would still be spitting fire. It was extremely comical.

Soon I was to know what Raymond was in for. Fraud! Perhaps I would never have known the extent of his fraudulent practices if he had not panicked. But panic he did when he met a young man who knew exactly why he (Raymond) was in gaol. 'Don't tell Mike why I am here . . .' he pleaded with Moss. Moss met me in the section corridor and he cupped his mouth with one hand to talk to me: 'Does Raymond tell you why he is here? Do you know what he is in for?' 'Yes,' I answered, 'he told me he is in for leaving the country without a passport'. 'Balls!' said Moss raising his voice with irritation and oblivious of the warder a few steps away, 'he was convicted for fraud. He used to work for Ephraim Tshabalala, the Mofolo tycoon . . .' Later Moss told me more about Raymond's case. He went on to warn me against him. He had information that Raymond was an informer. He was in the pay of the gatas (police). There was no need to change my relations or attitude to Raymond. From the first day he said 'Hi, Mike' without prior introduction I regarded him as a stool-pigeon. We shared a cell, exchanged innocent anecdotes and so forth, but I never dropped my guard. I kept him strictly at arm's length, and relished the discipline I exercised.

When we parted with Raymond, we shook hands, and at the cell door he turned dramatically and shouted, Amandla (Power): (the ANC slogan) while he raised his fist militantly. His boss, Colonel Aucamp, smiled amiably, unconscious of the anomalous nature of that smile. I could not respond to the farcical salute. It was Raymond's unwitting parting insult to my intelligence. I began to regret that I had not exposed him to himself. Too late now. He was out to do damage where damage mattered most – outside, where the epicentre of the struggle resided.

With Raymond gone, my stay in Pretoria was without potential. I had to be transferred. The prison transport service in South Africa has long big trucks to convey prisoners from court to prison or prison to prison. These trucks have three compartments: the first one I believe is for black females, the second one for white males, the third one for black males. White females do not seem to have a compartment of

135

their own, I suppose, because they are a rare species in corridors of prisons.

To prevent me from contaminating the common-law prisoners *en route* to Leeuwkop, I travelled alone in the white-male compartment. Leeuwkop prison was mainly a transit prison, a sort of distribution centre for convicted prisoners. Prisoners from most centres passed through Leeuwkop to be classified and allocated their final penal destinations. It had a terrible reputation: prison gang warfare was rife, personal vendettas arising from double-crossing and other falling out of ertswhile accomplices were settled here, at this junction of evildoers. Leeuwkop warders were said to belong to some of these gangs. Prisoners butchered each other with the connivance or active participation of the law enforcement officers. Leeuwkop was also notorious for filthy body searches. On admission prisoners were thoroughly searched – stripped naked and forced to thawusa – an acrobatic dance that exposed the rectum. Even after the thawusa warders' gloved fingers poked into the rectum to ensure that no cash, dangerous weapons or any contraband was concealed deeper down this most private organ, so anatomically screened from external interferences.

I dreaded prison gang-warfare very much. Non-gang members could be caught in crossfire, and I might be the one. But I dreaded more the rectum-search. I thought the day it happened to me I might suffer a heart attack and go the way of all mortal flesh. When the truck came to a halt in the prison grounds my heart was already pounding. I was opened up first and head-warder 'Magalies' Lansberg was already waiting for me. He welcomed me in Setswana, which he spoke fluently: 'Moloi ke wena, a gorogile (you witch, you have arrived)'. Although it was said in bantering tones I objected to the remark. 'I understand you have applied for permission to study and why did you not do it while you were outside?' 'Magalies' continued his taunts unmindful of my objections. I informed him that just before my arrest I had completed forms to study with the University of London. 'Forget about the University of London. If we give you permission to study it will be with Unisa (University of South Africa). We do not allow prisoners to study with outside schools here', he asserted with authority greater than his rank.

'Magalies' took me through the maze of Leeuwkop doors, corridors and sections, straight to the isolation section into a cell converted from a storeroom. Inside the cell were Siegfried Bhengu, Patrick Bapela, Norman Mmitshane and Jerry Rasefate. Only the last named was not a political prisoner, but I knew him from my Sophiatown days. Fabulous: I had escaped the humilating search and I was among comrades and an acquaintance.

Unbeknown to me Leeuwkop had had a face-lift in the immediate past. Obviously the passage of political prisoners through here had made an impact. The vanguard of the politicos beginning from 1962 had of course borne the brunt of the prison administration. Colonel Bouwer, who had died a short while before in a car accident, had been the Commanding Officer of Leeuwkop before his death. The prisoners agreed Bouwer had transformed Leeuwkop's lifestyle. In typical Boer paternalism, he referred to prisoners as 'bant'abami (my children)', and many believed he really loved the prisoners as his own children. Assaults on prisoners still occurred especially at 'phaka (dish-up time)'. Head warder Khumalo and others loved to see prisoners jog to collect their food from the kitchen. Our section was exempted.

Jerry Rasefate was a nice guy. But he was not one of us. We could not take the chances with him. Even during the day when he was out in the yard doing his 'staff' duties we were careful about what what we said lest listening devices were planted somewhere in the cell. We confined our conversation to general topics, the United Nations – on which some of us vented their frustrations and some of us defended – Indonesia – about which we all speculated concerning the Chinese role in the coup and the CIA counter-role in the counter-revolution of Suharto – Sino-Soviet dispute – in which sides were taken and neutrality observed. Patrick had been to both countries. He was strongly pro-Soviet and violently anti-Chinese. Norman Mmit-shane had been trained in several African countries and the People's Republic, he was pro-Peking and anti-Moscow. Bhengu seemed to be neutral on the side of the People's Republic. Mike maintained strict non-alignment in the debate. The arguments were forceful and interesting.

In the evenings, Jerry entertained us with the tidbits of the underworld, the who's-who of crime that does not pay. He brought up many names I remembered. One of them, I shall call A was my social and gambling friend in the early fifties. A and I had often discussed the plight of Africans and deplored the worthless existence we existed. Our minds vacillated between organised banditry or orga-nised insurrection. Later we had gone our different ways. A, a gun-toting bank robber and I, a public-square agitator. Both of us were in gaol doing 15 years each for our dissimilar crimes.

The atmosphere in our section was very relaxed. The rest of the cells in the section were single isolation-cells, housing some who were punished and others who were isolated for their own safety. One of these was someone 'renowned' outside as 'Black Car'. Black Car got his name from a mysterious black car he was driving around in Soweto to harass, mug, and kidnap Sowetan night lifers prowling the unsafe streets of the township. Black Car was in for his black car crimes and a spate of armed robberies. When Bhengu and I got an opportunity to talk to him, we wanted to know from him why he, a black man, had been persecuting and terrorising his fellow blacks in the townships. 'Simple,' said Black Car. 'Our fellow blacks are responsible for our being in gaol. You rob a rich white man in town.

137

When you appear in court, there is your own black brother testifying as an eyewitness of your crime, against you. What business have blacks to be siding with whites against their own brothers? I resent it. I despise it. That is why I do what I do to them.' We could not move Black Car from his logic and philosophy. He informed us he was due to appear in court in the Western Transvaal. He would escape en route and go back to Soweto to continue his dubious mission, he told us.

A big group of us appeared before a Prison Board, the body that is responsible for classifying prisoners into groups. The classification is arbitrary and punitively designed. Before we appeared before the Board an Alex acquaintance, 'Broadway' Baduza, had suggested that as a first offender I would be placed in Group B. He had a long gaol record but did not expect to do worse than Group C. He was overjoyed that we were likely to be together in Witbank Prison where prisoners were engaged in creative industry, tailoring, shoemaking, etc. My contention that I was bound for Robben Island, he dismissed with authority. 'Forget it! You are not going to Robben Island, you are going to Witbank. In 1963 I was there with Robert Sobukwe, the PAC president. Yes, politicos do go to Witbank.'
'Broadway' was shocked when the Chairman of the Board castigated me for misdirected ambitions and pronounced I would be sent to Robben Island with some air of pomp. 'This one,' said the jowl-sagging Board Chairman, pointing at me for all to see, 'wants to take over the seat of the Prime Minister. His wife is in Bechuanaland to continue where he left off – organising subversion against SA. She will never set her foot in South Africa, and if she does, she will spend half her lifetime in gaol like her husband. Although he is a first offender,' he continued, addressing the captive audience, 'he will start in D group. He will serve his sentence on Robben Island maximum security prison.' 'Broadway' was stunned and disappointed. In spite of his long record, he was classified as Group C, as he had predicted. Then there was a man who was doing 15 years for murder – a first offender like me. He was made Group B.
Three of us left for Robben Island, on Thursday 21 July 1966, Patrick Bapela, Norman Mmitshane and myself. Siegfried, for some unclear objective of the security police or the Prisons Department, remained in Leeuwkop. Norman and Patrick were handcuffed together. Besides handcuffs, my legs were in irons. I was expected to jump on to the back of a high truck in those fetters. It was an unalluring and impossible feat. 'Magalies', mouthing obscenities and implying that I wanted to escape and that was why I was thus handled, heaved me up the back of the truck with the assistance of two young escorts. I overheard 'Magalies' inform the two in Afrikaans that I was going to shit in segregation. That was bad news. It added to the discomfort of the handcuffs and the leg irons.

Michael Dingake — in Botswana in 1985. *Photo: Lars Tallert.*

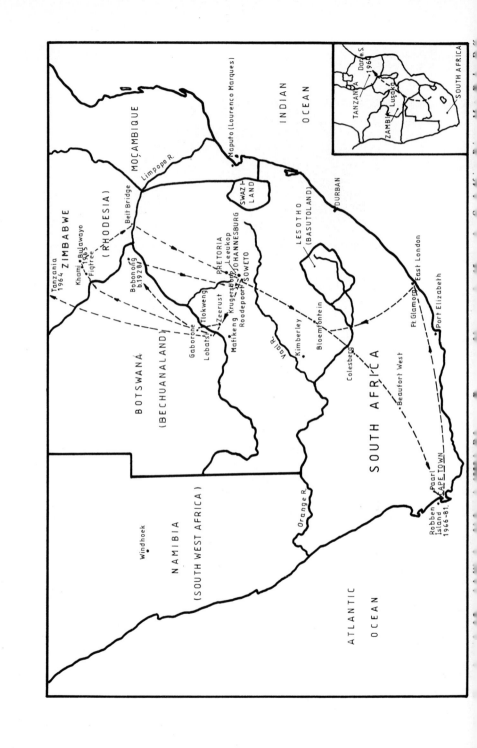

The church, in Bobonong, where Michael Dingake started his schooling. (See EARLY ENVIRONMENT in Chapter 1).

The pass office in Albert Street in Johannesburg in the early 1950s. What passes meant for those who had to carry them is described in Chapter 2. (See SOPHIATOWN AND ALEXANDRA and JOINING ANC).

The Johannesburg Fort, or No. 4 Prison. Michael Dingake's experience of the prison is described in Chapter 3. (Se
ON TRIAL).

Robben Island off the coast near Cape Town, where many of South Africa's political prisoners are held, and wher
Michael Dingake was imprisoned from 1966 to 1981. (See Chapter 4).

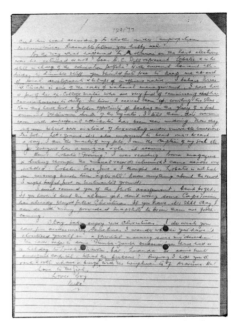

...xamples of censored letters, two of which Michael Dingake received mutilated. The third letter, by him, he was ...rced to rewrite with the underlined parts replaced before the prison authorities would post it. (See LETTERS AND ...ISITS in Chapter 4).

those hussies and fastworkers they will have no chance
with me around. I can sock too much.

It is rather difficult for me to tell
you anything of note because when I do you can be
sure of the fate of that missive. Anyway here goes
the humble stuff and blow me if it is not;
Agge had an operation for bunions and is not
feeling quite good one of her feet giving her a bit
trouble. I have not seen her for ages poor thing.
Peggy's kids may come and stay with me next
year. Rosejo and Mi-lai will be at college then.

The inhibiting effects of censorship on people writing to prisoners are illustrated in this letter from Michael Dingake's wife.

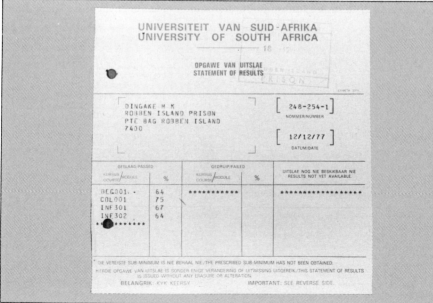

During his 15 years on Robben Island Michael Dingake obtained three degrees through study by correspondence. The certificate shows his examination results during the first year of a Bachelor of Commerce degree. (See STUDIES in Chapter 4).

is uncle greets Michael Dingake on his return home.   *Photo: Trevor Sampson.*

ournalists from the Botswana Press Association interviewing Michael Dingake at the border with South Africa after is release from prison. (See Chapter 5).

With his wife Edna shortly after his release.

With his daughter Gosego at the ANC's Solomo Mahlangu Freedom College in Tanzania. She was tw weeks old when he was kidnapped in Rhodesia an handed over to the South Africans who tortured, tried an imprisoned him. (See Chapter 3).

Michael Dingake greets SWAPO leader Toivo ja Toivo on a visit to Gaborone in Botswana. The two men had spen many years on Robben island together.

                                                                    Photo: Michael Kahr

At Colesberg Prison, across the Orange Free State border in the Cape, we picked up Govan Mbeki. He had been kept there for months in isolation to penalise him for giving evidence for the defence in Harold Strachan's case arising out of exposure of prison conditions. Govan was shocked to see me. He had believed that I was safe in the haven of my own country. I shared my handcuffs and leg irons with him for the rest of the journey to the 'Far Waters' as one of the escorts put it in Afrikaans: 'Verre Water'!

CHAPTER 4

Robben Island

I ARRIVE ON ROBBEN ISLAND

Outside the reception office, as we waited to be given our prison numbers, two prison officers, a captain and a lieutenant arrived. The lieutenant, looking more important than his rank, and the captain went into the office and came out again. 'Wie van julle is Dingake? (Which of you is Dingake?)' he wanted to know of the three of us. He went into the office after I had identified myself. Govan informed us the lieutenant was Lieutenant Naude, the prison security officer. His interest in me, according to Govan, showed I was designated for segregation. Sonny Singh, who was hovering at a moot security distance in the same corridor, had apparently overhead Lieutenant Naude's question and interpreted it as Govan did. At the earliest opportunity he sidled up to me to give me messages and news to the segregation prisoners. The news of going to the segregation section was bad. The news about the outside world was good, not necessarily in itself, but purely because it could penetrate the heavy iron gates I was surveying just then, with such a feeling of discomfort.

With my new identity as prisoner number 277/66 I followed the warder, together with Patrick and Norman, to the main section. Govan alone went to segregation. So he and Sonny had been wrong; 'Magalies' had been wrong too, when he predicted, in Leeuwkop, that I was destined for segregation. There were more prisoners in the communal cells section. Even in prison, I had discovered, there was a semblance of merriment in numbers.

Reunion with long-serving comrades, who were still in good spirits in spite of their poor physical condition, was invigorating. We exchanged news. News of unequal struggle outside, but nevertheless a consistent and determined one. Cowards might have fled, we told them, but the banner of the freedom struggle fluttered on, undeterred. In turn they gave us the lowdown on their more unequal struggle inside. Prisoners had just ended an epic hunger strike, lasting for a week. The details were sombre: prisoners had been driven to exert themselves at the stone quarry in spite of their extreme exhaustion from lack of nourishment, the collapse of prisoners at their tasks, stronger prisoners pushing the collapsed comrades in wheelbarrows back to gaol and the iron determination to continue the strike in spite of the dissipated physical strength.

The hunger strike had started in the communal cells section in protest against the poor and inadequate prison rations and for improvement of general prison conditions. Communication lines with the segregation section were officially non-existent but

140

unofficially alive, though a bit slow, underground. The segregation section learned of the strike a day after and joined in sympathy. Despite the attempt of the prison authorities to play off one section against the other by false reports, the solidarity of prisoners of different sections was never broken. The time lag at call-off of the strike, just as at the beginning, equalised the days the strike lasted in both sections.

The prisoners' strike was infectious. The warders who had their food at the officers' mess, mainly the bachelor warders, caught the virus of protest. Shortly after the prisoners' strike they too went on a hunger strike. In their case, diet improvement was instant. In the case of prisoners, the improvement in quantity was grudging and erratic. While the strike lasted, the unwanted food had looked good and appetising to lure the strikers back to the previously unappetising and meagre rations.

The strike, however, appeared to have been a gradual turning point in conditions on the island prison. Some prisoners at the end of it had earned themselves extra sentences for their role as 'ringleaders' of the strike. Although the selection of ringleaders was arbitrary, those who paid with extra sentences could be proud of their contribution to the prison community of the day and future generations of prisoners.

Two improvements were already in evidence as they reported on the strike. A dining hall was under construction in the main section. In the past, and at the time of our arrival, prisoners squatted in the open to have their food, when they returned from work. We squatted in long rows in the cold, gobbled or nibbled our food while the greedy sea gulls hovered overhead and augmented our cold meagre rations with their liberal droppings. With warders lining the fringes of the dining rows, their carbines at the ready, the picture of a classic gaol was complete.

The second improvement was the soccer ground. This innovation was however not completely welcome. There was a division in the ranks of prisoners. Some felt it was a necessary and appreciated recreational facility. Instead of being locked up the whole weekend in the cells, prisoners would have the chance of wider movement on the soccer field. Sport could reduce the immense tension that formed the inescapable environment of a prisoner. Others felt differently. The introduction of sports facilities was a propaganda stunt that could only benefit the enemy. As such it was to be rejected. Moreover, how can one play sport on a half-empty stomach? The food was still inadequate for the hard-working prisoners and until that was taken care of, soccer could go to blazes. The pros and cons of the argument seesawed and created an atmosphere of mutual suspicion and mistrust in the rival opinion holders. Eventually the ayes had it.

Besides the two major improvements mentioned above, from what comrades told me, other tendencies towards slightly improved conditions were discernible. The Kleynhans brothers, there were

141

three of them, had been transferred from the island. The Kleynhans brothers were brutes. Everybody talked about them. They were defendants in a number of cases of brutal assaults against the prisoners. Actually the reign of terror by the Kleynhans brothers on the island has still to be chronicled, and this is no place for it, nor am I the person qualified to do it. Here, suffice it to say they were gone. The island was nonetheless not completely free of warders who hated blacks, particularly the political prisoners. Some were to mellow a bit in the course of time eg Meintjies and Head Warder Delport. A seven-footer, Delport, was a slave driver at the stone quarry where I worked for two days. He could be seen towering above men and structures in the quarry. He could be heard bellowing: 'Hey! Laat daardie kruiwa loop, laat daardie kruiwa loop! (Hey! That wheelbarrow must move, that wheelbarrow must move!)' The wheelbarrows moved all the time and the hammers, big and small, came down on rocks and stones; still Delport made the quarry tremble with his slave driver voice and he took down names of prisoners his caprice judged as malingerers. It happened all the time and these prisoners were isolated and punished.

The morale of the prisoners was high in spite of harassment and trying conditions. Comrades buoyed each other up with the stories of the heroism of revolutionaries in social revolutions that had gone before, they helped each other with their studies and cheered one another with jokes and newsy tidbits about warders, the eccentricities of some officers and an occasional entertaining event in the officer community.

There was an incredible story doing the rounds when we arrived in section B of the communal cells section. We heard it the very first day we arrived. In a prison, in an abnormal society like South Africa the story was really juicy: the wife of warder Van Niekerk (Mhlonyane) had an affair with a prisoner, a common-law prisoner, and Mhlonyane apparently after a tip-off had caught them in bed. Immorality right in prison? How could it happen? I was incredulous. Easy, I was told. Common-law prisoners were privileged to do household chores in the officers' houses during the day while the officers were performing their duties in prison or at one of the quarries. During their hours of absence house cleaning took place – and more.

The immorality case was presided over by Lieutenant Naude. Of all the officers on Robben Island, Lieutenant Naude was the wrong man to preside over such a case. Naude's interest was the security aspect in prison; the 'immorality' aberrations did not interest him much. Naude sentenced the male offender to a few days spare diet and warned Mrs van Niekerk not to succumb to prisoners' amorous tendencies in future. All this I heard and could not believe. In the morning as we fell into line for the quarry, a comrade who knew I was a doubting Thomas pointed out the lover-prisoner and informed me that he was no longer allowed to work at the officers' village. While

142

we watched the man and talked, Lieutenant Naude walked down the lines with Mhlonyane shouting for all to hear: 'Where is that prisoner who . . . Mhlonyane's wife?' in Afrikaans. Naude was quite a clown. Many stories circulated about his ill-breeding. Anyway the lover-prisoner was kept aside to ensure that he did not slip into the house cleaning span.

I considered myself extremely lucky to be in the communal cells section. In the first few days I was hopping from section to section to meet many of the scattered comrades I knew. The communal cells section had a number of sub-sections, each divided into communal cells. Prisoners were supposed to stick to one section and cell. It was an offence to be found in the wrong cell. But the longing to see friends I could not meet at the quarry was too strong. Comrades helped by arranging swaps. If I went to spend a night in one cell in a different section, one inmate had to transfer from that cell to my cell. It was fun, flitting from cell to cell meeting old buddies under the grim circumstances and yet enjoying the physical togetherness. Although I did not fancy the segregation section I longed to see the comrades there. The story was that they were out of bounds. They were quarantined and inaccessible. The only way an inmate of the communal cells section could come anywhere near them was to be sent to the punishment cells, which were in the unoccupied wing of the horseshoe-shaped section known as segregation. From the punishment cells one could catch a glimpse of Mandela and his section mates if one was lucky enough to be locked up in one of the cells overlooking the common yard. Some luckier offenders had even managed to exchange a hello with Mandela or Sisulu or Govan or Kathrada and they spoke of the excitement generated by such a social bonanza. Well, if that was the case I was going to insult a warder and risk the punishment cells.

The Monday following our arrival we went to see the prison quack. The prisoners said so. All prisoners' complaints were hypochondriac or psychosomatic. He was either a quack or a prison officer. Prisoners would not budge from their opinion. We were examined and pronounced fit, which we were, fortunately. Tuesday and Wednesday I went out with the quarry span – the 'Bombela'. The prison population was more than a thousand when I arrived; the quarry span was the largest workspan, comprising more than 70 per cent of the population of the communal cells section. We marched along a route enclosed by a high security fence, with armed warders marching outside the fence and ensuring that the lines were not broken. At the quarry comrades played a protective role, keeping us as far as possible from the cussedness of the known 'quarry tyrants'. Two of the tyrants actually went round calling out for newcomers, ostensibly for induction sport. In that big crowd we could manage, with the invaluable help of older prisoners, to merge our identity with the

143

quarry mass. The call of 'new arrivals, new arrivals' went unanswered.

It was hard work at the stone quarry. Compressor drills vibrated the whole day shaking their operators like reeds in the wind. Some prisoners wielded huge hammers and pounded metal pins with all their might to split huge rocks embedded below sea level. The bulk of the prisoners sat in arranged groups to break the rock pieces into smaller pieces. Each prisoner had a daily standard quota to fulfil. Failure to fulfil the quota was punishable. The rest of the workspan carted the crushed stones around in wheelbarrows. Blisters and calloused hands were the hallmarks of quarry span prisoners, regardless of their specific job. Quarry work was tough. The comrades who laboured next to me did their best to assist me fulfil the quota. There was much concern that the span warders sooner or later might discover my bogus accomplishment of the quota. The quarry comrades conferred with comrades in non-quarry spans where the work load was considered lighter and span warders less of slave drivers. Through some elaborate juggling of positions in the line formations on the third day, Thursday, I joined Comrades Masala and 'Squire' Makgothi's span at the docks. The job was backbreaking, unloading coal from the cargo boat *Diaz*, but it was much better because it did not last the whole day. In the afternoon, the unloading was over and the span relaxed.

On Friday, the fourth day, the indefatigable comrades had managed to incorporate me in the brickworks span, which was a tremendous upgrading. Not only was the job lighter, it was constructive and sensible. The weekend we spent indoors, locked up, because the offer of soccer was still a hot issue among inmates. The one nutritious diversion was head warder 'Phumasilwe' Opperman's raids into the kitchen. Opperman was one of those few warders who were apparently affected by the prisoners' hunger strike. He knew, as political prisoners knew, that the scale and quality of official diet was not alone to blame for the undernourishment and malnutrition of prisoners. The cooks, common-law prisoners in the kitchen, were partly responsible. Some of the fat, sugar, puzamandla (a powdered drink made from ground corn), bread and meat, that was to be shared by the entire prison community ended up in the kitchen in the special pots for the cooks. They prepared most sumptuous dishes out of other prisoners' rations. Opperman knew this racket was going on. He conducted forays into the kitchen and discovered and uncovered dishes fit for kings. He carried the loot into our cell and distributed it. It was a feast.

Monday, back from the brickworks, we squatted in rows as usual to have our cold porridge. Some prisoners' names were being called and someone was handing out precious letters to the few who were

144

called. The name Michael Dingake was also shouted. Really? 'D' prisoners were entitled to one letter in six months at the time, did it mean I was a lucky exception? I followed the voice that called my name to where Lieutenant Naude was standing. He did not hand me a letter, instead he called a nearby warder and instructed him to take me to my cell to collect my meagre possessions. There was no time to say bye-bye to comrades as the warder led me with a battery of 'kom, kom! (come, come!); kom! kom! kom jong (boy)!' There was absolutely no chance to fall back under such verbal spurs. I followed him to the cell ignorant of the undesirable transfer.

The single cells section inmates were locked up already when my new single cell was opened. It was quiet in the section, an eerie sort of silence. Mac Maharaj broke it with a whisper that amplified into the whole corridor, after the warders had locked me up. 'It's Mike,' said the hawk-eyed, one-eyed Maharaj, 'we'll see him tomorrow!' The silence curtain fell again. 'Stilte in die gang! (Silence in the passage!)' It was the law of segregation.

In the morning comrades laughed at me as we squatted in the yard washing our ballies (sanitary buckets) because I concentrated on the outside of the ballie. 'It's the inside of the ballie you must wash more than the outside. Otherwise it stinks,' someone said giggling at my squeamishness.

The entire section of 30 prisoners walked to the lime quarry after breakfast. Along the route to the lime quarry spans of other prisoners had to give way to the 30 'lepers'. They were moved from our path and concealed behind the bushes and allowed to come back into the road after we had passed. Yesterday I had mixed freely with the path-givers, without contaminating them. Today I was among those certified as fit for quarantine and I was isolated. Prison is madness, human madness institutionalised. Communal cells section comrades had informed us that the segregation comrades were working with a very sweet warder 'Mazithulele (the quiet one)'. It was true. The whole morning I did nothing but give a report to Comrades Mandela and Sisulu. Three of us had our right feet on our spades and conversed. Mazithulele sat under a bush and never interfered. I continued my 'state of the struggle' message with other groups in the afternoon; Mazithulele maintained his sweetness. The lime quarry wasn't bad.

Over the week Colonel Aucamp was on Robben Island and he came on inspection. We all stood behind locked grilles displaying our prison cards, although unlike in the communal section each of us had his full name displayed next to the door. Aucamp instructed the warder to open my grille. He had spotted two books in my cell. I had not yet got formal permission to study. So possession of books was an offence. The two books were confiscated plus some borrowed goggles. One book belonged to Comrade Mandla Masondo, another to Comrade Billy Nair and the goggles to Dr Massler. Oh, what trouble

145

for the three comrades! I was going to be charged and they were going to lose their belongings and probably be charged for lending me things they were not supposed to lend me. I felt quite sad and everybody was depressed. Fortunately Lieutenant Bosch was lenient when I appeared before him. He cautioned and discharged me. The books and the goggles became prison property. Goggles were prison property in any case. I tried to argue for the retention of the goggles on the grounds that the lime glare was ruinous to the eyes. No, I could apply for permission to have goggles of my own from the hospital, but the confiscated ones were confiscated for good. Prison logic is illogical. 'There was the possibility that the prison hospital would give me the same goggles, so why can't I have them now?' 'No,' said Bosch. 'Unlawful possession was unlawful. Prisoners cannot be encouraged to keep it! Verstaan? (Understand?)'

Aucamp's cell raid was petty and vindictive. His stool pigeon Raymond Mnyanda had failed in his mission; Aucamp was nasty about it. Actually I had applied for permission to study while I was in Pretoria and handed the application to him. He had replied verbally that it was all right I could study when I arrived on Robben Island. Now he turned round and explained procedures to be followed; procedures he had glossed over when he still hoped I could be bagged by his scheming designs. For a man of his rank his behaviour was outrageous.

Things did not stay sweet and quiet for long at the lime quarry. Mazithulele was transferred from our workspan. A Van Rensburg, nicknamed 'Suitcase' by us because he arrived in the section carrying a mini-portmanteau, replaced Mazithulele. We noticed a swastika tattoo on his forearm. From the outset, Suitcase made it clear he wanted us to work hard. Unused to the work we failed to work as hard as Suitcase intended to make us work. Unlike Mazithulele, who stood at a distance, he stood next to us and egged us on: 'Come on, come on.' he shouted the whole day. He booked anyone who in his opinion was not exerting himself hard enough. Every afternoon several of us were taken to the lieutenant to be charged as malingerers. The prison administrative court became quite busy, trying cases of malingering. Needless to say the court believed Suitcase's evidence rather than the prisoners'. However, it was never smooth sailing for him. Every case was strongly contested by the accused. Our legal committee, composed of Nelson Mandela and Fikile Bam, both lawyers and the generalist, Mac, briefed the accused in the appropriate court craft.

Suitcase, unskilled in court procedure and formulation of charges, always left many loopholes which we exploited. The favourite one was to ask for further particulars which he omitted every time. Suitcase would be thoroughly bamboozled and very often the court adjourned *sine die* to enable him to submit further particulars.

146

Sometimes we rattled him in cross examination. The intellectual level of the section was in fact far above him. But like all men who must obey military orders, Suitcase never said die. He drove us hard and charged us according to his whims and his instruction. Every evening we went back to prison exhausted, covered from head to shoe in lime dust and looking a sight.

Back in the section our first duty was to have a bath. It was impossible to rid ourselves of the day's lime dust by any other method but a good bath. Our bathroom had two seawater showers. There was also a tap for brackish water in one corner of the bathroom and three 20-kilo buckets which we used as bathtubs. A group of four or five shared one bucket – we squatted around the bucket, soaped ourselves and washed off the soap by scooping water from the bucket. In winter the water could be freezing, but necessity demanded a bath. And we obliged with a brave face and even a jolly carefree attitude to being deprived of a proper bathroom.

Splashing ourselves and sometimes splashing each other mischievously with the cold water, we often broke into beautiful song: 'Auntie Dorah. She's a hell of a beautiful woman . . .' Auntie Dorah would have wept from sheer sentiment had she heard us sing praises of her beauty in such melodious voices.

One morning, while we stood in twos in two lines on the ramp in readiness to file through the section gate to the lime quarry, Lt Naude brought us an order from the Commanding Officer, Major Kellermann: From that morning on, the span was forbidden to talk on the way to the quarry and during work at the quarry. The only time to talk would be during the lunch hour when we had our cooked mealies and puzamandla. 'Rubbish!' cried Walter Sisulu standing next to the lieutenant. I tugged Walter's jacket reflexively, worried that if repeated it might become a cry to mutiny. Naude himself somewhat taken unawares by Walter's reaction turned round and enquired who had uttered the defiant expletive. Everybody kept quiet because Naude should have located the source better than most: it was right next to him. We marched to the quarry in mute communication. Our general reaction though unexpressed was spontaneous and accurately reflected by Walter's outburst. Rubbish! The order was crazy. It had to be fought. As we collected our picks and spades from the shed we briefly discussed our first line of action at the earliest opportunity. At lunch time we were to discuss our strategy: initially the order was to be obeyed. Whatever action was contemplated it had to be united. It was difficult for some of us to obey absolutely but whatever talking took place was on the sly and soft.

We unanimously agreed on a prisoners' committee to plan and organise our strategy as well as represent the section to the prison authorities. On discussing the precise action to adopt, suggestions ranged from outright confrontation to dialogue. In those early days on the island representation of prisoners by one or more other prisoners was explicitly refused. The prison authorities insisted that each prisoner had to air his own grievances not other prisoners' grievances. 'No ANC or PAC here! Verstaan?' they repeated *ad nauseam*. In a way the idea of organised representation was an attitude of defiance.

In the midst of our serious palaver Kellermann walked into our lunch shed smiling from ear to ear. No, gentlemen, it was all a misunderstanding. I, Kellermann, the Commanding Officer on Robben Island, never intended to turn you into deaf-mutes. I was merely saying you should not make too much noise. That's all. Please enjoy your lunch and don't stop talking after lunch. Talk softly. And with a smile and a polite manner unbecoming to the Island Commanding Officer talking to bandiets, Kellermann took his leave.

It was obvious that the OC was revoking his order due to some impending and yet unknown favourable event. There were more signs that something was in the air when we returned to our section in the evening. Comrade Nelson's name and effects had been moved from cell No.4 near the section entrance, to cell No.18 further down the corridor. We concluded that an important visitor was on the way and Comrade Nelson as a leader enjoying the highest national and international prestige would not be the most desirable person from the side of officialdom to present our case to the visitor while the visitor had the time. By the time the visitor got to the point where Nelson would be standing, the visitor(s) and the officers would be studying their watches and announcing 'time up' before he could say his say.

The following morning the newly appointed committee was on the ball. It recommended that inmates near the entrance should not delay the visitor(s) by raising trivial personal complaints. Comrade Mandela was to be our spokesman on general complaints.

To support our suspicion, at the quarry, before we started work, Suitcase asked us to fall in line – something unusual. 'Boys,' he said with paternalistic familiarity, 'I have withdrawn all the charges against you, all of them . . .' The third day we did not go to work and Mrs H Suzman, at the time the lone Progressive Party MP, arrived in the company of the Commissioner of Prisons, General Steyn. 'Have you any complaints?' enquired Mrs Suzman of the inmate in the first cell. 'Yes, I have a lot of complaints. All of us have. But our spokesman is Mr Nelson Mandela down the passage.' Because of threats that my wife would not be allowed to visit me while I served my sentence I was exempted and allowed to raise this issue. I requested Mrs Suzman to make representation on my behalf for my wife to be granted safe conduct to visit me. Otherwise all the inmates before Comrade Nelson had the same stock answer as the first man. Helen Suzman moved quickly down the corridor to cell No.18.

In the meantime Suitcase was scared and anxious. One of the warders had warned him: 'Hey, that swastika tattoo is going to get you

148

into trouble. These bandiets don't spare people like you when they have a chance . . .' Suitcase approached Dr Pascal Ngakane, a prisoner, for advice. He wanted to blame the fascist tattoo on his father. Could Pascal tell him how to explain it in good English? Apparently Suitcase expected to be dragged before an impromptu inquisition with Helen Suzman in the role of Grand Inquisitor. The longer Comrade Nelson stood reeling off our grievances to Mrs Suzman, the more Suitcase looked ready to amputate the arm that so eloquently proclaimed his fascist tendencies.

In the end, contrary to his unfounded fears, Suitcase was not courtmartialled nor interrogated about his tattoo. Our charges to the last one were reinstated again. 'But Meneer Van Rensburg you withdrew the charges!' we argued. 'Never!' said Meneer Van Rensburg unashamed. It was his word against ours, his power and authority against our powerlessness and vulnerability. Kellermann however did not reimpose his silence decree and the noise/loud talk at the lime quarry did not diminish, it increased despite Suitcase's persecution. One afternoon part of the span got involved in a heated debate: Do tigers exist in Africa? The debate assumed political overtones when the champions of 'the existence of tigers in Africa' charged that their opponents were brainwashed by linguistic colonisers who postulated that a tiger was not a 'nkwe/ingwe' (leopard), whereas 'nkwe/ingwe' was in fact vernacular for tiger. The debate revolved around a terminological misconception traceable instead to missionary/colonial translators who translated the word 'nkwe/ingwe' as tiger. Tempers ran high and voices were raised until a young warder who had brought his truck to be loaded with lime could not bear it any longer: 'Get on with your work; you talk too many and work too few,' he shouted in Afrikaanised English. That of course brought about raucous laughter from all sides. The warder did not like the noise and the humiliation, and his two-way radio brought Major Kellermann to the scene in minutes. Kellermann arrived strutting like a Goliath on a field of battle. 'Mandela! jy moet jou vinger uit jou . . . trek (Mandela! you must pull your finger out of your . . .)' he swore as he advanced belligerently to where Nelson stood dignified and unwinking. The major probably remembered that Nelson's favourite sport was boxing, for he halted a short distance from him as his foul language repertory tapered correspondingly.

Comrades Nelson and Mandla Masondo were singled out for a ride back to the cells. We knew it meant harsh punishment. Comrade Mac approached me: 'We can't allow this to happen to our leader, we must down tools.' Agreed: 'Let us consult Comrade Walter.' Walter was very cool: 'Know your enemy, know your strength.' This classical argument did not mean passivity. It implied that our actions had to be carefully calculated. Counterproductive steps had to be restricted. Impetuous actions could not be totally avoided, but they had to be pruned as much as possible. Every grievance was brought before the

149

newly elected prisoners' committee and appropriate action would be adopted by consensus. From the inception of the prisoners' committee real pressure against harsh jail conditions started building up. The main section also had its representative body working independently for the same objective. Whereas, de jure, we could not act in concert as prisoners, when it came to representation to prison authorities, a de facto recognition of our communal grievances and interests soon became the order of relations with the authorities.

The arsenal of our offensive and defensive strategy was limited but consistent: deputations, memoranda, representation to visitors sympathetic or hostile, hunger strikes, go-slow strikes. Besides our organised resistance, sideline-sniping played an important role. The major problem encountered by political prisoners on Robben Island was the extremely hostile attitude of warders. The prisons department, to ensure the success of their policy of brutal deterrence to black resistance, saw to it that Robben Island prison was a black political prison staffed by an entirely white staff indoctrinated in the superiority of the whites and therefore unscrupled by humanitarian considerations. The mainstream of representation took this up very strongly of course. But below the official level, individual inmates went on a systematic campaign to educate individual warders on our human dignity. At other times we acted through normal conversation on an individual level. This did much to change the attitude of many warders who were previously prejudiced and hostile. To circumvent this happening on a mass scale the prison administration adopted a clever policy of transferring staff from one section or prison to another on a regular basis.

The transfer and rotation of staff on Robben Island was an effective policy instrument to delay changes, bring them about or reverse them. For political prisoners to influence change was therefore extremely difficult. Nonetheless there was never a moment of despondency or disillusionment. Political prisoners like a good fight. I was very much inspired by this deliberate and relentless militancy of the inmates. The sojourn on the island was likely to be gruesome but it promised some interesting highlights.

Shortly after my arrival the security police paid me a visit to show their interest in me had not abated. They asked innocuous questions and left. They came again, asking not so innocuous questions which I declined to answer. Again they visited me with names of acquaintances outside and either said things about them or pried into their relation with the ANC. Under the 'shield' of my convict status I dismissed their importunities – Captain Viktor's visit left me uneasy. He became aggressive and threatening when I refused to answer his questions: 'Still the same old stubborn Mike, eh? Do you prefer to be taken back to Compol?' He gave me a malevolent look and left. It was in the middle of 1967, with my sentence reduced by one year.

150

On some hot shiny day in September head warder Bonzaaier of the reception office came for me at the quarry. 'Dingake, kom! (come!)' My inmates cheered and shouted 'kuyahanjwa (on the move)', a cry that greeted prisoners on transfer from the island on the eve of their release. Inmates had always been optimistic about my release in the near future. This optimism arose out of 'reliable sources'. The British government in conjunction with the pre-independence government of the Botswana Democratic Party of Seretse Khama was said to be negotiating with the South African government for my release. Personally I did not share the optimism of my fellow inmates.

Colonel Aucamp escorted me from the island. At Viktor Verster Prison in Paarl, Western Cape, we were joined by a number of prisoners due for release, among them Seretse Choabi who had served a three-year sentence under the Unlawful Organisations Act. I was completely in the dark as to my destination and told Seretse so when he wanted to know where I was going. At Beaufort West prison where we stopped for the night I was separated from the other prisoners after I had been informed by Seretse & Co that whilst I was in the toilet, the CO of the prison, who met me for the first time that evening, had referred to me as 'die gevaarlike gevangene (the dangerous prisoner)'. From the report I became convinced that I was going to Pretoria for a further charge. Well, let it be.

In Pretoria Local Prison I was again separated and isolated. The following morning the passage cleaners were active as usual: smuggling newspapers, conveying verbal and written messages from cell to cell and performing other clandestine duties. My previous experience in Pretoria Local was that among these corridor-messengers there were reliable ones and unreliable ones. The only way to differentiate between them was by a tip from someone who knew them or through bitter experience.

When I left the island we had news that ANC and Zapu were fighting in Rhodesia. Casualties had been reported in the press, and arrests of guerrillas had occurred in Botswana and even worse in South Africa. Naturally I was eager to know if any guerrillas arrested in the skirmishes were in Pretoria Local. My passage contact told me, no; only Swapo detainees and one Zapu member. I had left some of the Swapo detainees in Pretoria Local so the report of their presence was not exciting news. But a Zapu member in Pretoria was something. Within minutes of the news of Zapu's Ngwenya, an express postal service was in full swing. One had to be careful in the beginning about the contents of the notes we were exchanging. When the warder intercepted the third note it was still on a personal level, attempting to satisfy myself about the identity and authenticity of Ngwenya as a Zapu member.

It was during the lunch hour when the warder startled me by jingling the keys in my door. I shoved the newspaper I was reading quickly under the mats and pretended all was in order in the cell. 'Is this note from you?' asked the warder showing me the intercepted piece of paper. 'Yes!' I admitted feeling it would be futile to deny it and also wishing to expedite his departure from the cell. 'I will show this to the CO and you'll probably be charged,' explained the warder retreating from the cell. I strongly believed that the episode was not an accident. The cleaner was a prison decoy.

I appeared before Colonel Gericke, the Officer Commanding Pretoria Local Prison. The prosecutor was a young lieutenant who looked quite puzzled when in the true tradition of a segregation inmate of Robben Island Prison I demanded 'further particulars' of the indictment. Gericke was offended because I was 'trying to be clever' and disregarded his language overtures. He spoke Northern Sesotho (Sepedi) very well and without knowing it, he reminded me of Inspectors Franz and Eiselen, and of their arrogance and paternalism. Nonetheless he instructed the prosecutor to comply with my request. The case was adjourned for two days. When it resumed the two witnesses were the warder who intercepted my note and the decoy. Colonel Gericke found me guilty of unlawful communication in spite of my spirited defence. The court adjourned three days for sentence.

During my few days in Pretoria Local I had observed that I was directly under the jurisdiction of Prisons Headquarters, not the local command. Any complaint or request I made was referred to the headquarters. The adjournment of the court for sentence was unusual; it gave me an impression that my sentence was to come from the headquarters.

The sentence was six days, spare diet. For six days I was to live on rice water. After going through the formality of a medical examination my spare diet started. A voluntary hunger strike is not as bad as compulsory spare diet. The first two days were the most terrible. The gnawing pains of hunger kept me wriggling on the second day and night. On the third day I had a windfall. Gerson Veii, then Swanu Vice President and serving five years, by some stroke of luck and great personal risk, managed to smuggle some meal to me. I have never eaten as voraciously as I did on that day. The food sat heavy and uncomfortable in my tummy. The discomfort of an excessively full stomach bears no comparison to that of an empty stomach.

On the sixth day, the last day of my spare diet 'Rasie' Erasmus, my faithful escort, came to fetch me and take me to Compol. Swanepoel sat behind a long counter, a loaded revolver next to him. Next to the revolver two typed statements, bearing two names I knew, were displayed. 'Good morning, Captain,' I said trying to be civil to the uncivilised. 'What?' barked Swanepoel at me. I withdrew into my shell in the face of the vociferous antagonism. 'What did you say?' persisted Swanepoel. I shut my mouth and waited hostile developments. 'Dingake, I want a statement from you . . .' 'What happened to the one you took from me last year?' 'It was all a tissue of lies! A tissue of lies! We have been able to discover that you lied to us about what you did in Bechuanaland . . .!' Swanepoel was shouting at the top of his voice. 'Well,' I replied, shouting back in sudden temper, 'if you have discovered that I lied, why bother me since you have got an authentic statement of my activities from elsewhere?' 'I want confirmation! Confirmation! Confirmation from you!' he announced banging his fist hard on the counter. 'I am not making any statement!' I replied trying to match his determination.

A black cop, Silas by name, his mouth slightly open, sat next to me. I was standing. A white warder who escorted me together with 'Rasie' stood next to me apparently uncomprehending. 'Oumaat (old mate),' Swanepoel addressed himself to the warder, 'take a stroll. He is in safe hands. If he tries to escape, ons skiet sy harsing uit (we will blow his brains out).' The warder left and Silas remained, his gaping mouth a study of bewilderment and docility, mixed up in some amorphous meditation that was hardly for my comfort.

While Swanepoel was trying to persuade and intimidate me into making another statement I read parts of Ronnie Letsholonyane's statement lying on the counter. Ronnie had been involved with some ANC machinery in Bechuanaland when I was there in 1965, but I had absolutely nothing to do with him. Anything he might claim to know about my activities in Bechuanaland would be mere thumb-sucking. Yet there was my name in Ronnie's statement and I wondered what he said about me. Swanepoel saw me scanning the statement. He did not stop me. Instead he told me what he wanted confirmed; the allegation was the old one: namely that I had infiltrated and hidden trained guerrillas in Bechuanaland. Their original suspicion/information had been confirmed according to Swanepoel, now he wanted me to confirm the confirmation.

Well, I was not doing anything of the sort I told him. 'Well, if you won't do it voluntarily, we'll take it out of you,' said Swanepoel standing up and instructing Silas to lead me to another room. The room was familiar. It was the room in which I could not fall asleep after three nights of sleep deprivation. The cell in which I was tortured was adjacent to this bigger room. I thought it was back to the cell and the standing ordeal. I was walking resignedly in that direction when Swanepoel and Silas directed me to another part of the room. Before I knew what was what, the two policemen assisted by the third who had suddenly joined them, grabbed me, picked me up and hoisted me, hanging me by the handcuffed arms; my toes barely touched the floor. Swanepoel left Silas to watch over me. From time to time he stood up from his stool to tap hard on my knuckles with his stick, or to push the handcuffs back to position if they appeared to be sliding/inching down. For the first time in my life I knew fear. I was terrified. Terrified of the unknown. What was to happen to me? Would I be dismembered? Would I ever be able to use my arms again? On the wall next to me was a police poster depicting assorted weapons of war, presumably used by 'terrorists'. The poster warned the public to be on the alert against 'terrorists'. The pain was excruciating. I wanted to die. Desperately. I had always scoffed at suicides. Suspended on these handcuffs, I wanted to die. Life was worth living. So much undone. So much to be done. But under the circumstances life was agony. A worse alternative than death. I wanted to die urgently. Where was the power of auto-suggestion? I closed my eyes and concentrated my mental energies to my extinctive relief. It eluded me. The tea-maker who a short while ago was addressing Swanepoel as 'baas' came through the room on his way to his duties. He looked up at me disgusted: 'What is wrong with this one? If you don't talk you'll become a mogwapa (biltong), you'll dry up there!' The pain doubled at my own black brother's derision, moreover a Motswana like me: Is my struggle in vain? Am I in the lunatic fringe – unappreciated by my constituents? Simon, a friend of Silas, looking thick and dumb, joined Silas to give me a lecture: 'What do you think you can achieve with your terrorism? Yes, all you will do is kill innocent people. But the government will remain. You can never touch the government . . .' he concluded with a frown to underline my stupid and futile amibitions. Lieutenant Ferreira, the reputed murderer of Looksmart Ngudle, walked into the room stretching his neck compulsively: 'Dingake, you were unlucky I was not among your interrogators last year. You would not be undergoing your present ordeal. It would have long been over.' I did not know what to make of this.

The warder who had been asked to take a stroll strayed into the torture room. His eyes popped out when he caught sight of the dangling spectacle. He remained petrified at the door for a fleeting moment, then he beat a hasty retreat to disappear for good. The reaction of the white warder was anaesthetic to the tearing pain. If there was a token white South African, a warder at that, who could appear shocked on beholding police torture, then there was a glimpse of hope; South Africa and the human race might still be redeemed in spite of centuries of oppression.

Handcuffs were cutting into my wrists. The pain was unbearable. But more than the pain, the fear of permanent disability over-whelmed me. My mind could live death rather than incapacitated life. The third alternative was to swallow my pride. Like everything else personal pride is not infinite. I masticated it and swallowed it. 'All right, I'll make a statement,' I told Silas. He looked at me with half closed eyes and replied that I had wasted the Major's time by refusing to talk while he was still in a talking mood. (So Swanepoel was Major. Perhaps that was why he barked at me when I greeted him as Captain). Silas's truculent mood kept me hanging despite my ignominious surrender. To trifle with men in power can be hazardous. I had been dangling for over six hours. My death wish was still a dream. The pain and the fear were stark realities. How can men be

154

such brutes?

One white security officer came into the torture chamber. He went to fetch Swanepoel and a strong contingent when I expressed a wish to make a statement. The posse loosened my handcuffs and took me to an office for a statement. The statement itself was very short. All that was required was for me to agree that I had infiltrated guerrillas in Bechuanaland; then to answer how, and where I kept them. My lies were not challenged. I did not expect the police to challenge anything I said because any information about guerrillas in Bechuanaland in 1965 would have been completely obsolete in 1967 and their knowledge of Bechuanaland geography was poor. My hunch was that the police needed a signed statement from me which 'exposed' me as a danger to the security of Bechuanaland and a potential source of friction between my country of birth and South Africa. Armed with the statement South Africa's probable arguments against negotiations for my repatriation would be enhanced. I strongly believe that that is what the statement was meant to and did in fact achieve.

After I was forced to sign the statement I had dictated to the police, I was treated to the usual bravura of police propaganda. A long list of names of Umkhonto cadres, 81 in all, who were alleged to have crossed the Zambezi River, some to fight with Zapu in Rhodesia and others to proceed to South Africa, was read to me. I was asked whether I knew any of them. When I answered 'No' there were smiles all round. 'Of course you wouldn't: these are all pseudonyms.' After deciphering some they believed I knew, they proceeded to inform me that all the 81 had either been killed or captured by the South African police. What the police did not know was that I had already read in the press that some of the cadres they claimed were dead or in South African prisons, were in fact in Bechuanaland. Much later I came to know also that some of the names on the list had never been part of the invading force. However, I could not begrudge the police their mendacious onslaught, they had just scored a neat coup by 'persuading' me to lie so adversely against my own interests. Without lies, where would the white supremacists be?

It is not possible to imagine they could survive without lying. King Cetshwayo is said to have called the Afrikaners 'a nation of liars'. Their basic lie of course is that whites are a superior race. Around that lie they have built an almost impenetrable fortress of lies to safeguard and protect the basic lie. They claim to be Christians; it is a lie. They have a greater affinity to the Pharisees than to Christ. Here is a catalogue of their lies: their Dutch ancestors arrived in South Africa at the same time as the blacks in the middle of the seventeenth century; that separate development is not apartheid; that apartheid is dead; that the world is wrong and they are right; that there is such a thing as a pure race and they are one; that communists and liberals are behind black agitation and resistance – lies about many other things, theoretical lies and factual lies, gross and insignificant lies, big and petty lies, old lies and new lies, domestic lies and international lies, scandalous and malicious lies; every hue of lies.

The tragedy of it all is that their lies are believed by themselves and others inside and outside the country, including some of the oppressed. This leads to a lie to belie all their lies, that is the implication in their policies to the effect that they can deceive most of the people most of the time and oppress all the blacks all the time. To consolidate their lying propaganda they coerce their opponents to make lying statements: I was a victim of the total onslaught of lies.

After the reluctant signing of the statement I was taken back to Pretoria Local Prison. Chief warder Breedt welcomed me with the words: 'Jy lewe nog? (You are still alive?)' But how did he know I was hanging precariously between life and death? Was it advertised widely or did he get it from the warder escort who absconded from his duties when he saw me abused?

Back in my isolation cell my zest for life returned. My spare diet punishment was not over yet. I was aching all over, exhausted, hungry and depressed, but I no longer wanted to die. I wanted to live to relive this experience, to live and hope for an opportunity to hold a mirror before the face of humanity, so that humanity could study its Janus features and perhaps take action to redeem itself. That night as I lay on my pesticide-smelling blankets, depressed and hungry after the bell had gone, I was soothed by some piano music from one of the adjacent houses. In the past I had been aware that I loved music, any good music, foreign or indigenous, that I enjoyed it. What I had never known was its soothing power, its power to assuage physical pain and mental stress. If music be the food of life, sing on.

In the tranquil scene of the prison night, the sweet strains of outside music stole into my prison cell and wafted tender notes of precious life-sentiments. My spirits lifted and blended with the invading music. How could I ever have contemplated suicide? Life was not all torture. There was music in life, music that penetrated the prison walls and soothed the imprisoned, music that penetrated the hearts of the dejected oppressed and revived their spirits to die on their feet rather than live on their knees. Music pervaded human life. It was stronger than social perversion. I wanted to live. Ardently.

The following morning a cleaner smuggled a newspaper into my cell. I read it from cover to cover and worked out crossword puzzles. I read the obituary as well. Probably because I had wanted to die. I was depressed again. Life is a pendulum. What depressed me this time was the death of Martha Lowenthal in Rio de Janeiro, Brazil. Martha 'Muti' Lowenthal was the mother of my last employer in Johannesburg, K Lowenthal of Art Fur Company. Muti was an extraordinary woman. She was completely colour-blind and uninhibited by the prejudices (which she abhorred) of her white compatriots. Whenever Muti met me in busy Eloff Street she would stop in the middle of the pavement and give me a motherly handshake, and make all the dear noises of a reunion of a loving mother and her only son. The scowls and the mumblings of white pedestrians at the obstruction caused by our provocative conduct never affected Muti. She hated racial discrimination, though she was not a politician. At elections she voted for the United Party of Smuts. Muti often invited me for lunch at the hotel she was staying in. Jocelyn Hotel in Twist Street, like all the hotels in Johannesburg catered for whites only. Blacks entered the hotel as 'delivery boys' only and entered through the back of the building. They had to use a separate lift marked 'Natives and dogs'.

The first time Muti invited me to lunch with her at the Jocelyn I pricked my ears and wondered whether Muti was serious. She seemed to read my bafflement, for she said: 'Don't go through the back, come through the front.' It sounded like an adventure. I liked it. As I put my foot through the doorstep of the Jocelyn I could see Muti through the glass door sitting with the receptionist waiting for me. Muti shook my hand, held me at the elbows before she introduced me to her receptionist friend. We had our lunch in her suite. She had gone far enough, farther she could not go. So our lunch was for two in the suite.

I could go on and on describing Muti's extraordinariness in the abnormal context of the South African situation. Now suffice it to say her death in far away Rio affected me like a death of my own kinswoman. I remembered that Muti loved Rio where she often went on holiday. Her only daughter was married there. Muti used to talk of Rio in glowing terms: there was no colour-discrimination there, she said.

Now Muti was dead. An uncommon grief tormented me. I wanted to ask white South Africans, why can't you be like Muti. I also wanted to send a letter of condolences to her son, my former boss. I burnt to express a deep-seated sentiment about my image of a prototype of a human being, a civilised being. I drafted and redrafted my letter of condolences. Eventually I gave it up as a pointless exercise. I could not find the right words; the letter would have to be smuggled out; it could not go through the normal prison channels. Prospects for doing that were poor at that stage. For seven years I lived with this unexpressed sentiment of grief, struggling to be expressed. In 1974 I took my chance and succeeded. That letter was acknowledged after five months by Muti's son. He had received it after three months, covered with stamps of all descriptions. But he had received it. It was an unspeakable relief.

South Africa is a unique country to be able to engender such an intense and long feeling of appreciation for what could be regarded as average social impressions in other countries. Again, the tragedy of South Africa is that not every black would share my sentiments in similar circumstances. There is a very strong attitude among blacks expressed in extreme form in the words: there are no good whites except the dead ones. Blacks who harbour and express this feeling are not found only in the so-called 'black consciousness' organisations. They are to be found in the ranks of the supporters of non-racial organisations. The difference might be one of a degree. While within the BC groups the central tendency seems to be outright rejection of white overtures, in the congress group such overtures are encouraged.

The policy of the ANC expressed through the Freedom Charter is a vital beginning for future harmonious relations in South Africa. The final step, however, remains to be taken, and it must be taken by the whites themselves by shaking off the cobwebs of racial indoctrination and identifying themselves with the struggle of the oppressed. South Africa needs whites of more than Muti's calibre, tremendous personality though she was. It needs white activists dedicated to the eradication of the curse of their apartheid. It means whites will have to be revolutionaries committed to changing themselves in the first instance and changing their social order in the last. It is a challenge they must accept to avoid a bloody conflict.

A week after my torture I was back in our communal cell in Leeuwkop prison on my way back to the island. Who should I find among others in the cell? Seretse Choabi! Through him I was able to communicate with the outside about my latest torture. The report would upset my family very much but they had to know what happened from an authentic source instead of being fed by rumours. The first letter I received from my wife already rang with some alarm: why were you taken to Pretoria, the letter wanted to know. Obviously Seretse's presence in Leeuwkop was a godsend. I briefed him fully on my experience. M D Naidoo was also with us on his way to the island to serve a five year sentence he had recently collected from the Pietermaritzburg Supreme Court. He offered me a cigarette as he listened to the pathos of my experience. I had given up cigarette smoking two years ago. My abstinence of two years crumbled under the extreme craving induced by a surge of relief in the company of comrades. I puffed and inhaled the cigarette smoke and sensed a strong recovery of my flesh and my spirits.

At the Robben Island docks we found a big contingent of warders, led by Kellermann, the OC, waiting for us. Kellermann, who evidently was informed of my torture and relished the imagination of it, wanted to know from me how I had 'enjoyed' my stay in Pretoria, did I prefer it to Robben Island? 'Gaol is just like any other gaol,' I answered. He reacted very abruptly: 'OK if you think so we shall treat you the same way they treated you in Pretoria.' Boers are really bizarre. Or shall I say all agents of oppression. The problem is that I do not know all of them, only the South African Boers. I now became prisoner 130/67.

Kellermann effectively blocked my attempts to institute action against Major Swanepoel, the Commissioner of Police and the Commissioner of Prisons. I had managed after hard effort and devious

158

ways to communicate to my wife that I needed a lawyer to sue the police and prisons for torturing me. Kellermann in co-operation with the police blocked the lawyer's visit and refuted my torture allegation with a prison doctor's medical certificate suggesting that I had put on weight since my arrival on Robben Island in 1966 and was obviously in good health and untortured. The guilty minds, the pathological liars were, at it again, lying their way to their short term survival.

LETTERS AND VISITS

The first letter I received from my wife mentioned a photo that was enclosed – my daughter's photo. On opening the opened letter, however, the photo was not there. The censors had detached it from the letter and sent it back. My daughter was two weeks when I was detained in Rhodesia. By the time I received the letter she was 11 to 12 months. I was dying to see her even if it was only in print. Unfortunately the prison regulations forbade it so it was sent back – back to my wife. The good news was that mother and daughter were well, the mother missed me very much according to the letter and the baby, still dumb and ignorant, missed nothing and thrived in her babyish innocence unbothered by earthly woes.

I read the letter several times and informed my colleagues: my family is fine. All around there were expressions of delight. The most depressing news in gaol is unhappy news about one's family. Assuming a prisoner learns his family is in some trouble, what can he do but to suffer in his helplessness and suppressed remorse of unplanned desertion. But worse than the most depressing news is news blackout about one's family in prison. The mind never lives in a vacuum, it does not exist in a chasm, devoid of substance real or fictional. Where there is a void, the mind fills it up, stuffs it with images unimaginable. Why is my wife not writing? Is she in hospital? Out of a job, friendless and unable to pay for a postage stamp? Or is she in gaol like me?

In 1967 during my second torture in Pretoria, I received a letter from my wife reporting a burglary in our rented rondavel. Her best dress, the one I had bought for her in Johannesburg, the one we referred to fondly as the 'trump card' was among some of her possessions stolen. She sounded very depressed and lost. I felt depressed too, miserable and afflicted. When my mother-in-law came to visit me, instead of showing her my wrists bruised by handcuffs, I covered them with the sleeves of my jacket. I dared not inform my mother-in-law of what had taken place. How would my wife bear the news of my ill-treatment atop of her own ill-luck? The report of my torture could be postponed to a later date. I dictated a telegram to my mother-in-law to be sent to my wife expressing shock and tender sympathies at her misfortune. The telegram made her feel good. 'It was as if I could touch you. . .' she wrote. Letters are a prisoner's

159

lifeline, not only letters, visits and other channels of communication, photos.

In 1966 letters were rare in prison. Most of the political prisoners were still classified as D group. D group were entitled to one letter in three to six months. Few people outside knew of this privilege since the prison authorities did not always inform them as they were supposed to do. This ignorance meant that some prisoners could receive their first letters after a very long term. Towards the end of 1967 or beginning of 1968 D group prisoners were allowed to receive one letter and one visit a month. Three photos were thrown in to improve and complete prisoner-family contact. All this was more in theory than in practice. Letters coming in were thoroughly censored; lines were blacked out or cut out. At times the whole contents of the letter were cut out and only the salutation – 'Darling husband' – at the beginning, and the signature at the end were left. Prisoners of course complained and hissed at the senseless censorship. To no avail. Censoring of letters naturally delayed their delivery. A letter could take anything from one month to four months before delivery. The censors' office was deliberately understaffed. The small staff generally consisted of hand picked 'literary critics' who derived pleasure from making prisoners feel the pinch of being locked up.

Warder Pogaard (I am not sure of the spelling) was 'expert' in Xhosa and its idioms. Yet Pogaard could take days censoring one letter. He carried about a Xhosa-English dictionary and cunningly wheedled out interpretations of unusual Xhosa expressions from unwitting prisoners. From 1966 to 1969 as far as I can remember there were only two censors, Pogaard and Oom Jorrie. 'Oom Jorrie' was not as strict as Pogaard but he was a drunk, and because of this habit his work rate was not much better than Pogaard, the meticulous censor. During those years the prison population was more than 1000 prisoners.

If letters were rare, visits were rarer. Most prisoners came from Johannesburg, Pretoria, Durban, Port Elizabeth and East London. All these places are very far from Robben Island. The time of travel was long, the cost was prohibitive. Relatives in regular employment could manage a visit if they were allowed some time off to travel to Cape Town. Not many South African employers care about the welfare of their employees let alone the welfare of their employees' 'terrorist' relatives. The upshot was that most relatives could visit once a year when they were on their annual leave. The lack of employers' interest aside, the cost of travel from any of the points mentioned ruled out regular visits from any but the wealthy or the sponsored. Wealthy relatives who could afford monthly visits to Cape Town, I do not know. Sponsored visits by the International Committee of the Red Cross (ICRC) were a new phenomenon in the late seventies. Even then many prisoners were unable to benefit as contact with the relevant relatives was not always easy.

160

The duration of visits on Robben Island in the sixties and early seventies was half an hour. All visits of political prisoners were non-contact. A political prisoner's group did not matter, contact visit was not for him. Visitors stood on one side, in cubicles partitioned from corresponding cubicles in which prisoners sat facing them. Through the glass partition visitor and prisoner saw each other and chatted for a half-hour. At the announcement of time-up, visitor and visited interrupted their conversation, stood up, looked at each other wistfully and turned their backs on each other and the transparent partitions that divided them, maybe to see each other in another 12 months through the same glass dividers.

In later years visitors from distant places could be allowed 45 minutes with their dear imprisoned. Thousands of kilometres and hundreds of rands for a 30-45 minutes visit! It was worth all the trouble and expense. In gaol there is nothing as exhilarating as contact of any sort. Personal contact is golden. After a visit, the visited prisoner assumed an aura of unusual importance, he became an instant VIP with his fellow inmates pressing upon him and plying him with inquisitive questions. How is your family? How is so and so? Questions and questions. Most of the questions expressed goodwill and concern for the welfare of people outside the gaol walls. The one popular question expressing self-interest was: When does she/he think we'll get out of here? It usually came at the tail end of the interrogation when all the unselfish barrage had been fired. The self-interested question was never seriously meant. It was a flippant taunt in recognition of our own unchanging status. Many weeks after the visit the prisoner would still be talking about the visit and others would still be probing and searching for further information and news. What was the visitor wearing? Has she/he put on weight? With whom did she/he travel from Johannesburg? How did he/she travel? Train? car? airplane? Where is she/he staying in Cape Town?

The most consistent phenomenon was that newsbits forgotten in the initial report immediately after the visit would be remembered at a much later stage. It led to some prisoners switching their 'tactics' from rushing for news immediately after the visit to postponing their interviews until the overwhelming excitement of the visit had died down. Indeed the name for a prison visit is 'excitement'. An indescribable sensation that overwhelms the prisoner more than the event of political freedom will ever overwhelm the ex-prisoner. To me this is evidence, if evidence was needed, of the tremendous personal sacrifice a freedom fighter makes in the cause of the struggle. It is a demonstration of the superhuman effort involved in taking personal risk in pursuit of ideals that go beyond the interests of oneself and one's own intimate social circles. The recognition of the greater common good and the lesser personal good does help to strike the balance in this major conflict of personal emotions.

Visits on Robben Island were strictly supervised. Each visit was

161

attended by two warders or three, even four, depending on the degree of intimidation the prison authorities chose to apply. One warder stood next to the visitor and listened to the conversation from that side; the second warder listened from the side of the prisoner. In the earlier years conversation was through a hole in the glass partition. Later security was tightened and conversation by telephone was introduced. The supervising warders listened in through the same telephone devices.

Conversation at the visits was strictly controlled. Prisoners and visitors were warned what not to talk about and advised what to talk about. Politics was of course totally forbidden. Mention of non-relatives was banned; mention of another prisoner's name was prohibited; passing of messages from other parties either way was verboten; notes to help memory at the accurately-timed visits were proscribed.

Prisoners were allowed to talk about themselves – what they were studying or wanted to study, how much money they needed for tuition the following year, how much money they needed for books and relevant queries about family members. Visitors were also allowed to talk about themselves and other members of the family. Any deviation from the officially drawn lines might end the visit prematurely. The trouble was that the officers did not always know all the names of members of prisoners' families. An unfamiliar name of a member of the family might invoke a stern warning. By the time the prisoner finished the necessary explanation to convince the warder that the unfamiliar name was the name of a genuine member of the family, a good part of the precious visit time was gone. Warder interruptions at the visits were a veritable nuisance. At times a prisoner might lose his temper at the besotted interruption and the unruly temper might see the visit go up in smoke. One had to be placid. Not always possible. The intimidating presence of the supervising staff was not conducive to a relaxed conversation. How can one feel relaxed when there is some stranger breathing over one's neck while one is supposed to be holding a sacrosanct family tete-a-tete? Beg your pardon! Security is more sacrosanct than anything else. Whose security, is irrelevant.

When Jimmy Kruger was Minister of Justice and Prisons, he introduced a new restriction in the already restricted visits. Prisoners were to be visited by first degree relatives only. Besides 'first degree relative' being a ridiculously foreign concept to African culture, the concession that went with it was highly provocative. Kruger let it be known that those who wished to be visited by friends, second, third, fourth or twelfth degree relatives, could have such visits provided they supplied the prison authorities and ipso facto the security police with particulars of these non-first degree personages.

We were allowed to deliberate the merits and demerits of the concession. All prisoners naturally expressed the wish to be visited by friends and non-first degree relatives but the condition that went with the concession was uninviting. Jimmy Kruger the Minister of Justice and Prisons was becoming too clever. In the past some lucky prisoners had been visited by friends and non-first degrees. You can take a bet they were thoroughly investigated by the security police before they could be given permission to dock at the quay on Robben Island. Minister Kruger now was trying to conserve his security forces for other duties by making prisoners unwitting informers. We said, no thanks! In any case the idea was preposterous in another respect. How could prisoners divine who of their friends and non-first degrees would like to visit them? Prisoners might wish these people to visit but it did not depend on the prisoner's wishes.

Take my case. I wished with all my wishing power to be visited by my wife; but for all the 15 years my wish did not come true. Jimmy Kruger himself and his predecessors Pelser and B J Vorster, later Prime Minister of South Africa, were responsible for frustrating my visit wish. To say I wished for the visit is an inaccuracy, a half-truth. I wished and made representations whenever an opportunity presented itself.

The hint that my wish would not come true was given in Leeuwkop Prison when I was classified 'D' by the Prison Board. The chairman of the board had made it clear that I was gunning for the post of Dr Verwoerd, the Prime Minister, and for this reason I was to start my 15 years hard labour at 'D' group level. In addition, that my wife who remained in Bechuanaland to carry on where I left off would not dare put her foot in South Africa because she would meet the fate that had befallen me.

The threat was serious enough to warrant my representations at the earliest convenience. When I raised the matter with Mrs. H Suzman on her first visit to the Island in 1966, a prison officer was instructed to write down my complaints for her. Ostensibly these complaints were later to be submitted to her to make representation to the relevant authority, presumably the Minister of Justice or Parliament. Shortly after Mrs H Suzman's visit, Lieutenant Naude the Security Officer called me to his office and read out a garbled reply to my complaint and request in Afrikaans. Although I understood Afrikaans I asked him to interpret the reply. The gist of it was that my wife would not be granted safe conduct in order to visit me. The reply came from the Commissioner of Police, not from Helen Suzman.

The implication was that my wife was engaged in subversive activity against South Africa in Bechuanaland. It was a lie. And the efficient, vigilant, diligent South African Security Branch knew that it was a lie. But they had to lie to themselves and anybody who might probe their vindictive refusal to allow my wife to visit me. Their lie justified their action in the eyes of the world and salved their timid consciences.

At a later stage I raised the matter with Colonel Aucamp. When I

163

challenged him to substantiate the allegation of my wife's subversive record he spluttered and ended up by making the ridiculous excuse, that my wife was not allowed to visit me because she was outside South Africa. Aucamp was getting old. His memory was beginning to let him down. At that time I could quote a couple of visitors from outside. He was stunned. To get out of it all, he eventually informed me it was a case for the security police. It was a neat way out of a dead end.

The behaviour of the South African government in regard to my wife intrigued me very much. I did not feel bitter or frustrated by it, rather I felt infinite scorn for a whole big, strong government that showed itself in such a petty light (for, in brief, it was the government that directed the execution of their inhuman policies). Captain Swanepoel, when our 'business' talk fell through, had quipped: 'So you want to become a martyr . . .' Well I had never expressed the desire to become one, but apparently the government had a compulsion to assist me become what I did not want to become, regardless of my resistance.

The last time I raised the question of my wife's visit was with the delegation of the International Committee of the Red Cross (ICRC). They promised to take it up with the government. Whether they did I do not know. What I know is that when I raised the matter with them and informed them that I was a Botswana national, they expressed surprise. As far as they knew, and they had inquired specifically, there were no foreigners on Robben Island. The only foreigner who had by then been released and deported was Chirwa of Malawi. Apparently the South African citizenship had been conferred upon me at last. Without my knowledge. It reminded me that it was standard procedure in South African government practices. Seretse Khama's ban had been lifted without his knowledge. I did not know how to celebrate my new status, with an innocent wife in irrevocable exile.

In the 15 years I received three visits. One from my mother-in-law Agnes, in 1968, that was before non-first degrees were excluded from regular visits. The second visit was from Tim Maharaj, the wife of my fellow prisoner Mac Maharaj, in 1971 also before friends were excluded. The third visit was from Peggy, my sister-in-law, in 1980. This last visit was originated by Comrade Nelson Mandela. Nelson was one of the very few prisoners who on the average received one visit a month. The focus of public attention naturally was on him and so the goodwill and assistance that goes with it enabled his dedicated wife and daughters to visit him regularly. All of his comrades, including myself, were quite proud and happy that he, as our leader, was a focus of attention on the island in various ways, including visits.

What I did not know was that he felt very much embarrassed by the fact that while he was receiving all these visits about which we felt

164

grateful on his behalf and on behalf of the organisation, some of us were not receiving any visit to talk about.

So one day Comrade Nelson pleaded with one of the 'reasonable' warders who was supervising his visit to allow him to raise the question of a visit for me with his wife. Nelson suggested that a lawyer be briefed to handle the matter. The visit was clinched, and Comrade Nelson was, I believe, very happy that I sampled a third visit. This was not an isolated incident. It is the ethos of political prisoners to keep each other's morale high.

On Robben Island it was the normal thing to share with inmates some of one's correspondence, especially from children and friends. Even correspondence from spouses was shared in the sense that some of the news was disseminated orally.

One of the inmates informed us that one of his sons objected very strongly when he learnt that his letters were read by more than his father. He was so disgusted that he stopped writing to his father for a long time. It was typical of someone who did not appreciate the value of his services. Had he known what his letters meant to the less fortunate inmates who did not enjoy regular correspondence of their own, he would not have been as mad as he was with his father. In fact he would have been very proud to know how much he was contributing to the unbroken spirits of the community.

Nobody who has not had the experience can imagine the feeling of burning anticipation on the eve of the distribution of mail from outside, the ecstasy that wraps the receipt of a letter and the vast gloom that envelopes the non-receipt of mail.

Whereas I had only three visits in my 15 years on Robben Island I was very lucky in regard to letters. Altogether I received approximately 240 letters during the same period, an average of one letter every three weeks, which was pretty good. Nonetheless at weekends when I returned empty-handed from the mail I felt miserable. I felt the whole world was in a shameless conspiracy against me, attempting to destroy and bury me, colluding and conniving with the enemy forces, the apartheid maniacs.

To buoy our spirits Comrade Walter Sisulu and I invented a mischievously insinuating slogan, 'aban'awusenza nto (they won't do us a thing)'. When comrades asked, 'Who won't do you a thing?' we replied 'anybody who thinks he/she can break us by not writing to us, including the Boers who withhold our letters, aban'awusenza nto!'

Comrades would threaten to inform our wives that we were lumping them together with the enemy. Too bad if they did. But it was proper to try to make light of the wretched feeling of being 'unwanted and deserted' by the trusted ones. Letters were a mighty psychotherapy, particularly on the rare occasions when they were delivered uncensored. The problem was that the rare occasions were

165

much too rare.

In the sixties the method used by the censors was blacking out the lines they found objectionable. This method was not always water-proof and apparently the censors found that out. They then adopted the method of excising the undesirable lines. Where the letter was written on both sides of the paper, it meant innocent lines were due to suffer too. Some censors could be quite vicious; they seemed to derive pleasure from handing letters to prisoners that looked like they had been through a shredder. I kept a few such letters as souvenirs. Another form of censorship was withholding the letter, and having the audacity to inform the prisoner: 'There is a letter for you, but you are not getting it.' Such censorship was originally reserved for letters suspected of coming from active members of the liberation move-ment. This applied to relatives of prisoners. For a long time Comrade Walter Sisulu was not allowed to receive letters from his son, Max. Only after many years of complaints did the warders concede and devise some way of conveying some of the contents of the letter to Walter. Instead of cutting the letter, the censors copied what they were convinced were innocuous passages from the letters and handed them over.

With the passage of time withholding of letters became common and indiscriminate. Around 1975/1976 two of my wife's letters were withheld. I felt very much frustrated, particularly because she was not a very regular correspondent. It was absolutely distressing especially when I recalled that she had informed me that she stopped writing to her mother in Johannesburg because her letters took months in the post. In spite of my strong complaints born of frustration and panic, the prison authorities would not budge from their original stand. I might ridicule the improbability of all the contents of a letter being objectionable and suggest that surely the salutation, 'My dear husband' could not be deemed objectionable, but the censors, the head of prison, the CO, the security officer, Aucamp, the Deputy Commissioner of Prisons, General Jannie Roux, would not move. The letters were withheld. Full stop.

During the early years letters were censored both ways – those coming in and those going out. Somewhere in the course of time something must have happened. We suspected that relatives who received the mutilated missives might have complained and maybe they threatened to do something about it. We knew for certain that Phyllis Naidoo, Comrade M D Naidoo's wife, was giving the Commissioner of Prisons a tough time on some of the department's practices that reeked with vindictiveness of the first order. Whatever might have happened, the mutilation of outgoing mail was stopped, it was too vulnerable to outside scrutiny.

Thus it was that the Prisons Department acting obviously in concert with the Security Branch and the Department of Information devised a neat plan that initiated self-censorship by inmates.

As usual the censors went through our outgoing correspondence with a fine toothcomb. But instead of paring a fine tooth comb with a knife or a pair of scissors, they pared it with a pen, a red one. The censors underlined or encircled any word, phrase, sentence or line that did not meet the criterion of passable communication between prisoner and correspondent. The pen, the red pen, substituted the knife, the scissors, the sharp instrument. Cutting was a savage method, an antedeluvian relic of Neanderthals. The Prisons Department, the South African Prisons Department, became sophisticated and substituted the pen for the cutting instrument. What was underlined was to come out of the letter before it could be stamped with the Prison censors' stamp and passed for the Department of Posts to handle. 'Mr So and So,' the warders were becoming rather too sophisticated, they had dropped the insulting 'kaffir' and 'bandiet' in addressing prisoners; 'Mr So and So, please rewrite this letter . . .' and they showed you what word, phrase, sentence or paragraph to rewrite, underlined or encircled in red. If one argued or declined to rewrite the letter, the censor could not be bothered, 'Well, Mr So and So, your letter won't go, that's all.' What can one do? After the censor has turned his back on you in an eloquent 'it's up to you', the first reaction would be naturally to reread the letter and try to find the grounds for the censor's objections. Often you felt like giving a mighty kick up the backside to the censors and the whole crazy system that humiliated, and piled more humiliation upon humiliation upon you.

The use of the word 'we' was taboo in the censors' dictionary of usages. 'We' meant one had assumed, unlawfully, the role of spokesman for other prisoners. It did not matter that in that particular context the 'we' used was the royal 'we', it had to come out, the whole letter of 500 words had to be rewritten. 'Scratch the 'we' and I'll write 'I',' you might plead; the answer would be, no scratching or deletion, rewrite!

In the end you rewrote the letter because of the 'we', and only then could it go if it did not fall into the hands of a different censor who might find other objectionable words or passages. It was not unusual to be asked to rewrite one letter more than once. What particularly aggravated the nonsense of rewriting letters was that letters to be rewritten were brought in with the incoming mail. It is difficult to vouch whether it was deliberate or not; the upshot of it was the creation of false expectations because when the names of mail recipients were called, no distinction was made between 'rewrites' and others. On occasions when there was no compensating incoming mail, you felt like strangling a neck or two.

The policy of forcing inmates to rewrite their letters was a master plan which enabled prison authorities to pose as angels to the outside public while they behaved atrociously to the prisoners. Imagine a relative who had been receiving blackened or mutilated correspondence from gaol, suddenly receiving a 500 word letter uncensored. Many must have felt ready to vote Nationalist Party if they were given the vote.

As far as the essence of communication itself was concerned it is easy to speculate that it did not suffer. The problem with restrictions or prohibition of any sort is that they hardly ever achieve their purpose. Every measure has its own countermeasure, every weight has a counterweight, every action has a counteraction. The victims of self-censorship developed styles of letter writing that meant absolute nonsense to the censors and yet were sensible and informative to the correspondent. If 'we' was objectionable as the plural of 'I', many ways, varied construction in syntax and grammar existed to convey the same 'we' concept. In the long term self-censorship was self-defeating. It was an exercise in futility. Make no mistake, the psychological implications for the victim were real and painful.

One more important means of contact was photos. On the occasions I was blessed with family or friends' photos I usually just stopped short of resolving to build a monument to the man who invented the camera. People might think me mad trying to honour a stranger whose history I did not even know. Photographs, when they were added to our grudgingly bestowed privileges, played a role in mitigating our social ostracism.

Many photos were returned to senders before we could be granted the privilege of three photos of a given size. My first photo from my wife arrived in 1968. It was a Sunday morning and we were busy cleaning the passage floor. Letters had been received on Saturday and nobody expected a letter until the next weekend. And I remember so vividly how the sight of my wife's photo paralysed me momentarily. I just stared at my wife's picture bewildered; it could have been somebody I could not recognise, the way I stood in the passage mentally transfixed. On recovering my senses I put it to my lips and kissed it with unusual passion for my kind of personality. Contrary to some halfbaked theories personality is not a fixed immutable condition, status or characteristic, but a product of concrete conditions.

That night I put aside my studies and allowed my memory and my imagination a free rein. In the morning I was exhausted from nostalgia and dreams. The privilege of photos, like all gaol privileges, had come after a relentless struggle by us and it had been granted halfheartedly. Three photos was the maximum. We argued it was not enough. What about our many relatives? Our families are big and extended, three photos is child play, allow more. All right said the authorities we'll allow more – 12 photos; but you can only have three at a time in your cell to exchange at regular intervals. You see, you cannot have all the 12, they are too many and besides they'll make your cells untidy. What utter nonsense! Did they think we would trifle with images of our dear ones? What silly asses! These photos were as good as the living beings they represented, we idolised them, they were deities for which we offered ourselves on the altar of sacrifice.

Anyway if they seriously believed we were irreverent enough to strew our photos around, why not allow us photo albums? After persistent representation on the issue, the authorities granted permission for albums on condition they were bought through the prisons department. We argued and argued but finally conceded the security point.

Twelve from the original three was an enormous increase. It was not enough, we had photo albums, we could have more photos in one album and be allowed more photo albums to have an unlimited number of photos. What's wrong with that?

Photos, like anything that came into gaol from outside, were carefully scrutinised and censored. An inadvertent thumbs up sign or raised fist in the photo rendered the photo objectionable. In the beginning a photo depicting a mixed group was against the rules of racism. In the late seventies, the rules were relaxed, photos with white, black, brown, pink and other colours could pass the grade.

The most objectionable photos were those of known freedom fighters in exile. For unknown reasons prison authorities seemed to believe that a view of some of these people in print would lead to a mass jail break. So any photo of an identifiable ANC exile was not permissible. Comrade Nelson Mandela wanted a photo of his former legal partner in the law firm, Mandela & Tambo Attorneys at Law. Winnie, Nelson's wife, did her best to obtain O R Tambo's photo for him, it was sent back to sender. Comrade Nelson, of course, complained strongly against the senseless procedures. To no avail.

In 1979, Comrade Nelson was awarded the Jawaharlal Nehru award for outstanding services to humanity. He was not allowed to receive the award himself, nor was Winnie, his wife, allowed travelling documents to receive the award on his behalf. Under the circumstances O R Tambo the life-long friend, legal partner of Nelson Mandela and President of the ANC, was the logical choice to represent Comrade Nelson in New Delhi at the glittering ceremony. An album of pictures at the ceremony was sent to Winnie who naturally passed it on to her husband. The authorities refused to release the album to Comrade Nelson. Nelson questioned this decision and made strong representations for it to be reversed.

After he was informed about the award, Comrade Nelson had immediately applied for permission to acknowledge the conferment. The permission was granted, although the letter was later sent back by the Prisons headquarters for rewriting. (The original letter was much later reported to have reached New Delhi through other channels). The granting of permission to write an acknowledgement of the award and the refusal of permission to enjoy a pictorial view of the ceremony appeared to be an intolerable conflict in the attitude of the authorities. Nelson pressed the point home. Eventually the authorities made an amusing compromise concession. One evening after lock-up a warder knocked at Nelson's window: 'Nelson! Nelson!' and he pushed the whole album of pictorials through Nelson's window. In the morning another warder knocked at the back window of Nelson's cell and pushed his hand through the window to receive back the album. Nelson of course had studied the pictures very carefully and he gave us a good description, more or less, of what the ceremony looked like and who of those he could recognise were there. The incident illustrates what care and pain the authorities on Robben Island took to deprive prisoners of any communication that could even remotely boost their morale.

Lieutenant Prins, then head of prison on Robben Island, once made an irrelevant analogy to express the official attitude on the question of prisoner morale. I had gone to him to complain about some passage I was instructed to rewrite in one of my letters. The letter was to someone in Botswana. In the letter I had wanted to know about the results of the previous elections in the country (Botswana). When the letter came back with the passage underlined in red, I saw red. Prins was not ruffled. He told me: 'Look, Dingake, would you regard it as a sound policy and practice if the prisons department brought women into the cells of convicted rapists?' The analogy was farfetched. But the point Prins was trying to convey was that in prison, political prisoners were to be made to forget politics in any form. Mention of politics of any kind was dangerous, it was morale boosting. Prins said so in plain language when I ridiculed his analogy. Prins was naive in the extreme. Not his fault. He represented naive policies.

The same Prins once called Comrade Toivo to his office and ordered him not to write Namibia on his letters to Namibia. Toivo refused to change the address, he was not going to use the coloniser's name when they had their own name. 'Okay,' said Prins, 'then your letters won't go.' 'Okay,' said Toivo. 'You are in power, you can do what you like but you won't make me adopt a name I reject.' Toivo continued to scribble Namibia on his letters to make his point to Prins the naive.

Photos circulated among inmates more than letters did. Circulation of letters was in practice confined to more intimate social friends even among members of the same organisation. Some of the photos even crossed the section boundaries from the communal cells section to segregation and vice versa. In our letters we became photo beggars: 'Please send me your photo' or 'please send me more photos' became a common theme of letters. The presence of pictures of friends and beloved ones in one's cell made a difference, a welcome psychological difference. It helped one survive, without being able to account for the survival under the rigours and hardships of gaol life. Imagination under the circumstances was not an intangible abstraction, it was a concrete reality. Visits, letters and photos kept us going in spite of their frequent use by officialdom as instruments of mental torture.

At one stage the authorities got it into their head that our old letters should be taken away from us. We were to keep only three months' letters with us: the rest of the letters were to be kept in our properties until the day of release. 'Parcel up your letters and hand them over!' we were ordered. Parcel them up we did. Hand them over, no! We regarded our letters as our most precious possession in our cells. We were prepared to challenge the authorities in a court of law if they enforced their order. It was obvious that if we handed them over ourselves, in any subsequent inquiry, the authorities could turn around and say we handed them over voluntarily. Consequently we refused to comply with the order and the prison authorities appeared to have second thoughts. In due course we untied our letters and continued as before, reading and re-reading them to refresh our memories of past events at home during our absence.

Shortly before my release, there was another demand for our letters. It was ignored while I was there. I believe if the prisons department had insisted on having their way the order would have been resisted as strongly as before. The odds are always against prisoners in any contest with the authorities of course. Where they are determined to have a showdown, there is very little the prisoners can do except protest and continue to exert pressure for restoration of lost privilege.

STUDIES

'You mean, they actually allowed you to study while you were there? And you obtained three degrees? At least it is some consolation. It is a credit to them – the South African prison authorities . . .'

That has been the general reaction of people who have shown interest in conversations with me about gaol conditions on Robben Island. True. Give the devil his due. Study privilege although it was not enjoyed by all the prisoners mainly because of financial constraints was a boon in many respects, but not in an unconditional sense. In fact this privilege more than all the others needs to be put into proper perspective.

After the conviction and sentence of Comrade Mandela and his colleagues in the Rivonia trial, some sections of the public were anxious to know whether they were going to be allowed to study. The government, in the wake of their triumph against 'communism and subversion', had to show some magnanimity towards their downed opponents. Any meanness at that stage would have been extremely mean. The government thus readily said, yes, the prisoners will be given permission to study whenever they apply for it. In a sense the government had committed itself publicly. In the course of time it

171

seems the Prisons Department either regretted its step or it was plagued by serious dissension internally or it rethought how it could turn enjoyment of study privilege into a stick to belabour the beneficiaries and make them more amenable to prison discipline or alternatively turn the privilege into a psychological instrument of torture.

Study privilege on Robben Island Prison was entangled with strict conditions. The conditions were a subject of controversy among the original inmates of segregation section – the Rivonia trialists and members of the YCC (Yu Chi Chan Club). There was a strong viewpoint that rejected the privilege under the harsh conditions which the prison authorities proposed to impose on those who applied to study. The two most controversial conditions apparently were that a student would not be allowed to lend his books to a non-student and that students themselves would not be allowed to exchange books or lend each other books even if they were studying the same subject. The two conditions meant that only those who had adequate funds could enjoy the privilege reasonably and be in a position to sit for examinations. Assuming a prisoner had sufficient funds to register and pay for tuition fees, but did not have money for prescribed books, he could not borrow from his fellow inmate who would be only too willing to help. Meanwhile the policy of the University library was not to lend prescribed books to students, only recommended works. As for non-students the condition condemned them to an approved limited selection of books in the prison library.

There were other conditions, for example, that students could only enrol with two approved South African institutions, namely the University of South Africa, for those studying for a degree, and Rapid Results College for those who were still pursuing their secondary education. At first there were two exceptions, Comrades Nelson Mandela and Walter Sisulu, who were permitted to study under the auspices of the University of London. In the case of Comrade Nelson who was doing an LLB the privilege was actually a disadvantage in the end, because the University of London with a tradition of unfettered scholarly research often prescribed study material which did not meet with the criteria of approved literature in terms of South African prison regulations. The result was frustration for Nelson who could not meet the examination standards from the literature he was allowed. Eventually the privilege to study with the University of London was revoked; at a later stage both he and Walter lost the privilege for several years.

In spite of the controversy that ensued over the acceptance or non-acceptance of the privilege under the restrictive conditions, the inmates agreed finally on the wisdom of acceptance. The feeling and argument that swayed the majority was that the fight for the removal of the conditions would not be abandoned after the granting of the emasculated privilege – the fight would be continued and intensified;

if the prison authorities were attempting to provoke a showdown or an excuse to deny prisoners study privilege they must be denied this excuse. Indeed it was a wise decision, for the prison authorities, enjoying the monopoly of propaganda to the public outside, could easily distort the facts and misrepresent the objections of the prisoners.

That was the state of affairs when I arrived in single cells section in 1966. It is the reason why my cell was raided by Colonel Aucamp and why I was charged and comrades' books confiscated. The price of breaking the study conditions could be even heavier than confiscation of books. One could lose the privilege itself for a number of years.

I was granted permission to study in 1967. I enrolled for two BA courses, Political Science and Economics. Although the University of South Africa enrols students from October, students on Robben Island never registered earlier than February. The excuse was normally that those who had written exams at the end of the year could not be given permission to register with the University before their results were known. The results were usually received around Christmas. But permission, which had to be sought every year, was never forthcoming until the end of January. The point is that every year the Robben Island students registered late by four months or more. Although in 1967 I had not been waiting for examination results, I registered at the same time as those who were waiting for their results.

Our Economics class was a very lively class. Even Suitcase's 'Come on, come on!' could never curb its animation. The 'laymen' in Economics stood and watched as we argued noisily over our supply and demand curves and drew them on the ground to demonstrate their gradients and elasticity. I wrote my Economics Course One papers in Pretoria at the time of my second interrogation and I was praised for my B symbol. Actually people who deserved praise were my classmates. The discussions we held at the quarry were very helpful.

The lime quarry was, even at the worst of times, a site for intellectual stimulation. That is partly why their mood was so ugly on the morning of the shut-up decree. To a very large extent, while Suitcase was in charge our class discussions never interfered with our work. Except for Comrade Isubhai who was very fond of making his point at very close quarters, we had developed an amazing combination of work and talk. The absorption in our discussions probably did much to take our minds off the picking and shovelling we did so instinctively.

Our average span at the lime quarry was 30. Although we had a handful of inmates who were not literate in English, the average standard of education could be said to be at the undergraduate level. Classes were organised for all standards including beginners and

173

subjects, with teachers for lower classes being appointed by the 'head teacher' who was Dr Neville Alexander. University students arranged their own discussion groups when they were not teaching or helping others.

In the evening, in the cells, the preoccupation was always preparation of the following day's lessons. The few who had no permission to study had to go to bed with the bell at 8 pm. Students were allowed to study until 11 pm. A minute after 11 pm the night duty warder moved from cell to cell ordering: 'Slaap! (Sleep!)' At the order all study activities had to cease. Any disobedience could be penalised heavily.

Studying in the single cells section was uncomfortable and awkward in the beginning. There was no bench or stool, no proper table or desk except a square piece of slanting masonite secured to the wall by brackets. One had to stand and do one's reading and writing standing. The sub-zero temperature of the cells did not help our studious efforts. Our cells were extremely cold. I did not believe I could survive the temperature of the cell. When I arrived on Robben Island, prisoners were allowed four threadbare blankets, one sisal mat and one felt mat, no pillow, no sheets, no bed. The very first day I registered as prisoner No 277/66 I stole two extra blankets. The communal cells were warmer naturally. In the communal cells there was also the practice known as 'federation'. 'Federation' was a popular practice whereby two inmates pooled their blanket resources. Each member of the federation rolled himself in one of his blankets and the rest were federated and shared commonly.

In the single cells section, each in his narrow cell for ever, federation was impracticable. Moreover the cells, according to reports, had been built hastily to accommodate the Rivonia trialists. The result of the speed of construction was that the whole edifice was saturated with water. In the morning the bottom sisal mat was always dank with vapour from the dampness underneath. The walls would be worse, trickling with icy vapour.

Here too I became a blanket thief. The Section Warder of course made it a point to count the prisoners' blankets while we were at the quarry. Extra blankets were invariably taken back to the store. Another warder would have charged me for blanket theft, but Van Zyl seemed to be content with frustrating my efforts. To outsmart Van Zyl I had to steal one or two blankets after work and restore them in the morning before the span went to work. It was not always easy because access to the storeroom was a bit difficult except for the two non-political prisoners who were working in the section as cleaners. Only with the collusion of one of them, Andrew (he later identified himself with us and was regarded as such by the prison authorities), could my thieving be fairly successful.

Comrade Nelson Mandela had raised the dampness of our cells with Colonel Aucamp. The Colonel had showed very little concern

174

when the complaint was raised. 'The dampness of the cells will eventually be absorbed by your bodies . . . Alles sal regkom, Nelson, (Everything will be alright, Nelson,)' Aucamp explained airily.

By the time of my release the walls of our cells were dry and no dampness was oozing from the floor. Our bodies had indeed absorbed the dampness. At what cost to our general health? Pity, medical research will be denied this rich field of investigation. To attempt any studying in the cells we had to wrap ourselves with two or more blankets and stand on the rolled mats and the rest of the blankets.

In 1978 Robben Island Prison was opened to local and international journalists. They stormed our cells and took pictures of their interior, bookshelves packed with books, a little locker on the cell wall and a decent little table in the middle of the cell. We were not allowed to talk to the journalists; they got their stories from the prison officers and the dumb misconstruable furnishings inside the cells.

The bookshelves had been built by us against strong opposition from the authorities. Whenever we worked by the seaside we made it a point to collect some useful flotsam, planks mainly, for construction of our bookcases. It depended on the disposition of the warder in charge on the particular day. The next day a not so well disposed warder would not only refuse permission to bring any planks into the section, he might dismantle anything constructed already and charge the prisoner for unauthorised possession. The bookshelves the journalists photographed were an umpteenth attempt after genera- tions of aborted attempts and personal prisoner misery. Had the journalists interviewed the prisoners they would have heard the harrowing history of the subjects of their photo lenses' delights.

Up to 1968 or 1969 the prisoners who studied with the University of South Africa could feel somewhat indebted either to the University of South Africa itself or the Prisons Department – it is not clear which – in regard to tuition fees, which were only half the fees paid by other students outside prison. There was talk that prisoners were subsidised by the Prisons Department to study while in gaol. Some said this was just propaganda by the prison staff. Other talk was that the University of South Africa in the kindness of its heart had decided through its Council or one of its decision-making bodies and felt it incumbent upon itself to encourage prisoners to pursue and cultivate the virtue of learning while they were serving their long sentences. The anonymous benefactor did well while his/her benefac- tion extended to the students. Like all good things, however, the subsidy came to an end the same way it had started, sans ceremony, sans warning.

The termination of the much appreciated subsidy was the subject of some rumours. One rumour was that the Prisons Department was revising its policy on the privileges of studies for political prisoners. This was confirmed in a way when in 1969 all the prisoners who were

175

doing postgraduate studies were instructed to sit for their examinations in February 1970. Students who had planned their study programmes to culminate later than 1970 were admonished: it is 1970 February or never.

Nothing could change official attitude. The students had to cram two or three years work into one year. Fortunately they all succeeded – Neville Alexander (History), Andrew Masondo (Statistics), Govan Mbeki (Economics).

The cancellation of postgraduate studies was followed by excision of specific subjects – History, Law and Political Science – from the curricula of junior degrees. Those who had already been granted permission to study these subjects could carry on, but new applicants came up against a wall.

Those who were exempted by virtue of previous permission however came under systematic harassment by the prison section in charge of studies. Applications for library books were scrutinised as never before. If books were permitted to be ordered they were carefully censored and very often sent back to the library as undesirable before the borrower could see them.

It was during this period that I did my Political Science III. Tremendous effort was required to obtain recommended books from the library for assignments. For one assignment one of my recommended books was *Power Politics* by J Morgenthau. I believe the title scared the study officer even before he opened the book. The thickness of the volume must have been another disincentive to the warder's favourable disposition. He came to inform me that I could not get the book. It implied that I would not be able to qualify for my year-end examination because my tutor insisted that the assignment, which was a qualifying one, had to be based primarily on the book. Since I could not shift the study officer I requested him not to send the book back to the library while I appealed to the CO against his ruling.

The OC Colonel Van Aarde was a man of amiable disposition, a benign personality who could not be trusted with proper authority in a place like Robben Island. His presence on Robben Island was regarded by us as a purely nominal appointment. He could not take the simplest decision on the spot. All decisions minor or major were the preserve of Brigadier Aucamp (he had been promoted) at the Headquarters in Pretoria. My appeal to him might be decided in Pretoria by which time the loan period of the book would have expired. Nonetheless I had no alternative.

When he heard the title of the book he almost had a heart attack. '*Power Politics*!?' he queried incredulously. It took all my persuasive powers and latent charm to convince Colonel Van Aarde of the innocuousness of the book and that he should read it to prove my point. This time the decision came from Van Aarde himself. I could have it. It was two days before the expiry of the loan period, which forced me to ask for extension of loan period retroactively.

Generally the problem of adequate and suitable literature for students on Robben Island was perennial and endemic. No student, whatsoever his subjects, escaped the petty harassment by study officers – deliberate delaying of delivery of books, unsubstantiated objections to certain books, gross inefficiency in processing approved book purchase orders and many other pinpricks. And there was no stage at which the harassment ceased or abated. It was intertwined with study privilege. If you were privileged to study then you were fair game for constant pinpricks.

Another rumour or speculation that followed the termination of the subsidy was that the prison authorities were beginning to be extremely unhappy about the intellectual disparity between prisoners and warders. This disparity was growing rapidly and wider every day as all prisoners were enthusiastic about education while the prison warders were not. We did much to encourage them to study, because we believed that an educated man is a rational being in some ways. At the beginning, the response was very poor. 'Ek is lui (I am lazy)' was the average warder's confession and excuse. At a later stage the bug of learning did bite the warders. Many studied. Those who did not study expressed the wish to study, very often in absolutely superhuman idealism. For example, one young warder, who after investigation had not done well in his Junior Certificate, planned to do a BA in one year!

Whatever the motivation of the prison's latest policy directions on study privilege, prospects for the continued enjoyment of the privilege by prisoners were very poor. The 'Verkramptes' and 'Verligtes' in the Prisons Department and the Cabinet were obviously reviewing the wisdom of 'encouraging "terrorists" to commit acts of terror against the government, only to be rewarded or spoiled by further education in gaol'. The whole process smacked of absurdity to the ultra conservatives, the Verkramptes in government. The party liberals, the Verligtes, seeing one step ahead of their conservative 'broeders' thought the objection was shortsighted, and that foresight demanded the taking into account of international opinion as well as inevitable future change. The news of the infighting filtered through to us through unguarded remarks from senior officers and gossip from the junior staff.

At the end of 1970 Colonel Van Aarde, the CO, gave way to Colonel Badenhorst whose fame had preceded him to the Island. On arrival he was promptly christened Kid Ruction. Kid Ruction immediately suspended all legal procedures and processes in gaol administration. Gaol decisions, particularly those sanctioning punishment of prisoners, are at the best of times biased and arbitrary. Kid Ruction's administration added a touch of absurd drama to the bias and arbitrariness. Prisoners were stripped of their privileges without charge or explanation, they were locked up in punishment cells at the whim of the CO, completely denied access to the lawyers. Any prisoner who demanded an explanation of his fate was told: 'Jy weet! (You know!)' 'But I don't know!', a prisoner might try to remonstrate and plead; 'Jy weet,' would be the final answer when the punishment cell door was slammed on the prisoner.

To ensure full observance of his tyrannical regimen and instructions, the officers that served under him down to the section head warders and warders were a handpicked lot who shared his wickedness and his ruthlessness. Nozinja, Pollsmoor and Dictionary (nicknames of warders) were assigned to our section with a mission to put us in our place by inflicting physical and mental pain. The relative deference previously accorded our section in the context of prison attitudes was discarded in favour of unparalleled vindictiveness. We were made to eat in the rain, some of the section inmates were physically assaulted – something unknown in the section in the past – Comrade Nelson Mandela was threatened by the OC with retribution when he dared raise the grievances of our section with a powerful visiting delegation of judges (the threat was made in the presence of the judges). Our cells were raided frequently, our books tossed on the floor and trampled on by the arrogant all-powerful search parties. No chance was left to humiliate us and expose our prisoner status to us. Many of us were deprived of our study privileges during the full term of Badenhorst's administration. Events leading to cancellation of study privileges of some of us were swift and dramatic. I remember the day Kid Ruction descended upon the lime quarry walking like an all-conqueror at the scene of final battle. Even before his vehicle came to a halt Kid Ruction was holding the door open ready to jump out while he repeated to his driver, 'Kyk hoe staan hulle . . . (Just look how they are standing . . .)'

At that moment part of the span stood and chatted to the new warder who had just expressed his dissatisfaction at the rate of work. The prisoners were explaining the work norms that prevailed at the quarry and naturally were urging the warder not to expect more than the norm. Other prisoners were doing their usual stint at their normal pace. Billy Nair was busy cleaning the shed in which we took our lunch as part of his duties and I had gone to drink water at the tap near the shed. Without saying anything to the warder or to the span, Badenhorst climbed back into the vehicle and instructed his driver to radio for a truck to come and take us back to prison.

We were lined up outside the Administration Office and informed that thenceforth the 16 of us were down one grade in our classification. As became Bs, Bs became Cs and Cs became Ds while Ds remained where they were. We had always condemned the system of classification as ill-designed, spiteful and degrading. The downgrading meant automatic loss of certain privileges, the number of letters one could write and the number of visits one could receive.

178

Worse was still to come.

One morning the man who was in charge of studies came into our section holding a piece of paper in his hand. I was standing at my cell door ready to go out with the span when the study officer approached me and said: 'Dingake, pack your books!' He did not explain why, in the true style of the day, so I asked him. For once he did not say 'Jy weet (you know)', he said: 'Your study privilege has been cancelled.' 'Why?' 'Because you are a D group and D groups are no longer permitted to study.' Prisoners who did not study were not allowed to keep books in their cells except the Bible and books borrowed from the prison library—even the ordinary language dictionary was banned from cells of non-students.

Two cells down, the study officer stopped and told Comrade Billy Nair the same sad news he had told me. Billy and I packed our books and handed them to the inefficient and corrupt custody of the prison service. After two years, when my study privilege was restored, some of my books were missing and no one accepted responsibility for the loss. We were the first to lose study privilege in the section, Billy and I, but not the last. Many more inmates soon became victims of the same trend.

The loss of study privilege made the grim gaol conditions grimmer. Already I had read all that was worth reading from the censored collection of the prison library. Although prison regulations allowed prisoners to purchase fictional literature on condition it was donated to the Prisons Department after reading, this privilege was never implemented, partly because it was controversial and partly because the prison authorities preferred to ignore it. In the atmosphere of prevailing conditions, prospects for a quick restoration of the privilege were remote and bleak. The psychological strain imposed on the prisoner who had previously enjoyed the privilege is hard to imagine.

But political prisoners are a hardy lot. The motivation to struggle against odds is strong. The knowledge that one is fighting for a universal principle of human dignity and that progressive and right-thinking humanity is behind one works miracles towards counteracting overwhelming depression. This psychological attitude makes each political prisoner ready for extreme personal sacrifice in the interests of his colleagues.

Prior to the administration of Colonel Badenhorst we had won an important concession from the Prison Headquarters, namely the privilege for students to exchange personal literature. Although the concession was not extended to lending books to non-students on our own, in practice we had extended it to them. The loss of study privilege by a number of prisoners and the removal of books from cells of those affected implied renewed unlawfulness of possession of another prisoner's book if one was not an accredited student. The warders became vigilant. Cell raids and body searches in the cells became frequent and aggressive. These measures however did not stop the 'privileged' few from sacrificing for the 'unprivileged' majority in the section. To a very large extent the prisoners were always up on the authorities and casualties in the book-smuggling racket were few and far between.

It was during this interruption in my formal studies that I decided to redress my old disappointment. AML Masondo sacrificed with his maths books and time at the quarry. Maths was just the right thing to tackle at this stage because of the nature of the problems one solves. Mathematical problems have a unique power of absorbing the mind. In my experience nothing has ever concentrated my vagrant mind as did maths. It was just the ideal preoccupation under the circumstances. The danger however was that in such singular concentration one could be surprised by a snooping warder on the lookout for unapproved activity by non-students or after-time activity by the students – 11 o'clock was the limit beyond which students were not allowed to go except during the exams when extra time was conceded.

I found a way of getting round that one by working out my maths problems on my tummy under the blankets. I made sure my head was at an angle which was incompatible with clear vision from the cell window. Some warders of course objected to reclining positions that impeded full view. In that case one had to comply and try to have one's ear to the ground to pick up warning footfalls of the night duty warder in the passage. Then like a tortoise one withdrew one's head under the blanket shell and simulated a loud snore. The most dangerous warders were those who walked in their socks. Fortunately those who insisted on certain positions of sleeping were not always the same as those who walked in their socks. The dice were not always heavily loaded and one managed to survive warder vigilance by one's own super vigilance.

In 1973, thanks to my wife's intervention through a lawyer, my study privilege was restored on the eve of the university registration closing date. My lectures arrived in April which meant six months to prepare for my BA final exams.

With the ban on postgraduate studies I had to look around for another junior degree. I opted for B Admin with majors in Public Administration and Local Government Accounting. My BA majors had been Economics and Political Science. In 1976 I completed the B Admin degree. My second 'third degree' (I had actually been conferred the first one at Compol University, Pretoria) was B Com which I started in 1977. I was very lucky as usual to have got the permission when I did, because a little later in the year the prison authorities came with a startling announcement that thenceforth no prisoner would be granted permission to do post-matric studies. Prospective students on the Island, except the warders, would have to

180

be content with GCE, Senior Certificate or diplomas. Those who had permission to do a degree would be allowed to complete their courses.

It was a shattering blow to the prison community. Since the ban on senior degrees, we had never given up hope of their restoration; we had maintained persistent pressure on the authorities to rescind the decision of 1969. The announcement was a severe setback to our efforts. What would happen to lifers and others who were doing long sentences? There is nothing like three Senior Certificates in the curriculum of secondary school education. In any case, the authorities themselves would be the first to stop any enterprising prisoner who attempted to acquire three Junior Certificates or two Senior Certificates. Another discouraging factor was that prisoners were not allowed to engage in creative writing – poetry or fiction – or any writing for that matter, except the monthly letters which had to be rewritten according to the whims of the censors.

The denial of the right of prisoners to write creatively was to a large extent a negation of the seemingly important concession of granting study privilege to political prisoners. Over the years we made representation to the authorities to have this attitude reviewed. Instead, our cells were continually raided, our books ransacked for unauthorised scraps of writing. Should the search parties find what they were looking for, the penalty could be severe. One might lose his study privilege on a charge of having abused it. A few lines of unauthorised poetry might just be enough to see the privilege irrevocably destroyed.

The prison authorities were also beginning to implement a long-standing threat, namely, that after completion of any study course, the prisoner should hand over all the literature related to that particular course. This was absolute insanity. Thus far they had not been able to enforce the decree, primarily because of understaffing and our resistance, grounded on the irrationality of the policy as well as our fears that the safety of our books could not be guaranteed in the custody of the inefficient and corrupt prison staff. Some of us who had had our books taken away when we lost our study privilege could cite from personal experience what happened to books impounded. The authorities found an answer to the insecurity of books in their custody. Ship them home! Were the discretion of what to ship home and when to do it left to the prisoners, it would have been a fair compromise. It was not compromise the authorities were looking for but strict compliance. In the circumstances the outlook for prisoners was bleak and threatening to be more so.

There was yet an additional rider to the granting of study privilege: qualification for study privilege would in future depend on the previous performance of the prospective student. The University of South Africa was also introducing some such criterion for continued enrolment with them. One can concede that an institution of learning like the University of South Africa is entitled to set standards for its students and that they would be qualified to assess the true potential of their students. But what right and what qualification would the Prisons Department claim to have on this matter? This was unwarranted interference in the relations between the institution of learning and the student.

The good performance of students on Robben Island was not necessarily and wholly dependent on their IQ's. It could depend on the physical and mental capacity of the prisoner to survive the harsh, abnormal conditions of his surroundings and his adaptability to further strains imposed by inadequate communication with his family. A rational dispensation would be expected to take some of these disadvantages into account before formulating such threatening intentions. But no.

In four years' time I would be out of gaol. I had survived the 11 interesting but gruelling years. The four remaining years would be absorbed by B Com. I was almost home and dry. My colleagues? We continued to voice our grievances, concentrating on the deterioration in the study privileges and demanding improvement. The status quo ante, would do, but our ultimate target was restoration of postgraduate studies. At the same time we agitated for permission to engage in creative writing. The demand for permission to write creatively was a ticklish issue at the time, because a precedent had already been created with Breyten Breytenbach who was doing nine years for 'Okhela' activities.

Breytenbach had been obviously favoured, whether because he was a 'son of the soil' or for some more obscure reason, we did not know. But there was clear discrimination and we laid our finger on it. The Nats under P W Botha are still the same Nats who came to power under Dr D F Malan in 1948. They are the same. They practised apartheid under Dr Malan and they still practise it under P W. The only difference is that under Dr Malan they were blunt, frank and arrogant: Apartheid: Kaffer op sy plek (kaffir in his place). Hotnot op sy plek (Hottentot (Coloured) in his place) and Koelie uit die land (Coolie out of the country). Under P W Botha they are suave, dishonest and double talkers: Blacks to the 'homelands', Coloureds and Indians to the new dispensation of three parliaments, each parliament centred on eie (own) affairs. This approach enables P W Botha and company to say apartheid is dead. South Africans have ridiculed this artful dissimulation. Where is the corpse? If apartheid is dead, bury it, it is causing a stench!

The truth however is that apartheid is alive and well. The knowledge that P W Botha and Co do not like to call apartheid apartheid can be useful to a limited extent in dealing with the Nats. If you told them: 'You are discriminating in favour of Breyten Breytenbach because he is Afrikaner', they replied: 'No, we are not,

182

he is a poet, we have allowed him to write poetry'. 'We want to be poets too, allow us to write poetry,' you retort. 'No, he does not keep what he writes in his cell, he hands over to the authorities what he has written every morning,' they try to argue. 'We can do the same,' you answer, and they don the official armour of 'we won't be pushed'.

The problem with the Nats is that they have two skins. I am not talking of the endodermis and the epidermis. It is actually one skin but it is reversible, thick on one side and thin on the other – two-in-one. The thick skin is impervious to change, the thin skin itches easily, and suffers from scratches administered by pressures for change. Thus far the scratches have not affected the thick skin, it has not developed the itch. Elephant skin.

At the time of my release from Robben Island in 1981 the authorities were still unprepared to allow other prisoners except Breytenbach the privilege to write creatively. They had however restored both post-matric as well as postgraduate studies. Conditions surrounding the extended privilege were going to be tighter. The disposal of prescribed literature for courses completed was to be strictly enforced, the stationery used by students would be stationery printed by the Prisons Department and dissertations for Masters Degrees were to be screened and approved by the Prisons Department.

The stationery condition was meant to combat smuggling of notes (illegal communication) between sections. I never understood how it was supposed to do that. What puzzled me was what was to happen to the stationery supplied by the University. All Unisa (University of South Africa) students were entitled to a specific quantity of stationery for the assignments at no extra cost. The order for prisoners to buy prison stationery without a corresponding reduction in the University tuition fees smacked of a 'hold up' of defenceless victims. I wish I knew how the issue was resolved. The involvement of the prison authorities in the selection of a scholarly dissertation appeared to be a built-in veto for Masters Degrees in spite of anything to the contrary.

When I left, Comrade Govan Mbeki was battling to get permission to enrol for his MA in Economics. After numerous representations the dissertation had been approved by the prisons headquarters. There was a major hitch however, namely, another condition that sought to bind Unisa to sanction the ban of the dissertation even before it evolved. Even the conservative, loyal, Unisa seemed to view this as an unacceptable precondition of a scholarly effort. It was a mockery of higher learning. A deadlock appeared to be looming on the horizon between Unisa and the Prisons. Subsequently I heard a rumour that Govan was not granted the permission after all. After this precedent would a Masters be any prisoner's hope?

Without study privilege many of the prisoners would have atrophied intellectually and bouts of demoralisation might have superseded the general buoyancy of the community. Studies to a large extent played some diversionary role. It is true the majority of prisoners did not enjoy the formal privilege of study while they were in gaol for a number of reasons, the principal one being lack of funds. Informally, no prisoner who had an interest in learning failed to benefit from the intellectual atmosphere that prevailed. The privileged students took risks, 'abused' their study privilege to help their less privileged fellow inmates.

RELIGION

My disillusionment with Christianity in the late forties emanated from what I regarded as shameless hypocrisy and gross insensitivity on the part of practising Christians, in particular the white Christians, as evangelists of their doctrine and influential members of their so-called Christian society. White South African Christians acted completely contrary to their Christian principles. They did not love their neighbours, the Africans, they hated them. Africans were not human beings, they were subhumans. No matter how much the poor African converts tried to set an example of good Christianity by insinuating themselves into the white Christian society, they were rejected and kept at arm's length.

One of my fellow inmates on Robben Island once related a story which reflected a typical tendency of whites to reject Africans. I laughed when the story was related not because it was funny but because it was tragi-comic. A white member of one of the Dutch Reformed Churches had died in Kimberley. African members of the congregation did what they regarded as their Christian duty, they attended the funeral. As is the norm in South Africa on rare occasions when whites and blacks congregate, they segregated themselves in colour compartments. On addressing the mourners the predikant (priest) started: 'Dames en here (Ladies and gentlemen),' then he paused and faced the black side of the audience, and in a deepthroated unfriendly voice: 'en julle (and you)!' he said eyeing the blacks ungraciously. 'And you!' Ladies and gentlemen did not refer to Africans. They are 'you (julle)' – non-descript creatures, unwanted sycophants who embarrassed their lords/ladies by yes-sirring and yes-mumming when they were not called. 'Julle (you)': you non-humans, subhumans, children of the devil. If you are black and you knew some of these negative attitudes of some of the white section then you would be a dyed-in-the-wool optimist to imagine that white South Africa can change through constructive engagement and dialogue.

Somewhere I have said the churches, after the introduction of 'Bantu education', have never been the same again. According to my unresearched opinion, 'Bantu education' was the first government-measure against which the Christian churches generally, and the Catholic Church in particular, voiced their strong opposition and

184

even took a stand in an organised form. 'Bantu education' was the brainchild of the Calvinistic Nats who attempted to win the 'Bantu' from the embrace of non-Calvinist denominations and under the pretext of secularising black education were in fact creating favourable conditions for their own Calvinist hegemony.

The Catholic Church and other denominations were angry because they realised 'Bantu education' was meant to pave a way for a psychological coup of the black mind by the Calvinists. It was the mission of each Christian church to mould the mind, to indoctrinate the black child according to its peculiar interpretation of the gospel. The Calvinist clique was therefore looking for trouble when it attempted to monopolise the sacred duty of all the religious cliques. The Nats are their own enemy. Good thing.

The formation of the South African Council of Churches (SACC) in the sixties was a natural development after the trauma of a spate of apartheid legislation in the first 10 years of Nat rule. The Bantu Education Act must be given pride of place in this development. Even from the Calvinist fold, prominent theologians emerged to sound an alarm at the deviationism of their political leaders: Beyers Naude, Geldenhuys and others.

Leading Church figures in South Africa were becoming outspoken against unjust government policies in the sixties. Politics was no longer to be the prerogative of the cabinet ministers and parliamentarians but of the minister of religion as well. The government officials, accustomed to the docility of the churches, did not fancy the new sauciness of the pastors. Mr Ben Schoeman in 1962 attacked Bishop Knapp-Fisher of the Anglican Church and said he should 'keep his nose out of politics and like a cobbler stick to his last'.

Bishop Knapp-Fisher's reply was an accurate interpretation of the feeling whose unfulfilment made me shun the church. What he said in the words of the *Annual Survey of Race Relations* for 1962, was this.

> There is no warrant for such a view (that as a bishop he should keep out of politics) in the bible. The old testament prophets were outspoken in judgement about social and political life, fearlessly condemning what they considered incompatible with God's righteousness. Christians are not only heirs to this tradition, but should have concern for every situation in which human interests are involved. To fail in this response would justify the taunt of non-Christians that religion is only a means of escape and a vague promise of future compensation for present ills.

A message to the people of South Africa, drawn up in 1968 by an interdenominational Theological Commission, set up by the South African Council of Churches, was something of a landmark. It was drawn up by a Commission which included members of the Anglican, Presbyterian, Roman Catholic, Methodist, Lutheran, Bap-

185

tist denominations and also former and current members of the Nederduitse Gereformeerde Kerk and the Nederduitse Hervormde Kerk of Africa:

> The message declared that the gospel of salvation in Christ should be understood in a cosmic and universal sense. Salvation must be sought in the circumstances of the time and place in which Christians found themselves. It was the Church's right and duty to concern itself with political systems.

The statement did not find favour with the Prime Minister, B J Vorster. He issued one of the strongest threats ever issued by a South African politician against the churches:

> At a party meeting in Brakpan on 27 September, Mr Vorster repeated that people should not use the pulpit in an attempt to achieve political aims. He is reported to have added that there were clerics who were toying with the idea of doing the sort of thing in South Africa that Martin Luther King had done in America. 'I want to say to them, cut it out; cut it out immediately because the cloth you are wearing will not protect you if you try to do this in South Africa.'

Obviously the churches were beginning to drive the Prime Minister into very ungraceful political tantrums. It was a measure of the latent power and influence that Christian churches could wield in the context of South African politics.

The question was, why had they left it until so late? In spite of the axiom, better late than never, it is regrettable that the churches entered into the political scene at this late hour. It has led them to an erroneous interpretation of crucial political trends in the South African scene and an over-estimation of their own influence and methods of struggle. The churches represented by the South African Council of Churches, despite their profession that they understand why the liberation movement has resorted to violence, continue to condemn more strongly the occasional acts of violence committed by the liberation movement than they do the institutionalised violence that led to the revolutionary counter-violence of the liberation movement.

They fail to appreciate and distinguish the goals of the two types of violence. Institutionalised violence of government, besides being provocative, is self-perpetuating. This is so, because it is oppressive, and nowhere in history has oppression been tolerated. In order to continue with the oppression of the black majority the South African government cannot do otherwise than resort to violence in a myriad of ways. That naturally provokes resistance, which in turn provokes more violence to suppress the resistance. It leads to an escalating vicious circle: violence, resistance, more violence, more resistance.

The revolutionary counter-violence of the liberation movement has as its objective the ending of institutionalised violence which breeds a spiral of violence. It is violence to end violence and to create an atmosphere of peace in which the popular aspirations enshrined in the Freedom Charter can be realised.

An objective analysis of the South African situation must admit two important facts. The first fact is that the South African government has made some ideological concessions in the context of their original policies. 'Kaffer op sy plek (Kaffir in his place)' and 'Koelie uit die land (Coolie out of the country)' has been replaced by 'Bantus in the Bantu homelands' and 'Indian South Africans in a tricameral parliament'. In practice the substance has not changed but the shadow has, which exposes the substance and makes it more vulnerable. The naked advocacy of oppression is being denounced and the unity of bigoted Afrikanerdom is no longer guaranteed. It is necessary to recognise this fact in order to put the history of the struggle in proper perspective as well as to formulate relevant strategies. The second fact to admit is: the first concession would not have come about without the resistance of the masses, in particular their threat to use violence to achieve their goal of freedom.

Before the ANC resorted to the threat of violence (I underline 'threat' because the scale of counter-violence is still at an insignificant level) the so-called 'independence of the homelands' was not on the cards and foreign investment in these 'reserves' was specifically excluded. The threat of violence by the liberation movement brought home to the oppressors that the oppressed were determined to escalate their resistance unless some tangible concessions were made. 'Independence of the homelands' was viewed as such (tangible concession) when it was made. Events have not confirmed this initial major strategy to divide and rule the oppressed black majority. The fact that the strategy has misfired must not be construed as its having had no grand designs. It had. The only problem it did not take into account was the political consciousness of the people and the extensive campaign that had been conducted by the liberation movement internally and internationally. In the era of African independence, the oppressed were bound to distinguish between pseudo-independence and true independence. The partial success of the bantustans' 'independence' is due to the ignominious role of collaborators and the employment of cunning and violence by the oppressors to get their way.

The destabilisation factor that features so prominently in South Africa's foreign policy with its weaker neighbours, in spite of its success story, could not have been taken lightly by the South African government. It is quite probable that before the South African government opted for destabilisation, they asked for and received the green light from their imperialist allies, in particular, in Washington. To have undertaken a policy with such potential disastrous consequences is a measure of the immense fear the government has of the ANC threat.

In the past the ANC was never mentioned in parliamentary deliberations, today the Ministers of Defence and Police justify their actions on the basis of ANC threat. ANC is an important factor in the political situation in SA. The demands for which it stands are still far from being met but it can no longer be ignored in serious deliberations that concern the future of the country. The ANC has reached the position of recognition by threatening violence. This recognition has far-reaching implications in the long run for the interests of the oppressed.

White South African rulers despite their extensive use of institutionalised violence are terrified of counter-violence. Political violence and upheaval in a society that has known violence in one direction only is fraught with ghastly implications for the South African way of life – white affluence, white power, white status, white arrogance – all these will be affected should there be an eruption of real violence. The government is committed to stamp out violence in the country. Whether they succeed remains to be seen. But the lesson that violent oppression breeds resistance and counter-violence is not likely to be forgotten quickly. The immediate reaction of government, assuming violence is stamped out, will be to bring about 'gradual' reforms. What the government will not learn is that the people's aspirations cannot be satisfied by gradual reformation but by a sweeping immediate revolution. Gradual reformation in the typical tradition of SA politics ignores the voice of the oppressed. It is sterile. Sweeping revolution on the vehicle of counter-violence expresses the impatience of exclusion from decision making and the determination to be involved in their own destiny. Like any birth it will be accompanied by pains. But its fruit will be healthy and sweet. Reforms initiated by an oppressor government cannot and will never upset the status quo, only revolution in the form of mass uprising and counter violence can and will overthrow it and prevent it from resurrection.

The SACC is playing a progressive role in the struggle for freedom. Its voice inspires hope. Christian churches have undergone a radical metamorphosis since the day I began to disdain them for impious aloofness from the people's struggle. That point must be clear. Having come so far it is hoped that they will not revert to destructive criticism against methods of struggle dictated by the prevailing circumstances.

One of the fears of churchmen with regard to violent methods of struggle is that such methods will leave a lot of bitterness and make reconciliation very difficult. The Reverend Jones, a Methodist Minister, used to preach a great deal about reconciliation whenever he came for a service on Robben Island. It went on until one of us,

188

Eddie Daniels, told him that his sermon was misdirected. Reconciliation would have validity if preached to the white oppressors. The oppressed majority has always advocated reconciliation, and reconciliation is the central theme of the Freedom Charter.

The Rev Jones never dropped reconciliation from his sermon no matter how much he tried after Daniel's challenge. He suffered from nightmares of insecurity derived from the Congo experience. The Rev Jones was an eye witness of the Congo tragedy. He will live with it to his grave. But he was wrong to blame the tragedy on the former oppressed of the Congo.

On Robben Island members of various denominations came to hold services, and churchmen were therefore our regular contacts with the outside world. Needless to say they were issued with permits on the undertaking that they came solely to preach the word of God and minister to our souls. With warders attending the services and watching every movement of the men of God, compliance with the undertaking was more or less the rule. Of course the Ministers' presentation of the word of God varied on the basis of their personalities, denominations, sympathies and antipathies. Language skills also played a role in enlarging the restricted area of communication. Occasionally a minister's sermon might be judged to have exceeded the permit undertaking and the permit would be summarily cancelled. All the ministers who visited us were very interesting characters. They had their individual quirks and ways of expression.

There was the Rev Bosman who always looked lugubrious and preached doleful sermons. He was undisguisedly pro-government. He left the Island to become chaplain of the army in the Operational Area. Divine riddance! His sermons were not conducive to our morale let alone our tempers. His right place was in the Operational Area. There he would be good for the morale of the army by praying for them and by blessing their murderous deeds.

I have already mentioned the Rev Jones. He had a phobia. The Congo haunted him. Whenever he set eyes on us, he saw the living ghost of the Congo struggling for reincarnation. The Rev Jones' permit to preach reconciliation to the Congo apparitions seemed to last indefinitely. Shortly before I was released he was still visiting us, though he was mentioning his impending transfer.

The Rev Schaeffer of the Dutch Reformed Sending Kerk (Mission Church), one of the black sections set up by the white Dutch Reformed Church, for a long time avoided our section. Reports about him from the communal cells section were very bad. The comrades in the communal cells nicknamed him Zambia. Before returning to South Africa, he had been stationed in that country and apparently did not think much of the Zambians and their misbegotten independence. His sermons reflected his impressions mirror-like. It was hearsay. 'Baphuz'utywala, babema intsango bafun'inkululeko . . . (They drink liquor/beer, they smoke dagga, they want freedom . . .)' That is how the Rev Schaeffer's sermons went in the communal cells. Very abusive. 'They' might have meant anybody – the Zambians, the Timbuktuans. But the Zambians and probably the Timbuktuans had already got their independence. The clue to who 'they' were was in the use of the present tense 'want'. 'They' was therefore the captive congregation addressed. They got drunk on booze, got high on dagga, etc, and developed ideas about freedom! The Rev Schaeffer was cynical.

These reports about the reverend gentleman reached our isolated block. Some of us wondered why the inmates attended his services. If the Rev Schaeffer was on a mission, the main section inmates felt they too had a mission to proselytise the heathen missionary, the godless high priest. So they went to his services, to listen to the holy abuse and formulate their defensive offence. One Sunday, the Rev Schaeffer peeped into our section as he passed on his way from the main section. The door to our section was open as three of us were pushing our food drums back to the kitchen. We exchanged greetings with him and asked him why he never came to our section for service. 'Ndiyoyika (I am afraid)' he replied. 'Don't be afraid. Come!' we encouraged him. We were very keen to listen to the things he was said to be saying out in the main section.

It was in the seventies when the Rev Schaeffer visited our section. By then the missionary, the convertor, had been converted. The Rev Schaeffer was not a freedom fighter yet, but he no longer thought the demand for freedom was a pipe-dream, some remote hallucination suffered by the drunks and the dagga smokers. He recognised the legitimacy of black aspirations. In conformity with the 'other cheek' theory of the bible, and in agreement with the pacific statements of the other Christian churches represented by the SACC, he condemned the violence of the liberation movement. At least, it was a step forward by the Rev Schaeffer.

An interesting point about the Rev Schaeffer is that from extreme hostility towards freedom fighters he moved swiftly to a position of persona non grata with the prison officials. By the time of my release he was no longer visiting the Island. His permit had been withdrawn, we learnt. The Rev Schaeffer's case is interesting, not only because a rabid irreligious fanatic could change his views so markedly, but also because it disproves the notion that freedom fighters are just communists and anti-christs. If they could reconcile a missionary with his bible then it must show them in a new light to denigrators and propagandists.

Not all prisoners attended religious services on Robben Island. Some were completely prejudiced and cynical. The missionaries according to popular African analysis of African history, arrived with a bible in one hand and a gun in the other. They opened the bible, read a verse and asked the Africans to close their eyes in supplication. While the innocent, trusting, ignorant, poor Africans shut their eyes tight, the missionaries stole the land and the cattle. More than the politicians, the missionaries are often portrayed as sly foxes. For those suspicious types who doubted the sincerity of the missionary's prayer they were robbed at the point of gun.

My disillusionment with Christians had brought me to the brink of complete severance of ties with the Christian churches. On Robben Island, however, I resumed attending church services, for a number of reasons, taken together: As stated above the organised churches were to some extent revising their practices *vis-a-vis* the struggle for freedom. Belatedly though it was, it vindicated my expectations of seeing Christian churches play some role in the fight for freedom; secondly, for years, I had been mulling over the advice of a veteran freedom fighter, Moses Kotane.

One Saturday morning in 1959 in Alexandra I made an uncomplimentary remark to a group of worshippers. I was passing down the street when an acquaintance in a crowd of worshippers invited me to join them. I dismissed the invitation by observing that 'I'll join a similar throng the day churches stopped putting the fear of hell into the hearts of people already acquainted with its scorching heat, I'll attend a church service when priests started devoting their pious devotion to the cause of freedom.' Moses Kotane was not among the church crowd but he later learnt of the remarks. When he met me he criticised me for it. Said he: 'When I was a young man like you, whenever a friend or an acquaintance invited me to church I agreed and went along. Such a person would find it difficult to refuse an invitation from me to attend an ANC meeting at the Freedom Square the next time.' The point needed no elaboration. To lead the people one has to be one of them. Moses Kotane was one of the foremost South African Marxists. He probably believed as Marx believed that religion was the opium of the people. Nonetheless he was a pragmatist in distinguishing rhetoric from what is practicable.

Thirdly when I arrived on Robben Island conditions were grim. Officially, prisoners were entitled to one letter in six months, one visit in six months, no photos, no games, no sport and no other things. The weekend days, Saturdays and Sundays, were particularly hard in the single cells section. Inmates were entitled to a half-an-hour exercise in the morning and half-an-hour in the afternoon. The rest of the time we were locked up in our cells. On weekends when no priest came for service it meant we would be locked up in our cells for 46 hours out of the 48 weekend hours.

On those weekends when a priest was around it felt like a wonderful reprieve to come out of our cells to bask in the sun and listen to the priest. The more longwinded the priest was the better. Mean warders sometimes did not let us out of the cells, they simply unlocked the doors and left the inside grilles locked and expected the priest to preach in the long passage of 16 cells a side.

The last time that arrangement happened, Father Hughes was very cross. He walked up and down the passage like a caged lion, spitting fire – and quoting Sir Winston Churchill when he mobilised the British and the world to resist Hitler: 'We shall fight on the beaches . . .' Father Hughes was an Anglican priest, Welsh by nationality. He had been a submarine chaplain during World War II. Over the years, until his death, we always looked forward to his visit. He brought along a portable organ which he played very well to the accompaniment of our melodious voices. Father Hughes never tired of praising our singing. We reminded him of his own Welsh people.

As conditions improved and we were allowed to sit in the yard for a good part of the weekend the single-cells church congregation thinned, especially when the visiting priest was not Father Hughes. Many of us preferred consistency. Father Hughes was everybody's darling. His sermons were varied but always pertinent to the situation. One just had to have the ear for poetry and the Welsh accent. He could weave newsy tidbits into the sermon which completely escaped the attentive warder. During the Kid Ruction dispensation he was manhandled, his holy sacrament confiscated before he served communion and he was prohibited from playing his organ to us. It took some time before Father Hughes' privileges of preaching the gospel unmolested could be fully restored. One of his favourite quotations was: 'I groused and groused because I had no shoes until I saw a man who had no feet.' Father Hughes did not mean we should be contented with our situation and acquiescent. On the contrary he was exhorting us not to allow our spirits to flag.

In spite of his knack of infusing morale in an adverse situation like prison, Father Hughes was very careful not to antagonise authority. He treated all warders with deference although there were some he was not enamoured of. His mission was to be as long as possible with us. He knew his value to us in our circumstances.

NEWS

In 1980 political prisoners on Robben Island who were in Group One were accorded the privilege of buying newspapers. To the great delight of the privileged group, the newspapers were to be delivered uncensored. It was a historic breakthrough. Starting from 1978 all political prisoners had enjoyed the privilege of listening to censored 'canned' newscasts relayed over the intercom system. The first major news item on the intercom system was the report of the death of Mangaliso Sobukwe, the former president of the Pan-Africanist Congress of Azania. Shortly thereafter, it might have been the second day, another major news item was the massacre of 15 members of the BDF (Botswana Defence Force) by Ian Smith's troops along the Rhodesian border.

It appeared the news privilege had been granted to disseminate sad news. However it was a change we had fought for all the years of our incarceration, right from the beginning, and even the lopsidedly bad news was to be welcome. The uncensored newspapers were even more welcome in 1980.

The only blemish in the privilege was that it was not extended to all prisoners but only to prisoners of one group. In a situation where all groups, One to Three, mixed at work and at recreation, the classified privilege seemed fragile and transient. Anyone abusing it by unlawfully passing it to the non-privileged risked losing it forthwith. Fortunately in the beginning warders did not seem primed to go out deliberately to catch the offenders. In spite of the generally lax attitude of the warders, who turned a blind eye to the free circulation of newspapers among the unprivileged groups, by the time of my release at least one man had already lost the privilege because his paper was found with someone who was not entitled to the privilege. It was easy to identify the papers since all the subscribers were known and their names were distinctly marked on the first page of their papers.

The fear of losing the privilege of buying newspapers did not deter Group Ones from risking the loss by sharing their papers with Groups Two and Three. It must not be imagined that newspaper subscribers were defiant or careless about preserving their newspapers; no, they tried hard to circulate them by stealth, but the odds were always overwhelmingly against them.

During the 'news blackout days', prisoners once or twice managed to steal a newspaper from Lieutenant Naude himself. He was the security officer, charged among other things with enforcing the news blackout for political prisoners. An inveterate soliloquist, he was once overheard saying: 'The newspaper will not get you out of gaol! Yes, it won't release you!' Sour grapes, of course! But basically it was the truth. The privilege of reading a newspaper or hearing news of the outside world from any source would not free the prisoners from their island gaol. Nonetheless for approximately 15 years, since the inauguration of Robben Island as a political prison, the prison authorities had fought relentlessly to deny prisoners news of what was happening in the outside world. They continued to do this even when we told them it was an exercise in futility, for the simple reason that in spite of the security measures they adopted we were getting news clandestinely.

The prison authorities knew it was the truth. From time to time they raided our cells and came out with piles and piles of newspaper cuttings. They probably derived satisfaction from meting out punishment to the unlucky offenders whenever they discovered their 'news-dealing'. The Prisons Department policy of news deprivation to political prisoners had a clear motivation which we as prisoners understood very well. The objective was to demoralise the prisoners, to break our resistance to government manipulation and to impress us with their firm control of political events. The censorship of letters was meant to achieve the same purpose, so was the strict supervision of visits. For our part it was our sacred duty to discomfit the insidious attempts by the authorities to remould us in their own image. Newsgathering was a crucial engagement on Robben Island. It was practised with keen devotion and reckless determination. We had to get news or perish spiritually. We got news. We survived and flourished. To the chagrin of the tormentors.

In the early years, before the segregation of common-law prisoners from political prisoners, the source of newspapers was the common-law prisoners. They, with their special skill of charming and manipulating those in authority, enjoyed a special relationship with the warders; they could smuggle any contraband stuff into gaol, including newspapers. Although the original idea of mixing political and common-law prisoners appeared to have been to harass and humiliate the politicos, the idea boomeranged in the end. Instead, the political prisoners quickly assumed a position of influence and dominance, to the extent that the common-law prisoners were soon at the beck and call of their political fellow inmates. By doing us numerous favours for some time the common-law prisoners had managed to play a clever double role. Eventually the prison authorities discovered they were being double-crossed and wasted no time in building a completely separate section for them. Before that happened, the integration had been a real blessing.

After the transfer of the common-law prisoners to a separate section, the politicos were on their own. From the years of association with the non-politicos they had been inducted into useful methods of maintaining an erratic but steady flow of news. They did well— stealing radios, stealing newspapers from careless warders, smuggling newspapers through some of the 'nice and corrupt' warders, wheedling news from the talkative types, risking being shot by slipping out of work spans to raid the rubbish dumps, etc. Comrade A, popularly known as 'die main ou (the main guy)', was once caught with a sackful of newspapers from the rubbish dump. He paid for it with weeks of spare diet in the punishment cells. Comrade A of course was not to be deterred. He had been successful with the rubbish dump in the past, he was determined to succeed in the future. The capture was a challenge to plan the rubbish dump raids with skill, precision and daring.

News circulation from authentic sources, newspapers, radios and reliable 'sympathisers' never ceased. It might be disrupted for a while but it was never stopped altogether. Political prisoners, despite their official news deprivation, were generally far more informed than people outside gaol. The reason was that prisoners read any newspaper they came across from cover to cover. Besides that, they analysed any news item in depth and talked about it for days. Every newspaper was shared across organisational lines and all news items were discussed back and forth and correlated. Moreover, Robben Island prisoners were not choosy: we read any scrap of newspaper we could lay our hands on – English, Afrikaans, Xhosa, Zulu and Sesotho.

Neither were we choosy about the age of a newspaper. To us there was no such thing as stale news – a newspaper might be nine months or 12 months old, it was read from cover to cover and digested with relish.

For a community like Robben Island prisoners in the days before newspapers-privilege, our ravenous hunger for news was explained on two grounds. We needed to be informed on national and international events. Naturally, in our circumstances, our preference was for news of a political nature to bolster our political morale, but economic and social news in general were sought after and enjoyed, eg Elizabeth Taylor turning up late for an appointment with the President of the Republic of South Africa at Ellis Park or the same Elizabeth marrying Richard Burton for the third time at Chobe Lodge in Botswana. Secondly, where there is news blackout, rumours are likely to abound. In gaol we had two types of rumours: baseless rumours and rumours that basically were distortions of actual news, usually dubbed 'masala' by sceptics. Both types of rumours needed verification. Hence the urge to collect and read any old scrap of newspaper.

There were occasions when we received the day's news the same day. One such occasion was on the assassination of Dr Verwoerd. 'Verwoerd is dead,' someone announced in a whisper. It was lunch time and the kitchen span had just delivered our lunch drums at the lime quarry. 'What?' we all enquired incredulously. 'Verwoerd is dead,' the newsbearer repeated himself. In clear breach of news-gathering code – not to ask the newsbearer the source of news – everybody wanted to know where the news came from. We suspected a hoax, but the general scepticism did not overrule the probability of the event. Surprisingly the rumour did not generate a fever of excitement among the lime-quarry diggers. The 'rumour' circulated quietly, from one small group to another, without attracting the warders' attention. Did the warders in charge of us know? None of them seemed to be carrying any radio, and the news apparently had just been announced over the radio.

Whatever the case was, the warders like the prisoners did not seem to be a-flutter at the news, they all went about their jobs normally. Perhaps the composure of the serving politicos derived from the realisation that the event would not change anything in their favour, that the status quo at the lime quarry would survive, and even worse, that the apartheid system would long survive its reputed architect, the granite Dr Verwoerd.

In 1960 when an attempt was made on Dr Verwoerd's life by farmer Pratt, there was a wave of excitement in the townships. I heard the news as I was going from house to house trying to exhort township dwellers not to patronise the apartheid Rand Easter Show. It was at the Rand Easter Show that Pratt fired two non-lethal bullets into the head of the Herr Dokter. Verwoerd did not die. According to surgical diagnosis the second bullet deflected the first one from its lethal course! It was one of those 'miracles' that so often in history make tyrants legendary. In Alexandra, radio listeners who picked up the announcement: 'Verwoerd has been shot', interpreted it as Verwoerd has been killed. Sense perception is biased in favour of individual outlook!

Conscious of the flavour of optimism that usually dresses political news in the ghettos I rushed home to receive the news from my reliable transistor. I was quite excited. 1960 was dramatic and exciting. The political atmosphere vibrated with excitement. Sharpeville. Burning of passes countrywide. Banning of the ANC and PAC. The state of emergency. Detention of hundreds of political activists. Panic of foreign investors. Disinvestment fear. Fleeing of capital. Now the shooting of Dr Verwoerd, just as he was about to open the Rand Easter Show and crow to the world about South Africa's reliability as a trading partner, a safe haven of investment and a model of political stability in spite of the 'temporary' state of emergency! South Africa was in a state of flux and the fund of excitement expressed it. Dr Verwoerd did not die from the two bullet wounds. He survived the wounds, and apartheid suffered not the slightest bruise, only a mild shock from which it quickly recovered. Apartheid is tough and resilient.

In 1966, the knife plunged into the heart succeeded where the bullet in the head had failed. However the assassination did not induce excitement and false expectations, rather it impressed one as a futile act, strange and alien in the context of the state of revolutionary political activity of the period. The collection of some of the cream of black South African activists here on Robben Island had a sobering message: the struggle was a protracted one.

The assassination however became a theme of conjecture. Who was Tsafendas, the assassin? Why did he do it? How did he get the job that enabled him to creep behind Verwoerd with such ease to administer the fatal stab? Who was behind Tsafendas? We speculated and argued. The consensus was that it was an inside job. Dr Verwoerd had served the narrow Afrikaner interests very well when the whole of Afrikanerdom agitated for political expression at the highest level. And beyond any shadow of doubt he had projected the Afrikaner's hour of achievement on the domestic and international scene impressively.

South African withdrawal from the British Commonwealth, led by Dr Verwoerd, was a milestone in the history of Afrikaner nationalism.

The Republic of South Africa Constitution Act was the apex made possible by the dynamism and leadership of Dr Verwoerd. After these two milestones in the history of Afrikaner nationalism, did Verwoerd still hold trump cards up his sleeve?

Intellectuals in Afrikaner circles and 'dominees' in Dutch Reformed Church circles were starting to fret at the policies of the Nationalist Party led by Dr Verwoerd. Afrikaner capitalist entrepreneurs were beginning to eye the huge potential African market covetously and wonder whether the extremist policies of their leader could help them penetrate the market. The concept of Afrikanerdom no longer expressed the Africanness of the Afrikaners as the novo-Afrikaner-rich wanted to express it. They wanted to be recognised as African in conformity with the rhythm of the African image that expressed itself in the stampede of political independence. They wanted to be distinctly African, albeit white Africans. To achieve this there was need to build, not only economic, but political bridges with the rest of Africa. Dr Verwoerd also subscribed to this outward-looking policy but was he flexible or imaginative enough to see that the success of such a policy depended on parallel reform gestures in the domestic policy? He most probably had conceived the idea of the bantustans, but was he prepared to see it to its logical conclusion – granting of 'political independence' to these 'homelands'? Diplomatic relations with Malawi were on the cards, but was the Prime Minister of South Africa prepared to sanction a black ambassadorial residence in a white suburb?

At the time of my detention the debate on whether the black envoy from Malawi was to be set up in a white suburb or a black township was raging in the Afrikaans press columns. Dr Verwoerd was silent on the matter and his junior executives were embarrassed by the lack of clear policy guidelines from the philosopher-king. They too were silent.

Bantustan independence and diplomatic relations with black Africa seemed cut out for a symbiotic relationship in the ideal future of white South Africa. One without the other was inconceivable. The deduction could not be welcome by Dr Verwoerd with his fiercely apartheid logic. He had to be removed from the political stage to release the new forces of 'reform' in the policies of 'separate development'. Basically that is how many of us in the quarry interpreted the assassination event. It was not something from the outside but something from the inside – a laager revolt.

The lack of excitement emanated from this analysis. In order to avert a revolution from outside the Nats resorted to an internal revolt. The 'verligte (enlightened)' faction within the Nationalist Party thenceforth assumed a predominant role in pursuit of cosmetic reforms in the application of apartheid. Tsafendas was brought to the unoccupied wing of our section. His cell was walled off from the other cells to prevent contact with occasional inmates in the

197

punishment cells.

We caught a glimpse of Tsafendas, the only white prisoner to be detained on Robben Island, through our cell windows, exercising on his side of our common yard. He moved up and down the yard, meditative and relaxed. Occasionally his hands moved in calm gesticulation and from the movement of his lips one could deduce a definite soliloquy. Communication with him was made impossible by the close surveillance that accompanied his morning and afternoon exercises. An opportunity to get the motive of the assassination from the horse's mouth, or more accurately, the assassin's mouth, never presented itself.

Tsafendas was later transferred from our section and from Robben Island to an unknown destination to be detained at the pleasure of His Excellency, the President of the Republic of South Africa. The court had found Tsafendas insane and not responsible for his actions. All political assassins are either insane or agents of foreign intelligence – it is an unwritten law.

This news of Dr Verwoerd's death was the fastest news to come our way in all my years on Robben Island, including the last years of my incarceration, when A-group prisoners were officially allowed to buy newspapers. Apparently what happened was that some 'nice' warder heard it over the radio, whispered it to one prisoner, who relayed it to the next prisoner until it reached all workspans and every prisoner on the Island.

News of other dramatic events took much longer to penetrate our insulated habitation. There was the 1976 Soweto uprising. The prison authorities did their best to keep us in the dark about this event. And they almost succeeded. Unfortunately prison policy and practice did not reckon with police duties of quelling the uprising and bringing 'culprits' to book. Since Robben Island was the destination of some of the 'culprits', in due course the news filtered in, carried by the perennial stream of 'agitators' and activists. Obviously the police and the prison authorities were at loggerheads – the one agency was undoing the good work of the other. It was to our benefit. Generally, and in principle, as serving prisoners we were very much against the arrest and conviction of more freedom fighters. Every time a freedom fighter was caught it was a setback to the struggle. We wished sincerely such setbacks would not occur. When new prisoners arrived on Robben Island, however, they were heartily welcomed mainly for their 'newsy stories'. There were even times during a long dry spell when one would hear a wish that some new prisoner might arrive to relieve the inmates of the unabating darkness.

For a political prisoner news from the outside world was a lifeline. That was why as political prisoners we became specialists at news-gathering. It was common talk among the warders that political prisoners could stake their lives to steal a newspaper, yet the same

198

persons could starve to death next to some delicious food belonging to someone else. It was true. We stole newspapers from warders, from doctors while busy with examination, and priests while they closed their eyes tight and prayed for our salvation and release from gaol. In practice priests were not allowed to bring in newspapers. But occasionally a new priest might innocently bring in the *Sunday Times*. And if the warder in charge overlooked the pastor's briefcase, it was no guarantee that the prisoners would do the same.

Another dramatic event whose secrecy was maintained for a long time by the prison authorities was the armed attack on the Sasol oil refinery plant. A very faint rumour did circulate after the bombing. But it was just that — a faint rumour! We all tried frantically to get confirmation of the rumour. Some of us tried tactfully to coax confirmation from the 'nice' warders. It did not work. All the warders, the hostile, the less hostile and the 'nice' ones, were under orders not to breathe a word about the oil refinery sabotage and they obeyed without dissension. Other confirmation-seekers risked having their precious visits cancelled by probing their visitors. Since the investigation had to be couched in devious language which was meant to be understood by the visitor and not the warder, fruitful communication was never achieved. The communicator and the communicant could not communicate. The warder's presence ensured it.

Eventually one prisoner picked up a business page of one English language paper. On this page there was printed an annual report of some subsidiary company of Sasol. In this report the financial loss arising from the act of sabotage was estimated at several million rands. This was the first confirmation after many months of rumour and speculation. More details came in later with the arrival of another batch of newly sentenced prisoners. They had taken inordinately long to arrive. If we had had our way we might have induced one activist to commit some political offence and expedite his transfer to Robben Island, in order to come and serve our insatiable curiosity of the goings-on in the outside. Such was our eagerness for news from the external world — the world we knew before we came to grace our temporary limbo.

The third dramatic event that kept us on tenterhooks at its rumour stage was the Great Escape of the trio, Jenkin and Co. That was really up our alley. Because of the nature of prison conditions, it is the ardent desire of every prisoner to escape from gaol if he/she can have the opportunity. On Robben Island chances for escape were almost nil: the prison is an ultra-maximum security structure, ideally situated. Collusion at the highest level of authority would be essential to break out of the cell and go through the maze of gates leading out of the prison section. Such collusion was extremely remote due to the inborn prejudice and hostility of warder to prisoner. Even assuming the collusion was feasible, the escape would be confronted on the next stage by the daunting facts of swimming 10 or more nautical miles across the cold current of the Atlantic and the likely prospect of being picked up by a patrol boat in mid-sea. Escape from Robben Island was rare and perilous. Makana, the Xhosa chief and warrior, attempted it and drowned in the process.

The heavy odds against escapes from Robben Island Prison did not mean that all prisoners completely resigned themselves to their deplorable fate. Few prisoners can ever accept the prison situation. Non-acceptance of that situation implies a wish, a burning wish, to escape it. In spite of the apparent impracticability of escape from this ultra-maximum prison many prisoners dreamt of escaping, a fair number mooted it and a few even made ingenious attempts.

The rumour of the three white prisoners' escape from Pretoria jail was the fulfilment of a prisoner's dream. It created a lot of excitement that overpowered the doubts that wrestled with it. Pretoria Prison, although not as strategically situated as Robben Island on structural security arrangements, was just as well secured by interminable corridor of doors and grilles that required maximum collusion or technical ingenuity to unlock. Whether collusion or ingenuity prevailed, only the escapees know.

The event was by any other name a supreme feat, fit to be celebrated by the entire prison population regardless of colour or creed. It reflected the spirit of resistance against evil in all its manifestations and a desire for freedom and life. In our section we toasted the event with mugs of coffee when confirmation eventually came.

The prison authorities in South Africa have adopted a new policy of refuting ex-prisoners' allegations about conditions that prevailed in gaols. It is quite probable that after reading the allegations of deprivation of news from outside in the sixties and seventies on Robben Island they may challenge these allegations and produce 'facts' to substantiate their statements. In that case I must pre-empt their move by making an important concession.

Strictly speaking we were denied news from independent newspaper sources and the radio. We were not denied news from the government-sponsored publications, although they too were not delivered whole to us all the time. These publications were churned out by three departments: the Department of Bantu Administration and Development, the Department of Coloured Affairs, and the Department of Indian Affairs. In line with the Afrikaner Nationalist policy of divergent and plural 'ethnicity' among the Africans we had about seven publications, each directed at a specific language group, all with a number of common features: they were published by the Department of Bantu Administration and Development as already stated, they were monthlies, they were published exclusively for the particular language group, they bore different linguistic names: *Tswellopele, Intutuko, Inqubela*, etc, but the names meant the same thing in English, 'Progress'.

It is a blatant misnomer. The last thing to be associated with the publications was 'progress' in any size, form or colour. The editorials extolled bantustan policy and bantustan leaders *ad nauseam*, the articles harked on the virtue of traditional values and 'ethnicity', and the letters to the editor, obviously written by school children, systematically fed the poison of 'Bantu education', reeked with drivel about self-government and the new era ushered in by the bantustans.

The propaganda in these publications was unprecedented. There was no subtlety about it, it lied, omitted, distorted and misrepresented the facts without let or hindrance. Outside prisons these publications circulated in schools. The teachers and primary school children were the main targets. Those in the urban areas had to be wooed to the bantustans with prospects of better life and colourful new developments in the new found 'homelands'. Those domiciled in these 'reserves', currently earmarked for separate development and independence, were to be persuaded to stick to them and to view the urban areas as a white man's island in which the black man could be at best a sojourner on temporary employment.

Many of us had known about the existence of these publications before we were imprisoned, but organisationally we had never made an attempt to study them with the view to counter the insidious propaganda strategy. Reading the propaganda in gaol one could see the main thrust of government propaganda efforts – to sell apartheid cheaply and extensively. The problem was that outside gaol walls, where there was a variety of reading material, an organisation needed extreme discipline and consciousness to read the insultingly gullible propaganda with consistent effort. In prison we were a captive audience. In the absence of more stimulating reading material any printed matter was better than no printed matter. We read the bantustan propaganda – not avidly but we read it all the same.

Now and then we gleaned valuable information from these publications, particularly when new legislation applying to Africans was passed. These publications were also quite informative in that every now and then they exposed (not out of malice but in self-exaltation) former members of the liberation movement who had crossed over to the 'homelands'. It was amusing to see these renegades posing grandly in these self-congratulatory publications. Whenever the government authorities 'won over' a waverer from the freedom struggle, naturally they made a great song and dance about it. There was Bruno Mtolo whom they sponsored to 'write' a book against communism, based on his carefully coaxed and guided statement during his detention. The publicity given to Bruno's evidence in the Rivonia trial and his book was of the kind usually reserved for visiting celebrities. Bartholomew Hlapane also hit the headlines when he assumed the mantle of expert witness on communism in South Africa.

These two were not the only ones who were elevated on publicity pedestals. There were many others, perhaps not elevated to the same heights on the propaganda stilts, but they were there and took their poses in bantustan publications. It could be demoralising to know that former colleagues in the struggle were now supping with the devil while he barbecued you for sport in his dungeon. Nevertheless it was good to know who these sell-outs were. The bantustan publications did a good job in this regard. We were able to know some erstwhile comrades who were now mortal enemies. Know your enemy, know your friend. The dark potential loss of morale was thus countered and compensated by the light of information gained.

From reading these government publications it was also possible to make intelligent deductions as to what the political situation was in spite of what government propaganda purported it to be. One way of doing this was simply to stand the news on its head, so to speak. If an article in the government publication went to great pains to 'prove' that the 'Bantu' now accepted 'Bantu Education', then you concluded that in fact the 'Bantu' were showing continued resistance to 'Bantu Education' or some important academic had written a strong criticism of 'Bantu Education' and the self-congratulating article was an indirect reply. If one bantustan leader was receiving unstinting praise, then you knew that he was the arch sell-out, and that the one who was referred to with scant comment was raising awkward questions – embarrassing to his masters. If the issue was censored, then we surmised one of their proteges, for example Gatsha Buthelezi, was acting to the black pavilion at their expense.

For all the above reasons we read this 'poison-to-the-unwary-mind' and even complained when occasionally some of the issues were delivered to us censored. It struck one as an absurd practice until one remembered that Robben Island prison was the culmination of an absurd practice.

Inmates on Robben Island were among the foremost freedom fighters in South Africa. Wasn't it absurd to throw them in gaol when they asked for the exact opposite? It reminded one of the biblical hypothetical question: who of you would give your brother a stone when he asked for bread? Robben Islanders would have chorused, 'The Nats' in answer. Now for the Nationalist Government (the Nats) to be censoring their own propaganda in pursuance of their perverted policy of keeping prisoners uninformed was an absurdity to outdo all their absurd policies of the past. Did the Nats know where they were going to? It did not seem so. Theirs was a trial and error government. Apartheid was an emotive word. It was coined as a magic catch-word to win support for racist bigots. It would rally the Afrikaners, make them a supreme nation among sub-nations and non-peoples of South Africa. That seems to have been the initial origins of the word. And if the magic did not work? Well, experiment with the blacks, the non-peoples, the guinea pigs . . . ! It had to.

Robben Island was a laboratory of a major political experiment. Here a major test of the political fibre of the oppressed was to be conducted. When the oppressed spoke of freedom, did they mean it? Were they prepared to make the sacrifices the freedom struggle entailed? All the ingredients of a laboratory experiment were there: the constant conditions and the variable conditions – the latter divided into dependent and independent variables. The main constant condition was the prison population itself, of course. The independent variables as the name implies changed independently of the constant. They were manipulated by the experimenter – the prison authorities. In the early days there were the 'carry on' inductions, the inadequate food and clothes. The variables were both independent and physical. The 'carry ons' stopped and there was some improvement in the quantity of food and the quality of clothes.

Later a new set of variables was introduced: withdrawal of study privileges on flimsy excuses, vindictive censorship of letters and the absurd censoring of government's own official propaganda, in the form of *Intutuko/Tswellopele/Progress* series of publications. It was psychological. The relatively physical variables had produced negative dependent variables, namely ineffectualness. It was hoped the more psychological conditions would show more positive results. The experimenter most probably is not yet ready to answer 'yes' or 'no' to the question of results. The experiment is not over yet.

However, one experience of 15 years says 'no', the positive results hoped for by the experimenter will not materialise. Can the experiment be expected to succeed in accordance with the bias of the experimenter when the experimenter himself is not quite convinced that it can succeed? The implication of the censorship of government's own propaganda to me was that in spite of all the massive battle for the mind of the oppressed, the government was beginning to accept that its efforts were futile and transparent as far as some section of the oppressed was concerned.

That the form of psychological torture did not work as expected does not imply that it did not work at all. The fact that I underline it so much, means I am still smarting under its effects. The common characteristic of torture whether physical or psychological is that it is painful to every sensitive victim. The psychological pain is more painful for, having to do with human dignity, it lingers in memory long after the physical pain has gone and as long as it has not found equitable redress. After outlining the form and content of official source of news in gaol what more can one say about it? I do not believe even the SA policy makers can say anything except to do the unwanted and agree with me. After all, the reforms are in the air, Nkomati is hugging the South African borders and P W Botha is twitching from unspontaneous backslaps in the European capitals.

FOOD

A favourite question from visitors to Robben Island was the food question: 'What sort of food do they give you?' Our food was poor and unappetising. The authorities knew it. Consequently warders never allowed prisoners to answer the question. Yet the prison authorities insisted in their propaganda that prisoners enjoyed a balanced diet. The allegedly 'balanced' nature of the diet did not stop prisoners from going on hunger strikes in protest against both the quantity and quality of the diet from time to time.

Food, on Robben Island, was one of the unredressed grievances at the time of my release, in spite of major improvements in preparation, and promises of revised diet scales. In the mid-sixties when common-law and political prisoners were still mixed in the communal cells sections, the cooks were drawn exclusively from the common-law groups. The preparation of food was perfunctory and left much to be desired. The warders who supervised the kitchen were equally indifferent. After all, the food was for 'Kaffer bandiets', 'hotnots' and 'koelies'. One chief warder was nicknamed 'Kaffer pap (Kaffir porridge)' from his habit of asking whether the 'Kaffer pap' was not ready yet.

The common-law cooks prepared better meals for themselves, from the same ingredients in separate pots. Corruption in the kitchen was encouraged by the warders who, according to reports, were themselves corrupt. They were thieves, engaged in stealing some of the prisoners' food for their families. One warder was an exception to the corrupt kitchen practice: Warder Opperman, 'Phumasilwe (Come let's fight)' from his pugilistic challenges to his colleagues, was different. Every time he was on duty over the weekend, he took it upon himself to raid the kitchen. He invariably uncovered specially prepared dishes for the cooks. These, he would carry to the cells to distribute among the rest of the deprived inmates. Fried chickens, fried potatoes, puddings and other special dishes of which prisoners were not aware would come out of the kitchen on every raid by Phumasilwe. The kitchen staff was always caught unawares since they never knew in advance when he would be on weekend duty.

The major grievance against the prison diet however was that it was discriminatory. Coloured and Indian fellow-prisoners had one diet scale and the Africans, another. This, despite the fact that they were not segregated in the communal cells, nor were they, in the single cells section. How were the Coloured and Indian comrades to feel, when they enjoyed preferential food while their African fellow inmates sat next to them force-feeding themselves on boiled mealies? In the single cells sections, the initial reaction by Coloured and Indian prisoners was to reject this base discrimination and boycott any food that was not shared by all prisoners. The humiliation and embarrassment was palpable and prompted this strong reaction.

After much discussion by all the inmates of the single cells

204

sections, it was felt that the boycott was unlikely to achieve its purpose. The authorities would either ignore the protest completely and reduce the privileged diet scale to the less privileged level, or segregate the two groups and continue to enforce the discriminatory diet scale. All prisoners demanded an improved diet. Downgrading of existing official diet scales would not be in the short-term nor the long-term interests of any group of the prisoners. Moreover the principle of segregation of political prisoners was unpopular among the prison population. The correct strategy was to fight for uniform improvements without jeopardising existing privileges in spite of their sectionality. Africans were not entitled to bread. Coloureds and Indians were entitled to a 'katkop (cat's head)', about one quarter of a standard loaf for supper. After extensive discussion, Coloured and Indian comrades decided on a compromise of sharing their bread with their African fellow inmates.

A formula for sharing varied with gaol conditions. In the beginning, each 'D-diet' (privileged group) prisoner was assigned to cater for specific 'F-diet' (ie African) prisoners. The ratio of D-diets to F-diets was not conducive to equitable sharing. Some D-diets had to share with one other person, while others had to share with two. Not much could be done to arrive at a fair distribution, because at this stage sharing one's food with another prisoner was not only against the prison regulations but warders were vigilant, and would not hesitate to punish food-sharing culprits.

The sharing formula ensured that it could be done with the minimum of detection. Later when conditions improved and the warders relaxed, a more convenient and fair formula was found. The bread slices were distributed from door to door by one member of the 'phaka span (dishing span)'. In that way the number of slices one received changed from day to day. One day it might be one and the following day two and so on and so forth. Although the warders' supervising visits would not allow visited prisoners to answer questions on diet, the Minister of Prisons could not evade such questions when they were put to him in Parliament.

According to the 1970 *Survey of the South African Institute of Race Relations* here is a summary of his reply on prison diet (daily unless otherwise stated):

Item	Whites	Coloureds/ Asians	Africans
Mealie meal or mealie rice or samp	4 ounces	14 ounces	12 ounces
Mealies	—	—	8 ounces
Bread	20 ounces	8 ounces	—
Meat or fish	7 ounces	6 ounces (4×weekly)	5 ounces (4×weekly)

Item	Whites	Coloureds/ Asians	Africans
Dried beans	—	4 ounces (meatless days)	4 ounces (on meatless days)
Vegetables	16 ounces	8 ounces	8 ounces
Soup/Protone/ gravy powder	1 ounce	⅘ ounces	⅘ ounces
Fat	1 ounce	1 ounce	½ ounce
Milk	3 ounces	—	—
Coffee or tea	Twice daily	Twice daily	Once daily
Puzamandla	—	—	1⅞ ounces
Salt	1 ounce	½ ounce	½ ounce
Sugar	2 ounces	2 ounces	1½ ounces

The scale is interesting for its fine distinction on both quantities and qualities. These fine distinctions, especially on quantity often led to controversial arbitrations when complaints were lodged by prisoners. On looking at his sugar, puzamandla or soup, an F-diet prisoner might honestly believe it was not the right quantity. Warders, generally, did not take kindly to prisoners' complaints. But just to demonstrate that he was keeping within the regulations, he might order the food-scale from the kitchen to weigh the item complained about. The result of such exercises invariably proved the prisoner wrong and authority right. The food the prisoner regarded as less than the right ration might be reduced further, on the basis of some deft manipulation or deliberate misreading of the scale. It was meant to intimidate prisoners against complaining about food. Prisoners were never intimidated however. They complained. They struck.

One wonders what criteria dieticians used to determine and distinguish nutritional needs of various groups. The prison authorities explained the differences in diet scales on traditional diet tendencies of the groups. Apparently on that basis, traditional Coloured, Indian and African diet did not include milk; Africans did not eat bread nor jam; Africans ate less meat than Coloured, and Coloureds and Indian less than Whites, etc, etc. Only an apartheid practitioner can follow the logic of this web of racial-diet theory. Of course it was never the policy of prison authorities to give honest and intelligent answers to prisoners. Prison officers from the lowest rank to the highest, are not trained nor do they have the inclination to discuss prisoners' complaints about policy – they respond in terms of unfamiliar regulation, prison practice, ideology and orders from above. The regulations says so and so! These are OC's orders! An order is an order, verstaan (understand)?

The new type of prisoner who complained and argued for his

206

inalienable rights as a human being was 'hardegat (cheeky)', a 'terrorist', 'poqo' or a 'communist'. The vigorous and sometimes aggressive manner of laying complaints or making requests was to pay dividends in the end. We delegated Comrade Raymond Mhlaba to take up the question of fruit for prisoners on one occasion. Ray was in his aggressive element: 'Look here,' he addressed the head of prison, 'we demand fruit. It is an essential food ingredient, even baboons in the wilds eat wild fruit . . . And we are not baboons whatever you think of us . . .' We did not get the fruit immediately. But the swelling representation to the authorities for fruit over the years was soon to have results.

The first consignment of peaches arrived without prior warning. We might have been a colony of Adams in the garden of Eden tasting the forbidden fruit. Perhaps the original Adam knew when to stop, before God and the rumbling tummy warned him of his transgression. Many of us did not know when to stop after all the years of deprivation and abstinence. Our overindulged tummies had good reason to rumble and run. Guavas followed later. It tasted like a new era in prison. The snag was that fruit rations were not regular but highly erratic. The authorities, to be fair, had indicated we could only get fruit when it was available. It was difficult to know what that meant. We had to guess that the supply would probably depend on the yield from Victor Verster prison orchard or some other such prison.

Occasionally we supplemented our food deficiencies from the veld, during working hours. Whenever we were out on time-killing weeding on the Island, we usually came across guinea fowl eggs. Except with very wicked warders, a friendly conversation in Afrikaans with the warder generally managed to secure the guinea fowl eggs for consumption by the work span. For pots, we used the same ones that brought our lunch from the kitchen. These had to be thoroughly scoured after the cooking so that they left no tell-tale remains of the day's contraband.

Along the sea-coast, correct approaches to warders also used to yield mussels and even crayfish. One day Lieutenant Terblanche, then head of prison, caught our pot of mussels on inspection. Unlike previous heads of prison he never seemed to trust his warders with prisoners. He suspected they smuggled things and did prisoners many favours. He personally body-searched night-duty warders to ensure they did not conceal newspapers and other contraband for prisoners. Moreover he was the only officer who seemed not to have a routine hour for his inspections. All this was deliberate and meant to catch warders during their fraternising moments with prisoners.

When Lt Terblanche appeared on the scene and walked to our steaming pot of mussels we were all petrified. He opened the pot, pulled one mussel out, tasted it and pronounced it 'smaaklik (tasty)'. And that was it. There was no confrontation with anybody.

207

Unbelievable! From then on the consensus on Terblanche's personality was undermined. We no longer spoke in a single voice about him. He was still a pig to some. To others he was reasonable, even wonderful. Food 'supplements' from the veld and the sea coast were of course niggardly and far between.

Robben Island diet was monotonous. Extremely so. But contrary to my primary school lesson that 'monotony in diet leads to indigestion', I would not say the food on the Island led to such tummy malfunction. Tummies in Robben Island had to learn to squeeze nourishment from the least nourishing products. One got tired or had little time to masticate half-cooked mealie grains, and half the time one swallowed these grains chicken-style. Unendowed with the gizzard like a chicken, the prisoner relied solely on his one stomach to do the job.

Even over the Christmas festive season, the food remained the same. Monotonous. The little extra the prison department spoiled prisoners with was a mug of black coffee. Black coffee for Christmas in a Christian country! Some said it was not even real coffee, but something that looked like coffee without tasting like it. South African prison regulations however have some provision for the prisoner's palate for Christmas. Provided a prisoner could afford it, the regulations said he/she could buy three pounds of some delicacies: one pound of sweets, one pound of dried fruit and one pound of fruitcake or biscuits. For many who had no funds, nothing could be done. Officially, they were supposed to watch those who could afford, enjoy their three-pound purchases. Whether one prisoner was prepared to spend his own money on his fellow prisoner was immaterial to the authorities; the regulations stipulated that a prisoner had to spend his own money to enjoy the privilege, and that was it. It meant that any prisoner who dared share his Christmas buy, was breaking the prison regulations and subject to appropriate discipline. The prisoners as usual shared in defiance of the regulations. And perhaps in the spirit of Christmas, the warders turned a blind eye to the wholesale defiance. The three-pound limit on prisoners' Christmas shopping has not been amended as far as I know. At least up to the time of my release it still applied in its original form.

The resourceful prisoners were for practical purposes able to increase the Christmas eats a hundred-fold, without interfering with the regulation as it stood. Quite early on, the crop of our legal pundits discovered some loophole in the regulations. According to this loophole the officer commanding had some discretion on certain matters in his Command jurisdiction. He could for instance authorise the purchase of 'prizes' where prisoners were permitted to organise game competitions.

Major Kellermann, Fat Mob, as he was known by the prisoners, was

208

caught in one of his occasionally 'charming' moods while Commanding Officer. He granted permission for purchases of 'prizes' for Christmas game competitions, which were then organised on a very small scale because of the small number of games which were played then.

The precedent opened up an avalanche of requests for games, outdoor and indoor. Draughts, dominoes and ludo, the only indoor games then, would not do. We applied for chess, scrabble, card games, tenniquoits, table tennis, lawn tennis, volley ball, carrom, monopoly, etc. Official reaction was very amusing. At this juncture the authorities had no objection to games in principle. From the security aspect they were inclined to be cautious, especially with the games they knew little of.

'Scrabble?' 'Yes, scrabble.' 'What sort of game is it?' 'Major, it's a word game, major. Players build up words from letter blocks on a board.' A pause. 'Then it means you can play words like "war", "violence", "kill", etc?' 'Oh, yes, Major, all English words are playable.' Major Kellermann was not happy. He pondered the 'violence' that could be wreaked by a game that had the freedom of spelling all the known violent actions in gaol. It took Lalloo Chiba's persuasive tongue and unflagging stamina to convince Major Kellermann that violent words do not always do violence. Some dogs have barks worse than their bites.

As permission to play more games was granted it became necessary for the prison communities, in both the communal cells section and the single cells section to be organised under sports committees. The committees had as their tasks, among others, organising recreation on a permanent basis, liaising with the prison authorities for the purpose and more importantly organising Christmas sports competitions at the end of the year and negotiating reasonably substantial prizes for this purpose.

At the quarry the games served both the recreational need as well as some psychological condiment for the monotonous diet of boiled mealies. With the mind concentrating on the game, the munching of the grains became a more automatic action. The joy of temporary reprieve from hurling inaudible curses at the apartheid monster, with every spoonful of mealies swallowed, can only be vaguely imagined. Yet there was no mistaking the ecstasy of the players in the domino game in particular. The players challenged and teased each other: 'Kom! Ek lê. In die mix!'

At the end of the game there was lightheartedness, banter and all-round sporting bonhomie. That light mood changed instantly into bickering and confrontation as soon as head warder Suitcase started his slave driving shouts: 'Come on, come on.'

The controversy that raged in the communal cells in mid-1966 on whether to accept the soccer facilities offer or not did not hinge on the recreation principle as such, but on priorities. Recreation facilities before some improvement in sustenance was a travesty of logical priorities. It was cheap propaganda to disguise the quintessential conditions in Robben Island. To reject recreation facilities outright, nonetheless, would have been a serious blunder in the circumstances. The correct strategy was to accept the offer conditionally and proceed to use it as one of the levers to press for other improvements, including food. Generally that is what happened.

Through sports, prisoners managed to purchase extra clothing, which they often used, albeit illicitly when necessity arose – for example in winter when the prison uniform was inadequate to provide warmth. The purchase of the prizes, like Christmas, came once a year. It was something to look forward to during the long year of tasteless 'balanced diet'.

Our single cells sections, like the rest of the prison sections, felt starved in spite of official statements about the balanced diet. But our section, unlike the other sections, was starved more of the gaol news and rumours. We were isolated from the bulk of the population. This was a disadvantage. For smuggled tobacco during the prohibition days we depended on the communal cells sections who smuggled the tobacco to us in various ingenious ways. The news from newspapers came the same way. Unfortunately we were starved of rumours. Rumours in gaol can be more juicy than the cold, uninteresting events of the newspaper world.

The main section, as we called the communal cells section, was lucky. Most of the new arrivals landed in the main section, loaded to the brink with news and rumours. There were many more warders there too. Amongst their large number, it was not unusual to find a loose talker, a gossip, a rumour-monger. However we were lucky one day to have Samson Fadana transferred from the main section to our section. Why Fadana was transferred from there to our section after four to five years, we do not know. Fadana himself did not appear to know. Most likely the authorities considered him troublesome and, therefore, a bad influence.

Certainly there was an occasion when Samson Fadana did insult the Prison Board, by almost telling them to shove their 'classification'! However after a year or two he had relented well enough to ask the same Prison Board why they were not promoting him. 'Remember what you told us?' the chairman reminded Samson. Samson argued that the Board had misunderstood him because although he had spoken in English his language was actually Xhosa. 'In Xhosa when you say "no", you mean "yes".' The Board forgave Samson and promoted him to a higher grade. All the same here he was, demoted to our section.

One good thing was that he came bearing a rumour. Juicy as usual, but incredulous. Samson informed us we were about to eat eggs in gaol. 'Eggs? Eat eggs in Robben Island? Are you off your rocker or something?' What saved him from physical harm was probably his

210

physique. Big, black, big-voiced, red-eyed and aggressive, he was not the man to think of venting one's disagreement on physically. All who listened to Fadana's egg-dream stopped at ridicule, and only a few dared verbal abuse. 'Look here, don't talk shit. Why don't you tell us we will be released tomorrow!'

More optimistic inmates tried to probe the source of Samson's rumour. According to Samson, the source was someone, a prisoner or a warder, from Victor Verster Prison. There, prisoners were eating eggs already. That was dismissable. It might have been a temporary surplus from somewhere. Were it part of prescribed prison ration, prisoners would have been informed. Why in any case does it not start simultaneously in all prisons? The rumour, appetising as it was, was dismissed along with its monger, Samson Fadana. The rumour-monger had the last crow when it became true eventually. 'What did I tell you?' bellowed Samson, when our eyes bulged at the sight of the fowl eggs instead of the precarious guinea-fowl eggs. Those first two eggs tasted extraordinary. We could have done with 10 times the ration. Things seemed to be looking up. Three days of meat, one day of fish, one day of eggs. The quantities were still niggardly and miserable. But . . .

The improvement in the prison food situation came when the preparation was improved. This happened after the transfer of the common-law prisoners. As a result of this transfer the political prisoners did their own cooking. Those selected for the kitchen had to undergo on-the-job training. The large-scale corruption of the past disappeared from the kitchen. Every ounce of fat was accounted for. The mealies became edible with the new magic touch of fat. The meat began to taste like meat. The only problem was one bit one's lip and fingers more than the meat because of its quantity. Vegetables became a delight to the palate, potatoes came mashed, fried or in their skins. Eggs were fried, scrambled or boiled. Although the quantity did not change, the better-prepared rations were more filling. Hunger-strikes still occurred from time to time but not as a protest against the food but against other grievances.

Eventually complaints about the diet centred around its discriminatory nature. The denial of certain food categories to some groups of prisoners did not make sense. Here, we lived together, played together, and worked together; so whence the discrimination? The argument that the food which Africans received in gaol was the sort of food they enjoyed in their homes was so much bunk. A deliberate lie!

In 1979 we were informed non-racial diet had been approved in principle by the policy-makers. It was not certain when full implementation of the decision would take place. There were disturbing reports that the transition from a discriminatory to a non-racial diet would be gradual. The Boers are firm believers in

211

Darwinism. It does not matter that Darwin based his theory on the natural process, and they based theirs on the apartheid process, they believe if Darwin was right, they are right too. Things must take time. Evolution, not revolution. The equating of natural process with social process is a prostitution of analogies. Shortly before my release, the process of phasing out the apartheid diet was beginning to assume some amorphous shape. It was a shape without a shape.

The F-diets, ie Africans, had gone as far as one slice of bread in the morning. We continued to pool bread and distribute it in the old way. The morning F-diet slices were kept until the evening when they were thrown in with the D-diet slices and distributed on the arithmetic formula of X slices divided by Y inmates. The quotient did not rise sharply but rise it did by one. The sugar-scale was levelled at the bottom rung, ie the Coloured and Indian sugar-scale fell from two ounces to one and a half ounces. The same axe fell on the D-diet meat. I do not know whether the puzamandla was extended to Coloured and Indian prisoners because our section had imposed an indefinite boycott on this fortified apartheid diet.

The puzamandla boycott was forced upon our section by some authoritarian officer, without good reason. There was a time when puzamandla used to be mixed in the kitchen for us. We complained that the mixture was not to our taste. Since the amount of puzamandla powder each prisoner was entitled to was fixed, why couldn't the prisoners be given the powder to mix according to their individual taste? The prison administration then listened to our complaint and puzamandla came in powder form. Most of us preferred to accumulate our daily ration of puzamandla until we felt it was sufficient to make a delicious mug of drink. The arrangement seemed to suit everyone concerned.

Suddenly, here comes this new head, his head full of baaskap. Puzamandla to be mixed in the kitchen from now on! We tried to make this guy see things our way; no, he was adamant. His word was to be final. Okay then, can the quantity of water be reduced so that we get half a mug of thick stuff instead of a full mug of watery stuff; it is tasteless. No! The man was determined: a full mug was to our taste and flavour. To hell then! The puzamandla boycott was on. It went on for a long time. It was still in progress when I was released. The D-diets originally did not get milk. Somewhere before the talk of non-racial diet they had started getting milk. The F-diets joined them after the announcement of the principle of non-racial diet.

It seemed the process of implementing the new diet was to be multi-phased and slow. Moreover it was clear it would be at the expense of the privileged groups. The preoccupation of the prison administration appeared to be to juggle around with estimated figures of the various prison population groups without tampering with the total estimates in the prison food vote.

When we complained about the slowness of the experimental

212

process, we were advised, 'have patience', for the dietician was busy, very busy, doing his best to expedite the whole process. We suspected that with so many departments likely to be interested, the process was going to evolve pitifully slowly. Imagine the accountants working out the budget, economists wary about rising government expenditure, racist anthropologists probably sceptical about the 'imposition of western dishes on primitive Bantu', ideologists arguing about the politics of introducing equality through the prison kitchen door. Mercy!

NELSON MANDELA

On Robben Island, the bell, up to the late 1970s, or the music in later years, woke up every prisoner at 5.30am. The bellringer, that is, the night-duty warder, clanged the bell with such vigour, it could raise the dead. The soundest sleeper, except for one or two comrades, could not outsleep the racket of that bell . . .

With the passage of time many of us did not need the bell or the music, the routine was in our system, and we jumped out of the blankets without effort. The cell doors were opened at 6.45 am. The next hour and a quarter was devoted to a number of routine duties: rolling up the blankets and the mats, tidying the cell, greeting fellow inmates in the opposite cells (those who could see you through the window) with a raised clenched fist, doing physical exercises, and washing one's face in the upturned lid of the sanitary bucket, or 'ballie'.

When the doors opened, everybody rushed out to empty and wash his ballie. Those who did not fancy washing in the small upturned ballie lid inside the cell had their chance to wash in the limited wash-basins provided in the bathroom. Everything moved fast after the unlocking of cells. Joggers at varying paces circled the small prison section yard. Those whose turn it was to 'phaka' got on with the job.

Breakfast done, the shout 'Val in (Fall in)' brought us in twos to our first gate. Then it was the next gate and the next. Each had its own attendant warder. Before each, we halted, usually accompanied by orders of 'Stilte in die gang (Silence in the passage)!' and 'caps off'!

The 'caps off' order irritated many prisoners. Cloth caps for African prisoners and black, cheap felt hats for Indian and Coloured prisoners, soon vanished as part of prison uniform, because prisoners stopped wearing them on the way to the quarry.

The walk of one and a half kilometres to the lime quarry was usually interesting. There was a possible glimpse of some communal section span, hidden in the wood along the road to give us a clear passage. The lovely morning breeze of the sea contributed to the buoyant morning conversation along the route. 'Mind the landmine!', someone would sing out, on sight of dog shit on the road, and the orderly marching line broke slightly to avoid the danger.

213

Past Mangaliso Sobukwe's cottage, we strained to catch a glimpse of the PAC President. Robert Sobukwe, after completing his three-year sentence in 1963 for PAC activities, had been detained on Robben Island for another six years under some special law called 'the Sobukwe clause'. He was kept alone and allowed occasional visits from his wife, who stayed with him in the cottage while she visited. 'The Sobukwe clause' was a definite psychological torture to many political prisoners who were doing short-term sentences. Under this law, anybody could be detained indefinitely after completing a sentence imposed by a court.

Each lime quarry day had a full (unofficial) programme for each prisoner, along with the hard labour. Each prisoner's programme varied from day to day. In the morning one might be busy with something in one group, and in the afternoon with something else, in another group. The main preoccupation was 'study classes'. The more subjects one studied, the busier one would be.

Generally, discussions in class carried on without notes. Where notes were unavoidable, then they were held in such a way that the warder in charge would not notice, otherwise there might be trouble. Picking, shovelling and loading the lime had to go on without obvious interference from the classes.

Another preoccupation was political discussion. When I arrived in the single cells section, ANC members were discussing the history of the ANC. Needless to say we had no written guides, but Comrade Walter Sisulu, who led these discussions, was a walking history of the organisation. Comrade Walter's memory was phenomenal. Not only did he remember events, and the names associated with them, but also the circumstances under which they occurred.

Political discussion was prohibited on Robben Island: it flourished notwithstanding.

After the history of the ANC, which took a vast period because of its richness and the complexity of its evolution, other topics were tackled: nationalism, Marxist theories, and current national and international topics. Consensus was never the object in discussions of a general political nature. The aim was to learn from each other.

Comrade Nelson among all the inmates was the most tireless participant in discussions – in formal discussions restricted to ANC members and in informal, bilateral or group discussions with members of other organisations.

Some of us, whenever we could, preferred to engage in 'Mlevo (palaver/idle talk)'. Not Comrade Nelson. Every day, but every day, in addition to his organisation's programmes, he had numerous appointments with individuals, always on his own initiative, to discuss inter-organisational relations, prisoners' complaints, joint strategies against prison authorities and general topics. Nelson Mandela is an indefatigable activist for human rights.

Two book titles *The Struggle is My Life* and *No Easy Walk to Freedom* summarise his political perception, commitment and dedication to the struggle for liberation of the oppressed masses in South Africa. 'Madiba', as he is respectfully addressed (using his clan name), is a man who lives for nothing else but the struggle of his people, outside gaol and inside gaol.

Nelson is a forceful debater, some say controversial and dogmatic. The opinion appears slanted when you get to know him better. Perhaps it is his direct, fiercely candid approach, which depicts him in an unfavourable light with some contrary opinion holders! In argument against someone with insubstantial facts, Nelson can be vicious, by adopting a modified socratic method. Very few people like to be cross-examined and exposed in their vagueness and ignorance.

Quite a few times I have come out of an argument with Madiba 'bloodied' and humiliated. None the less, I have found such experience fruitful in the long term.

For it has taught me to look at both sides of the question, to attempt to give an objective and honest answer to it. An objective approach to social questions, in particular, sometimes brings one to unpopular conclusions. Frankly, it is better to know the unpleasant truth than delude oneself with popular fallacy. Such conclusions might form a precarious base for future programmes and plans.

Those who have read the two books referred to above will have a good image of Mandela, the man. Forthright in his condemnation of government oppression, unequivocal about the society he is striving for, and forceful in his pledge to fight for a better society. He has not changed in gaol. On the contrary, his daily contact with the most extreme forms of repression, in the heart of the ultimate in state machinery, inspires him with tireless militancy and dignified resistance.

Whenever I have watched Madiba present his own general complaints to the prison authorities, stressing every word and every syllable of every word he uttered, I would be reminded of Chief Lutuli's favourite precept, 'Let your courage rise with danger.'

In the early 1960s, when gaol conditions were atrocious, Nelson played very much the role of a battering ram. He was one prisoner whom officers could not ignore, not only because of his status, but because he would not 'let them do it'. Comrade Mandela's attitude and conduct was that physically he was in prison, but psychologically he was free. That is why he could seriously tell Colonel Aucamp, the head of security in gaol, that he demanded the right to correspond with O R Tambo and exchange views on the liberation struggle!

The Commissioner of Prisons (COP), General Steyn, also came under systematic pressure from Comrade Nelson. To start with, the COP, to give his officers an unimpeded opportunity to institute a rule of terror on Robben Island, made it his policy to stay away as long as possible from the prison. Mandela, as the popular spokesman of prisoners, took up the strategic absenteeism of the COP from Robben Island strongly, by correspondence.

In reply, the COP usually stated as his excuse not to visit Robben Island that he was too busy, and pressure of time. To move from the defensive to the offensive, as befitted the COP in the apartheid state, General Steyn constantly warned Nelson to stop speaking on other prisoners' behalf. Each prisoner had to raise his own personal complaints and not assume the mantle of spokesman. 'And Nelson, you are a prisoner!'

This theme was taken up by all officers, junior and senior. The COP's attempt to enforce the injunction on Nelson was unacceptable. It was simply ignored. Similarly, the officers on the spot were also ignored.

In his correspondence with the COP, Mandela defiantly continued to describe general conditions. The rest of the prison population resolved to make it a duty of each prisoner to lay personal complaints at every opportunity to demonstrate the unfeasibility of a single warder taking down each prisoner's complaint at the weekend! It soon became apparent that it was just impossible for the limited staff of warders over the weekend to cope with the taking down of complaints from every single one of the more than a thousand inmates.

Officialdom is generally coy to admit retreat from previously held sacred lines. Consequently, the rule that each prisoner had to be his own spokesman, even on common grievances, was repealed by practice. Individuals or groups of individuals from respective sections were simply mandated to present their section's grievances. Since they were not turned back nor reprimanded for acting the role of spokespersons, the practice developed into a tradition and replaced the former misguided official policy.

The victory, therefore, over the 'each-prisoner-for-himself' prison strategy belonged to the combined effort of the whole prison population. The objective of the strategy was to intimidate prisoners, to isolate troublemakers, to identify the pliable ones and employ them in the nefarious efforts of the Prisons Department to divide the prisoners and undermine their morale.

The attempt failed due to the concerted effort of the prison community. Nelson Mandela's role in the success of the campaign deserves a special place, none the less.

As soon as it was evident that deputations were tolerated by the authorities, Comrade Nelson was the first to encourage appointment of inmates other than himself to represent prisoners on some occasions. Where the issue was regarded as urgent and weighty, especially when the officer to hear it was of senior rank or a visitor from outside, Nelson was invariably appointed alone or with a couple of other inmates. Generally, outside visitors requested to interview Nelson.

Nelson Mandela was among the very first modern political prisoners in South Africa to be incarcerated on Robben Island, in late 1962.

In those days, says Nelson, the conditions were mixed. Bad and not so bad. It was before the flood of arrests and convictions triggered by the passing of the Sabotage Act and the report of Justice Snyman's Commission, appointed to investigate the Paarl unrest said to have been initiated by Poqo, the militant group within the PAC. The report, while connecting the immediate unrest with Poqo, warned that the more experienced and resourceful ANC was more dangerous in the long term, and to be watched.

According to Nelson, when they arrived two notorious prison officers, the Kleynhans brothers, were already there. Nelson pays glowing tribute to the unintimidated attitude of his pioneer comrades. It is the standard of his extreme modesty that he will often underplay his own role while he highlights that of his comrades.

However, it appears that during those early days, the harassment imposed by the Kleynhans brothers was mitigated by the covert sympathy expressed by the Coloured warders. These warders would smuggle tobacco, newspapers and any little contraband comfort to the political prisoners. Their contrast with the naked Boer brutishness was a psychological balm.

Unfortunately, these black warders had to be transferred from Robben Island when the avalanche of prisoners inundated the place. Robben Island became a maximum security prison under all white warders, whose racial prejudice and political indoctrination ensured that they dealt with black prisoners without mercy of any kind.

Back from the Rivonia trial with his six other colleagues, Walter Sisulu, Govan Mbeki, Ahmed Kathrada, Andrew Mlangeni, Raymond Mhlaba and Elias Motsoaledi, Nelson found a 'refurbished' Robben Island, designed to intimidate and demoralise. The seven were segregated on arrival in some old section of the prison, while a new, specially built section was under construction.

Later, some members of the YCC and a few leading PAC and ANC members from the communal sections were transferred to join them.

The policy of segregation was designed to keep the prisoners considered influential away from others, ostensibly for effective administration. That is why the theme of prison administration was, at this juncture, each prisoner for himself. Organised representation might upset the gaol applecart; the authorities might find it hard to maintain order and discipline. Was it not as organised entities that the prisoners made a nuisance of themselves and landed in the mess they were in? Well, they were not going to be afforded the opportunities that misled them while outside. 'Die plek se naam is tronk. (The place's name is prison).' 'No PAC or ANC shit here!'

Shortly, it transpired that General Steyn, the Commissioner of Prisons, had been a prisoner of policies which were somewhat alien to his suave personality. A frequent visitor abroad, he showed himself more cultured than he appeared to be when he barricaded himself in his ivory tower at Prison Headquarters in Pretoria. Neat, in his expensive shoes, suits and fashionable shortbrimmed hat, which he doffed gracefully to prisoners, he soon won himself some personal regard from prisoners. His visits to the island still lagged far behind our demands, but they were beginning to be regular, as they coincided with the parliamentary sessions. Occasionally when some foreign visitor called on the island, the COP played the role of escort.

Before the presence of such visitors, General Steyn's etiquette could be dazzling to inmates more acquainted with abuse from junior officers. While the COP was not changing his essential policies, his manners were improving.

'Gentlemen', he addressed us one day, as he introduced advocate Henning of the American Bar Association, 'will you elect your spokesman to place your complaints before Mr Henning, if you have any'. 'Mandela', responded several voices to the rare offer. 'Mr Mandela, the floor is yours', said the COP, bowing slightly while making a hand gesture towards advocate Henning.

The advocate soon revealed himself as being to the right of the right in the American Bar Association. He seemed totally inexperienced with regard to aggrieved political prisoners, who made it their duty to challenge orthodox prison practices. Moreover, he had apparently been briefed in advance on the sort of complaints to expect. As a result he was a very bad listener. 'No', said Madiba, slight exasperation in his voice, 'you do not listen. I did not say we 'dunna wanna chup wod'! What I am saying is that chopping wood is a temporary occupation, our permanent work is the quarry work, the monotonous, backbreaking, picking and shovelling of the lime.' Henning looked stumped and obviously in need of a handy spittoon. He continued to counter every complaint raised by Madiba with comparisons from backward penitentiaries in the USA. He missed the burden of Madiba's representation, namely that as political prisoners we demanded rights and treatment commensurate with our political status. Our demand was for human dignity, right inside the gaol walls. In a nutshell, that was Madiba's message to Henning.

Although the COP looked absorbed in the argument between advocate Henning and attorney-at-law N R Mandela, he kept his peace and declined to be involved.

Representations by prisoners to visiting dignitaries hoped to win sympathy for the point of view of the prisoners. Since the visitors were considered to have the government's ear – otherwise they never would be given permission to visit – they were expected to comment favourably on prisoners' demands to enable the government or the

Prisons Department to reassess their prison policies. The openly unsympathetic visitors, of the kind of advocate Henning, had to be humbled for their support of primitive practices in a civilised world. None could better Comrade Nelson when it came to performance of that task. He was the expert. His handling of the conservative Henning thrilled us.

Comrade Mandela is articulate, confident, factual, assertive and persuasive. His representations did not always yield immediate results but they were never without lasting impact. He was a great inspiration in our campaign for improvements in gaol.

Comrade Mandela was also a shrewd tactician in dealing with prison administration. He made it a point to size up every Commanding Officer who was posted to Robben Island prison. As soon as the new OC arrived, he sought an interview with him. At such an interview he might get a slight insight of the man. More important, he made it his duty to outline prisoners' pending grievances, and acquaint the new OC with some of the unfinished programmes of the previous OC which were to the advantage of the prisoners.

Colonel Badenhorst, alias 'Kid Ruction', alone, as far as I can remember, declined Madiba's request for an interview. It transpired later that Kid Ruction was an appointee on a special mission to 'discipline' our 'undisciplined' section.

Entrusted with that sacred mission, Kid Ruction suspended prison regulations and instituted a rule of terror, particularly in our section. Whenever he came on inspection he walked through our lines with head bent. He had no time to greet or be greeted by a prisoner, let alone to pause for a prisoner's complaint.

The only time Kid Ruction spoke to a prisoner was when he pronounced punishment: isolation, spare diet, straitjacket, downgrading from a higher to a lower grading, loss of study privilege, etc. He dealt ruthlessly with strikes. His warder thugs were mobilised against our section one night to demonstrate their disapproval of the hunger strike that was going on.

Armed with batons, they raided our single cells in batches of three or four. 'Teen die muur (Against the wall)! Trek uit (Strip)!'

A number of prisoners in the segregation section were assaulted. They had their balls twisted, they were punched and kicked. Andimba Toivo ja Toivo, the SWAPO leader, was one of those who were severely beaten. After the assault, like the other victims of that 28th day of May 1971, he was forced to clean his blood-spattered cell. It is typical of habitual criminals to destroy any evidence or exhibit that might be used against them in future investigations. The South African police torturers and prison warders have developed the expunging of evidence to a fine art. Afterwards, in court or administrative enquiry, they can deny the allegations and lie with innocent faces, thankful that their consciences will not betray them.

Colonel 'Kid Ruction's' regime of terror lasted for two years. During the two years, on the average half our number were locked-up in punishment cells. This made it very difficult to organise any effective inside counteraction. Although it was not so easy to mobilise the outside, because of harassment of visitors (including the clergy), curtailment of the privilege of legal visits and stricter censorship of letters, slowly the harsh events of our existence filtered to the outside. Relatives of some prisoners, through legal representatives, instituted enquiries about the systematic harassment and arbitrary withdrawal of study privileges.

Then one day, a strong contingent of judges visited us at work, accompanied by senior prison officials including Kid Ruction. During their interview with Comrade Nelson, Kid Ruction butted in and made threats to Nelson: 'Nelson, did I ever order you to be punished, since I arrived here?' asked the OC, emotion in his voice. 'No', said Nelson, 'not me personally, but what you have been doing to some of my colleagues affects all of us. You are persecuting us.' 'Nelson!', interjected Kid Ruction, fuming and shaking his finger at Nelson, right before the eyes of the judges, 'You'll pay for this!'

Nelson in an eloquent dumb expression turned to the judges. It was an invitation to the judges to corroborate the oral evidence just interrupted.

One of the judges was Justice Steyn, the director of the Urban Foundation – the organisation concerned with black urban conditions, particularly housing. He seemed to take strong exception to the OC's outburst. There was a minor commotion as some of the judges who had been chatting with other prisoners on the side overheard Badenhorst's threats. The judges' expressions appeared to invite Kid Ruction to repeat such utterances inside a court of law. Unhappily for them, Robben Island was not a court of law, but a notorious prison where Kid Ruction and his ilk ruled supreme, in defiance of the judiciary and the rule of law. In fact, had Badenhorst decided to be nastier, he might have told the judges they authorised his administrative conduct. After all, it was the judges who sentenced the prisoners under the apartheid laws and he was merely implementing the apartheid legislation on victims of apartheid courts in a typical apartheid fashion. Authority was conferred on him by the legislature and the courts.

However, the favourable international opinion of the South African judiciary appears to have some desirable influence on some of them. After the Madiba-Kid Ruction encounter, we believed the OC would not wag his tail much longer on Robben Island. Whether by coincidence or the logic of events, indeed, Badenhorst's contract was not renewed for the second term. In spite of his harassment, oppression and persecution he had dismally failed to break us. That was his sacred mission, to break us: to humiliate, undermine our morale and force us to surrender our principles.

Like some of his predecessors he failed and left – that is what some of us long-termers used to say, 'Warders/officers come and go, we stay on!'

In his relations with prison officers, Comrade Nelson's conduct, whether by design or by instinct, differentiated between senior officers and junior officers.

With junior officers who knew their position, Nelson was charming and fatherly. Many young warders were friendly to him, occasionally soliciting advice from him in connection with their jobs or social problems. Some brought him greetings from their parents, who wanted very much to meet him, and envied their sons who were privileged to know this great man in person. Afrikaners, like all groups, are not homogeneous in character.

The top officers constituted Madiba's target. They not only had to answer his attacks on the rotten administrative practices, they had to field critical questions and allegations against their government. 'Why are you oppressing us?'

'The colour of your skin does not make you superior. We are all humans. We demand political status. We demand to be released from gaol. Robey Leibbrandt the traitor and Nazi sympathiser was amnestied. We are not traitors. We are patriots. Allow us to write our memoirs.' They might deny some of the allegations or refuse to accede to Nelson's demands, but he persisted and rubbed it into their thick skins until they squirmed in embarrassment.

Often these top officers and ministers exasperated him with their ignorance. Jimmy Kruger, then Minister of Prisons, was one such ignoramus.

When he visited Robben Island in 1978 he had a long interview during which Madiba raised prisoners' demands as well as discussing topical questions. Madiba came back from meeting with Kruger very much disappointed and shocked. The Minister, according to Madiba, was completely blank on the history and policies of the ANC. He could not argue on the Freedom Charter of the ANC, he had not read it. This of course did not stop him from condemning it as a Communist document! What justice could one expect from such a Minister of Justice and Prisons?

Obviously only prisons and imprisonment!

Comrade Mandela, though disgusted by ministerial ignorance, urged Jimmy Kruger to study the history of the ANC and the Freedom Charter. He probably tried, for he lost his portfolio thereafter! Who knows, one of his ambitious security officers might have caught him reading the 'banned document' and opened an unflattering dossier under his name!

Comrade Mandela's relations with the middle rung of the officers were uneasy and poor. In their aspirations to climb the hierarchical ladder, they behaved more top than topmost officers. Madiba made

221

short shrift of them whenever they assumed such airs: 'Look here, you are a junior. You cannot take such a decision. I want to see your seniors . . .!'

Lieutenant Prins, the head of prison, who once stopped Andimba Toivo ja Toivo's outgoing letters because they bore the name Namibia rather than the official name 'South West Africa', was typical of the middle-rung prison officers. He was never tactful, always blurting out the first thing that came into his mind, without weighing the implications of such a gaffe.

Nelson went to see Lieutenant Prins in connection with his wife's application to visit him. The application had been turned down on the unheard-of grounds that Nelson did not want to see her. Nelson did not want to see his wife? Preposterous!

Without investigating Nelson's complaint, Lieutenant Prins put his foot in it, by alleging that Winnie was just seeking publicity. Publicity, my foot! The constant persecution of his wife by the apartheid system, and this absurd remark by a prison Jack-in-office, made Madiba lose his head. He told Lieutenant Prins off in untypical intemperate language, shook his hammer fist at him, and stormed out of the office banging the door behind him.

He was still panting when he came back into the section. Someone whispered that he needed tranquillisers in view of his blood pressure.

The prison administration soon indicted Nelson for his misconduct against the head of the prison.

Ironically, Comrade Nelson looked forward to this case. It became his preoccupation. He prepared a counter-indictment against Lieutenant Prins, against his superiors, against the whole prison administration and against the source of all the black man's woes, the apartheid system.

His defence lawyer was not happy with that line of defence. It was likely to antagonise the court and the administration. Antagonising the court or the administration was not Nelson's bother. In any case, the white administration as well as the white court was antagonistic and hostile to the interests of all blacks. The antagonism was enshrined in the attitudes, policies, constitution and programmes of the white government. The line of defence Madiba opted for was necessary to show that blacks had passed the crawling stage. Blacks were on the 'standing-up' stage. Everywhere, outside or inside gaol, it was time to stand up against the tyranny of white supremacy. To stand up and let white racists see our height. Gaol, the institution made specially to cow and force blacks to crawl on their bellies and chant 'my baas' every minute of the day in South Africa, was the very place to stand up and show the stature of the black man.

Thus Comrade Mandela's line of defence. There were to be no apologies, but counter-accusation and bold challenge.

Unfortunately, the case did not come off. It was withdrawn, after the authorities had got scent of Nelson's line of defence.

They were not supposed to know, but they did, by bugging the room where Nelson consulted his lawyer. The client and his lawyer had actually discovered that some listening device had been installed to monitor their conversation.

The discovery led to another contest, when Nelson challenged the unlawfulness of the prison administration's effort to meddle in his legal consultations.

The prisons headquarters had to amend prison orders to legitimate their illegal action retroactively.

Shortly after the authorities had discovered Mandela's line of defence, there were attempts to confiscate the documents he was drawing up for his defence. All attempts and intrigues had failed, however, due to Nelson's alertness and long experience with the strategy and tactics of the enemy right in his own base. Nelson's familiarity with legal principles, prison regulations and his tremendous guts in awkward terrains, helped him to win exciting temporary victories.

The prison administration with its overwhelming advantage and resources was plotting a dramatic coup. After the bugging incident, Nelson's consultations suffered a setback. Every application of his lawyer to visit Robben Island was deferred by the authorities to some unsuitable future time. An attempt to proceed with the case without Nelson's lawyer was successfully challenged by him.

Then suddenly one day, things seemed to look up. There was a letter from the lawyer stating he would be arriving on a definite date for the case. The prison authorities also confirmed that the case was to take place on the day mentioned in the lawyer's letter, and permission had been granted for him to represent his client. Without informing Comrade Mandela, a few days before the set date for the case, the lawyer was told not to bother to come to the island as the case against his client had been withdrawn.

Meantime Nelson had not been informed. Only on arrival in court did he learn his lawyer was not around.

The court proceeded with its sham formalities of withdrawing charges against the accused.

Hardly had Madiba recovered his shocked breath when he was surrounded by officers demanding his defence documents. It was a neat administrative ambush. Since the case was over, the authorities had the right of access to any prisoner's property. Nelson handed the papers over under protest.

If the prison authorities believed their ambush was a 'coup de grace' they had another think coming. In spite of the dispossession of the papers, Nelson argued that the documents were his, and he instituted action to recover them. After a long legal contest the documents were returned to him.

Nelson's objective all the time had been to have the documents reach the outside officially through his lawyer. The prison authorities knew this, that is why they were compelled to withdraw the case.

After the return of the documents Nelson continued to insist that his lawyer had the right to see them and keep them on his behalf. Alternatively, if the authorities disapproved of the suggestion, his wife could keep them while he was in gaol.

Needless to say, the authorities were not prepared to let such dynamite fall into 'irresponsible' hands. It was quite safe with Nelson in his cell. There it could do no harm, being defused by the narrow space.

Comrade Nelson has not given up the fight to get this time-bomb outside to explode. It might do damage to propaganda and lies about the duckling-to-a-swan 'reformed' apartheid. Nelson never gives up. He thinks the struggle twenty-four hours per day in his life. His dreams and actions reflect his thoughts.

He has amazing stamina for discussion, too. In our section he never missed an opportunity to draw each of his fellow-inmates into some political discussion.

In discussion he is a wonderful listener. He never misses any point raised in a discussion. His capacity to retain what he hears made him an excellent reporter after interviews with authorities. He could be detailed not only in the substance of the point made, but in reporting expressions and innuendos of the participants.

Comrade Nelson's tendency to examine all aspects of a question sometimes sets him off as a controversial figure on topical events. Moreover, he is not a man to leave any important discussion hanging. He prefers to arrive at a principled conclusion. This tendency does not necessarily emanate from the desire to dominate an argument, but rather from the natural desire to see behind the other man's argument – to learn from a contrary viewpoint.

Comrade Nelson does not consider himself a political genius nor an extraordinary leader within his organisation. He believes that his organisation is a contribution of diverse talents now and in the past. He is very much conscious that he is a creature of South African conditions and, in that regard, a creature of his own organisation, the ANC. He speaks with the greatest admiration of all his former colleagues and the present ones. Moses Kotane, J B Marks, Chief Albert Lutuli, Dr Yusuf Dadoo, Bram Fisher, Lilian Ngoyi, Helen Joseph and others.

He has amazing confidence in all his colleagues now leading the struggle outside. He was very much offended at one time to receive a letter from one of his non-ANC admirers in exile, which insinuated that, had he been free, the struggle would have been on a different level. Since the letter had come through unofficial channels, it had to be answered through the same channels. It implied indefinite delays, which kept Comrade Nelson tense and unhappy. Only after he had answered the letter did Nelson relax.

To place him above his colleagues, those in the leadership, was blasphemous to the image of the ANC, a misconstruction of its history. ANC and its leaders are a reflection of the concrete conditions in South Africa. As long as the conditions remain what they are, there shall always be the ANC and the right calibre of leadership to steer it through a particular phase. That is Mandela's firm belief.

Again, there was a period when the international press 'appointed' Comrade Mandela as the President of the ANC (recently I have even heard him referred to by the media as the 'life president' of the ANC). Well, such unofficial appointments do not flatter Comrade Nelson. To Nelson, more than any of us in prison, these reports were wild and far-fetched. Were they true, they might betray some internal strife within the organisation or a loss of perspective. This was a source of anxiety to him.

One of Nelson's great virtues is his simplicity. Like all the leaders of the ANC, there is no image of cultism around him. In prison he could easily have used his national and international image to amass personal privileges from the authorities. All Commanding Officers including Kid Ruction would have been happy to be in the good books of Madiba. That is why Kid Ruction was so offended when Nelson exposed his fascist tendencies. That is why, in the beginning, General Steyn the COP did his best in an attempt to coerce Nelson to speak for himself. In the process, Nelson would have destroyed his image in relation to his colleagues. No leader of principle, let alone of the calibre of Nelson, would compromise himself that easily.

A true revolutionary leader must be one with the people. Thus, in gaol Nelson sought no personal privileges and participated fully in all common duties in the section. Each one of us of course cleaned his own cell and washed his own clothes. Besides the cells there were the section yard, the corridor, the recreation hall and the shower room to clean. For these duties we divided into a number of work spans who rotated the cleaning of these areas weekly. Nelson belonged to one of the spans and performed all the duties involved just like anybody else.

In the 'phaka' spans Nelson featured like everybody else too.

At work, there was our toilet bucket to clear and wash. We all did it in turns, including Nelson. None was exempted.

Ever since the first sentence of Madiba in 1962, the demand for his release has been growing. As I write this chapter P W Botha has made a conditional offer to release him. The US administration, the British government, along with some members of the white Progressive Federal Party in South Africa are almost falling over each other in their praise of the statesman-like gesture of P W Botha. This happens after Mandela has been in gaol for more than 22 years!

The noises these governments and parties have been making in this connection expose their misconception of the liberation struggle in South Africa, as well as the role and commitment of Nelson Mandela in it. Winnie Mandela, the revolutionary wife of Nelson, hit the nail on the head in answer to P W Botha. Says Winnie, 'Botha talks about the freedom of my husband, but my husband talks about the freedom of the oppressed!' Why isn't there a single spokesman in some of these establishments who can grasp this simple truth?

The answer is that they do not care. They do not know what it is like to be oppressed. Nor can they imagine what it is like to yearn for freedom. The liberation struggle is about unconditional and absolute freedom of the oppressed masses from the tyranny of apartheid. It is about equal opportunities, freedom from exploitation of man by man, and human dignity. Offering conditional release to Comrade Mandela is an insult to his revolutionary image. It is an attempt to discredit him by implication. It implies that during all his years of struggle and sacrifice he was misled and that he must now admit that the concept of freedom he has fought for is an illusion, a political mirage, some Utopian dream of the never-never.

The challenge to progressive mankind today is to apply pressure on P W Botha to stop insulting Comrade Nelson and the oppressed masses of South Africa, to force him to abandon his political gimmicks which threaten to engulf the whole of Southern Africa in a blood bath. Nelson Mandela must be free to lead his people and South Africa to peace and prosperity.

CHAPTER 5

Release

Nineteen-eighty came to an end on December 31 in line with the Anno Domini calendar years before it. Nineteen-eighty had been the year that stood between me and freedom more than all the years put together after 1966.

The exit of 1980 was the entry of 1981. 'Woza 1981! (Come 1981!)' I had been shouting, in half jest and half earnest, since Justice Viljoen sentenced me to 15 years hard labour on May 6, 1966. It was the fashion for political prisoners to invoke their year of release. The lifers made light of their indeterminate sentences and adopted every year as the year of their possible release.

I had done well in gaol, if one can do well there. I was leaving Robben Island in one piece, unbroken in spirit and in flesh. Not only could I boast a PG (Prison Graduate), I could boast three academic degrees obtained through correspondence with the University of South Africa. During my 15 years I had served our prison community through a variety of committees.

I had also served in all the underground structures of the ANC, from the committee responsible for drawing the organisation's study programme to the highest committee entrusted with day-to-day administration and organisational discipline in the section.

I had lived a full life in a 'basement' devoid of natural life.

Although I had lived every day of the 15 years for 1981, I now felt lukewarm on the threshold of my home-going, mainly because I was leaving so many of my dear comrades behind. Excitement in me was also being smothered by thoughts, vague, uncertain, confused, speculative and tremulous about my future. Where was I going to? What was to be my role in the unfinished task ahead? Would I be allowed to join my family? Which homeland was I destined for? Was I to be restricted, banned or house arrested? The excitement of waiting for a remote favourable event petered out with its approach.

At 12 midnight the prison walls shook and reverberated with a cacophony of sounds: thumping of the walls, clanking of grilles and iron bars, rattling of mugs, spoons and any instrument, all sort of percussions capable of making a racket, accompanied by revolutionary slogans and songs, bade bye to the old year and greeted the new. Comrades shouted Mike, and 'Woza '81' in tandem. They were obviously more excited than I was. It was a sign of deep empathy that only co-sufferers can reflect.

Instead of excitement I was thinking sober thoughts. Was humanity changing for the better? Was there social progress outside? Or were the richer still getting richer and the poor getting poorer?

Of course, the situation outside was not static. Social life was in a state of flux. The curve of positive change in human relations, in spite of its troughs, showed a definite upward trend. After years of senseless and vindictive vetoes by one of the permanent members of the UN Security Council, the People's Republic of China had eventually been admitted to the UN body and Taiwan, the usurper, had been booted out; the war in Vietnam had ended with victory for the Vietnamese people and the reunification of their colonially divided country; in Nicaragua the arch-dictator, oppressor and exploiter of the masses had fled the country and conceded defeat to the popular Sandinistas; in Africa, Portuguese colonial arrogance had fallen on evil days – Cape Verde, Guinea (Bissau), Mozambique and Angola had achieved bloody independence; and Ian Smith's dream of 1000 years of 'white rule' had been nailed by the patriotic forces of Zanu and Zapu.

South Africa alone looked like a granite in a sea of change. But South Africa too was changing. After years of glorifying apartheid dogma, apartheid ministers and their agents were beginning to wince at the mention of apartheid. 'Apartheid is dead,' they announced to the world. In practice, of course, apartheid was alive and in the best of health. Officially, at least in theory, a strategic retreat was discernible.

In prison, Robben Island in particular, the retreat was tangible and could be measured in leagues. From one letter per prisoner in six months to one letter every month, from cold sea water showers in winter to fresh hot water shower during all seasons, from news blackout to uncensored newspapers, from indiscriminate physical assaults to hospitalisation of deserving cases in mainland hospitals – the list could go on and on. In the early sixties Robben Island prison, more than any South African prison, was hell. In the late seventies and the time of my release, Robben Island was not a five star hotel, as government propaganda liked to depict it, it was still hell like all prisons, but a hell mitigated by small 'blessings'. One had to be grateful and proud of these 'mercies' particularly when one remembered how hard one fought for them. These were concessions wrung by dignified resistance on one's feet not by humble prayer on one's knees.

The granite was crumbling right at its heart. Prison is the heart of oppression in any oppressive society. And once any 'heart' assumes a new complexion or gets a 'pacer' then some life is in danger – the end is in sight. Imprisonment, thou has lost much of thy sting!

That did not mean anything could be gained from sitting in prison if one could afford an honourable discharge. One needed to be out where life was relatively unfettered, where precious time could be translated into useful action to pay one's debt to society for precious life. One needed to get out of the paralytic existence, the regimenta-

228

tion of limb and soul, to disperse the physical and psychological cramps. The dreary routine was killing: the bell to get you up, the rattle of keys to open you up, 'Phaka!' to get you to dish the food, 'Fall in!' to get you in line for work, 'Fall in!' to dismiss you for lunch, 'Fall in!' to get you back to work, 'Fall in!' to announce time-up for the day, 'Fall in!' to get you in line for the march back to the cells, 'Phaka!' to order you to dish for supper, 'Fall in!' to get you into the cells, the rattle of the keys at the cell door to bid you goodnight. Over the weekend, it was 'klaagte and versoeke (complaints and requests)!' to invite prisoners to air their inevitable lot – complaints and requests. Prison life is a life of complaints, and requests, which are another version of complaints. 'Klaagte and versoeke!' for every prisoner, and for a few lucky ones, it might be 'besoeke (visits)'. 'Versoeke' and 'besoeke' were often confused by the many who did not speak Afrikaans.

'Staan op! (Wake up/stand up!), Phaka! Fall in! Phaka! Fall in! Klaagte and versoeke! Besoeke!' These few commands summarised life in gaol. The human capacity to adapt to any situation is phenomenal. There is rhythm in any social life and social beings fall in step for survival. Survival, however, is the lowest rung of life. Humans strive for the highest rung, the sublimity of the stars. I scrupled about my remaining comrades and worried about my unknown fate outside. All the same I wanted out. It was a new adventure.

My uppermost anxiety was the difficulty of predicting the whims of my captors. No prisoner leaving Robben Island in those days could predict his destination and social circumstances with certainty. Some prisoners were released to their original homes, with or without a ban. Others, like Comrade A M L Masondo, were dumped into strange surroundings, in unfurnished houses, banned and confined away from their families.

Shortly before my release I had declined to complete certain official forms which we suspected were meant to enable the Department of Co-operation and Development to classify prisoners to be discharged by 'ethnicity' and settle them in the 'ethnic homelands'. Such lack of co-operation could spell trouble at the best of times, with the Department of Co-operation.

My anxiety seemed to be justified. Then a few days before my transfer from Robben Island, *Die Burger*, a Cape Town Afrikaans newspaper, reported that I was to be repatriated to Botswana. Since it did not give any background to the pending repatriation, I remained sceptical. In 1965 the Rhodesians had officially informed me I was to be repatriated to Botswana. Instead, I was illegally handed over to South Africa. Repatriation, in the context of minority regimes, was associated with hazards in my mind.

229

Despite the scruples and anxieties that nagged me I was getting ready for my departure. I had to, willy nilly.

I would miss my 'tea club' – Ahmed 'Kathy' Kathrada and Wilton 'Bribri' Mkwayi. A-group prisoners were now allowed to buy monthly groceries – tea, milo, coffee and biscuits. The three of us pooled our resources and organised this 'exclusive' club. Over the weekends, when we were in, we whiled away time by relaxing in one of our cells with mugs of some stimulating beverage. It was generally an occasion to reminisce about the past and our long-missed common friends. Nostalgia blended with a sweetened beverage could ever be so sweet!

I would miss Walter 'Tyopo' Sisulu the incorrigible 'scrounger' and 'parasite' at our tea club sessions. 'Tyopo', was always unwelcome and welcome. 'Tyopo! Who invited you here?' the three of us would pretend to harass Tyopo. 'I invited myself!' Tyopo would reply smiling affectionately and sitting down to enjoy the tea with us. Our tea could never have been sweeter without Tyopo. He is the sweetest man alive.

To sweeten the tea more, our uninvited guest usually proceeded without our permission to invite passers-by in the corridor: 'Madiba! (Mandela), Zizi! (Govan Mbeki), don't you want some tea? Come in!' That was Tyopo. Generous to a fault.

I would miss comrade Billy 'Monna' Nair. Ever shooting his clenched fist skyward in Amandla salute whenever our paths crossed in the constricted section corridors. 'Bamb' isibindi (Pluck up)!' he would exhort, plucky as ever.

I would miss Lalloo 'Isubhai' Chiba, the near-perfectionist, and ever on edge due to the elusiveness of perfection, his ideal. Isu was only less generous than Tyopo because he gave away only what belonged to him.

Comrade Elias 'Mokone' Motsoaledi was another I was going to miss. A chronic asthmatic and incurably humorous he was forever spinning illuminatingly poignant anecdotes about the lives and experiences of the oppressed. A formidable debater particularly whenever he prefaced his argument or counter-argument with 'hence I say . . .' which he did as a matter of course. I would miss him.

I would miss Govan 'Zizi' Mbeki. We called each other 'swaer' (brother-in-law), I don't know why, but that's how it was, 'brother-in-law'. Zizi, the most senior (age-wise) of our section, belied his age by 'befriending' the youth and participating in their frolicsome games, monopoly and ludo. Always full of beans, Zizi.

I would miss Raymond 'Ndobe' Mhlaba, his military gait and his uproarious laughter. Hear Ray laugh and you'd laugh at his laugh. Absolutely infectious. The sort of laugh that dissolves the bottled-up tensions inherent in the gaol atmosphere. Even in less tense situations one could do with such a laugh. I would miss Ray and his laugh.

230

I would miss James Mcedisi Mange, who had desperately wanted to die because he had been sentenced to die at the Pietermaritzburg trial in 1979 where he appeared with others. His sentence was later commuted on appeal. Before that happened, he had wished to die. When his lawyer visited him in the condemned cell to consult him on the appeal he had chased his lawyer away and told him he wanted to be left alone.

We talked him out of that mood when he arrived in our section. At the time of my release his despondency had completely vanished. He wanted to swap sentences with me. He was younger and he would be more of a long-term asset to the on-going struggle! It was a reasonable bargain. I had no objection provided it could be clinched with all concerned. I would miss him.

I would miss Kwedi 'George' Mkalipi, my short PAC friend. Fellow-inmates called both of us 'George', because we called each other George. Both of us were fascinated by Charles Dickens' characters. George is one of those pathetic Dickensian characters. I started calling Kwedi, 'George', and he retaliated uniformly. So we became the short and the tall George. George was tremendous. He was doing 21 years. He appeared least bothered by it. Ever cheerful and boyishly mischievous. George would miss George.

I would miss Andrew 'Clox' Mlangeni stressing his bandyleggedness by his walk down the corridor. Generally regarded as difficult, Clox's 'difficulty' was his difficulty in interpreting other people's attitudes and intentions correctly. Often, other people's attitudes appeared confrontational to him and he reacted confrontationally. His co-accused in the Rivonia trial called him 'robot' because the prosecutor called him so. It was a misnomer unless it was meant to underline his unswerving loyalty to the ANC. I admired his allegiance to the movement and was bemused by his personal relationships.

We were friends. I would miss him.

I would miss Comrade Nelson 'Madiba' Mandela. This implacable fighter against apartheid in all its aspects, yet warm and friendly and unspoiled by human prejudice that attempts to pervert and belittle him. Racial prejudice begets racial prejudice. Mandela is an exception. He is prepared to fight racial prejudice long and hard, using any weapon conceivable except racial prejudice.

I would miss him, comrade, friend and brother.

I would miss Andimba Toivo ja Toivo, the stalwart of the Namibian revolution. He was the only one of the Namibian comrades in our section. The isolation from his compatriots was to spite him for his aggressively uncompromising attitude towards Afrikaner colonialism.

As far as comrade Andimba was concerned the spite was a futile exercise, akin to water on the back of a duck.

We struck up a very warm friendship with Andimba the moment

231

he landed in our section. 'Neighbour', we addressed each other affectionately because our two countries were contiguous.

In conformity with the hallmark of genuine friendship, we saw eye to eye on matters of global as well as personal interest. But whenever our perceptions distinguished our personalities on an issue, we pulled no punches against each other in expressing our differences. Our mutual candour made us very close and inseparable. I would miss him. Very much.

There was hugging and shaking of hands all round as I took my leave from my section colleagues.

Major Harding, the Head of Prison, escorted us in the boat to Cape Town. There were three others transferred to Leeuwkop with me, Amos Masondo, from the new segregation section, David Nhlapo and another from communal cells section. Major Harding mentioned a big welcome that awaited me. When I asked where? he became evasive.

From Robben Island we stopped at Fort Glamorgan prison in East London. Many years before I got acquainted with police stations and prisons, Fort Glamorgan was one of those gaols that sent a chill through my spine – the stories of its atrocities and prison gang warfare almost made me vow against all transgressions of the law. A one-night stop there showed no evidence of its publicised notoriety. The warders looked far gentler than typical gaol warders in a harsh prison. The prisoners were quieter, less scared and less tattooed. Perhaps I had seen worse prisons by now.

The next day we arrived at Leeuwkop Prison. All applications to see my in-laws and friends from Soweto were turned down. It appeared the prison authorities were taking certain precautions unbeknown to my fertile imagination. The general practice was that prisoners on the eve of their release were not restricted in their visits. I slept a dreamless sleep on 4 May 1981. I was awakened early to get ready on the morning of 5 May. I discarded the prison uniform and wondered who would inherit it. In my new civilian garb I walked into the reception office, a free man bar the exit from the prison yard. Major 'Someone', a security officer, handed me the release and the repatriation documents and a letter from my wife written several months back. The letter explained the background to my repatriation. W G Mosweu, MP for Bobirwa and a relative, had initiated the whole thing by raising my impending release, and asking what the government were doing about my future prospects.

Without the intervention of the Botswana government, it is difficult to guess what the kidnappers might have decided. That is, of course, now academic. What intrigues me is the secrecy of the repatriation exercise. Why was my wife's letter withheld until the day of my release? Would it in any way have jeopardised the security of the land? Was the short article in the Cape Town *Die Burger* a security leak? Maybe the obsession with security by the SA authorities served its purpose by keeping me anxious.

After signing the papers, I was handed my private property. And there was a new item in my property bag—a gold watch! 'Rotary quartz!' Battery operated! Hadn't seen such a beautiful watch before. It was a present from my sister-in-law, Peggy. She had tried to visit me the previous day with Dr Nthato Motlana but was refused permission to see me, presumably because they would have tipped me off that I was due to be repatriated. I learnt later that Dr Motlana had offered to drive me to the Botswana border. The offer was turned down. The police were not interested in saving a few tens of rands' fuel when they had thousands of millions of rands to burn on enigmatic security to keep the blacks down.

In Zeerust, about 70km from the Botswana border my taste of freedom turned sour as I was jolted back into the reality of encrusted white prejudice. Accompanied by the black security officer who was part of the escort force, I walked into a shop to buy something. We waited at the counter, and waited while the white shop assistants served white customers who had found us waiting. My patience was wearing thin: 'How long must we wait before we are served?' 'You are going to be served!' she shouted. 'You, must wait!'

I stormed out of the shop, rather than leap over the counter and another spell in a prison cell. The security officer followed me, muttering, 'ja's' (yesses). After I had cooled down, I told him I was lucky to be deported to Botswana. Otherwise my new freedom would be shortlived. 'Ja,' he answered, bewildered, 'Ja!'

We arrived at Tlokweng (Botswana) border with 15 minutes to spare for the political transaction. At 2 pm when the immigration office opened I was the first 'immigrant' to be processed. The processing went quickly in spite of my lack of papers. My status seemed to be 'above' the normal VIP status. Everything was 'chop-chop'. I was west of the border, Gaborone way—home and dry!

As I struggled with my carton of books across No-man's-land, my eyes were searching for my wife in the cluster of welcomers outside the Botswana Immigration Office. Where was she? The immigration officers did not give me more time to search for her as they welcomed and ushered me into the office for immigration formalities, or was it for a waiver of immigration formalities?

Everything went fast, with my escorts watching the proceedings with interest and a sense of duty. Major 'Someone' on being asked whether I was now a prohibited immigrant (PI) in South Africa replied in guarded language: 'Not to my knowledge. What might be necessary for him, whenever he wants to visit South Africa, is to let us know beforehand.' So I was not a PI! How South African security force had come of age! Total onslaught required a total strategy. I remembered one security officer who was lurking in the corridor of Compol Building when I arrived for one of the torture sessions saying

233

to me: 'Dingake, julle wil Boere baklei (Dingake, you intend to fight the Boers)?' and he eyed me with contempt before he completed his message: 'Ons is nie meer die ossewa Boere nie (We are no longer the oxwagon Boers).' I had understood him clearly. Here at the Botswana border gate I also understood this unusual decision not to declare me a PI. The 'plaas japie' (the farm bumpkin) had grown. Not big and tall enough to notice that the 'mine jim' had also grown!

Botswana Press Agency (Bopa) reporters swooped on me the moment immigration formalities were over. I did not even notice my wife had arrived late. They exposed her inadvertently in the press the following day.

The reporters insisted the interview be conducted in Setswana ostensibly for the benefit of all Batswana. After many years of neglect in favour of more common South African languages, my Setswana was unimpressive. There were more er's than sense in the interview. Impatient asides from my wife did not help my fluency. When the interview ended I felt exhausted, dehydrated and a publicity flop. This did not stop the radio and press later making capital of the story.

W G Mosweu headed the party of relatives and friends who welcomed me at the border. The passage of time had distorted the appearance of many a relative or friend. Recognition came slowly in relation to some faces. Then there were the nephews and nieces I knew only from photographs, those were more recognisable, because studying of photos was a speciality in our incarcerated community. Otherwise many faces looked strange. Over the years I had become used to the faces of 30 fellow-inmates. Every day I saw these same faces. I could recognise each one of them with my eyes blindfolded. These many faces were now different and strange. To make recognition even more difficult, the faces back on Robben Island intruded and blurred my vision. I suddenly suffered double vision. Familiar old faces back on the Island, superimposed on the new strange faces at the border of Botswana and South Africa. I struggled to keep my memory and vision in separate orbits. It was not easy.

The chief Immigration Officer Mr Maopare and his deputy Mr Mabeo were the next to welcome me in their Gaborone office. Then it was the Office of the President, and tea with the President, Q K J Masire! The transition from gaol seemed complete. In welcoming me the President explained that my illegal arrest had happened before the country gained independence. This had prevented Botswana securing my release. I thanked the President for his words of welcome and in turn conveyed the condolences of Nelson Mandela and other comrades on the death of Sir Seretse, the former President; greetings and best wishes to the Batswana.

In Lobatse where my wife lived, we found a crowd waiting to welcome me. My 80-year-old father and my sister, Khutsafalo, were among the crowd. She had come all the way from Zimbabwe where she is married. I had expected a very tearful reunion with her, judging from the two letters I had received from her in prison. To my surprise she was just smiles and no tears. The old man explained that he had admonished her against crying. 'Your brother is resurrected. Don't cry. Rejoice', he had explained to me.

Khutsafalo confirmed the statement, but added she would not have shed any tears in any case, because she had cried herself dry during the years of my imprisonment. Moreover her daughter Keneilwe's involvement with Zipra forces during the liberation war in Zimbabwe had hardened her against suffering. Parents known to have their offspring in the liberation army were subjected to continuous interrogation and systematic torture by the Selous Scouts, Smith's special unit against insurgency. This harassment and torture immunised the victims against the tendency to lacrimony.

My father, old and ailing, had suffered tremendously. He had wandered from place to place, from office to office, from kgotla to kgotla, trying vainly to move those in authority or in circles of information, to act or cast some light on my circumstances. The old man found himself knocking at a row of barred dooors. Some offices spurned him, others sympathised but pleaded powerlessness, subordinate kgotlas passed the buck to superior ones and the latter moralised and railed against the renegade subject: 'Your son is a renegade. He should have concerned himself with the political and other developments of his country. Instead he goes and meddles in other people's affairs . . .' The old man had the right to be hurt, to be bitter and despondent. Now, I stood before him and he beheld me like a welcome apparition: 'My son,' he said in his small husky voice, 'it's you!'

The crowd of well wishers swelled as the evening progressed. All the available space in the house was occupied and the crowd spilled into the stoep and the yard. The telephone rang and rang with congratulations to my wife and promises to come and visit me. My wife hardly rested. The telephone rang, more well wishers arrived, the radio bored her with the refrain of the ex-prisoner from Robben Island. I overheard some reckless enthusiast remark that if I stood for elections for the highest post in the land, that night, I would win. She was sharply rebuked by a friend. The night wore on and the crowd dispersed reluctantly in dribs and drabs.

The climax of my welcome occurred in Bobonong, where I was born. The big welcome was not publicised. Attempts to publicise it flopped dismally. The media representatives, assigned by the 'newsreel programmers' of Radio Botswana to cover the event were pre-empted by the inebriating atmosphere that engulfed the village. Big pots bubbled with potent foamy home-made brews; gin, brandy, whisky, beer, could float the old man's donkey cart parked outside one of the rondavels. My teetotaller uncle, Keobokile, suspended his biting sarcasm and moralising against booze and drunks. He joined the bartenders to ply the boozers with their favourite booze. It was time to celebrate! Small wonder Bopa reporters' lights were dim when we arrived.

The celebrations were almost marred by our late arrival. We had been expected on Friday night but through no fault of ours, we arrived 24 hours late. Telephone lines between Gaborone and Bobonong happened to be down that weekend, and we failed to communicate our change of schedule. The organising committee, headed by cousin James Maruatona, managed to keep the villagers optimistic and in a celebrating mood.

When we arrived at dusk in our VW Beetle, we were immediately spotted by the villagers at one end of the village. A driver jumped into his bakkie (van) to lead the way to the venue of celebrations, my old man's place. His horn attracted other drivers. A convoy formed as we proceeded through the winding village roads. The honk of motor horns brought back some of the crowd who had given up and dispersed or were about to do so.

Before our VW could come to a proper halt I was dragged out and hoisted shoulder high. The women ululated, pranced around and recited clan praises. Children danced and sang newly composed welcoming songs in my honour. It was a very touching reception. My friend Dingaan Maleka, who accompanied me on the trip, was visibly moved.

The speakers, programmed to speak on the occasion made speeches castigating South Africa, and exhorting me to lay off my past roles. 'You have fought a good fight. You are a hero. It is time, however, you devoted some time to the welfare of your family and your country . . .' That was more or less the theme. Contrary to those who imputed I was a renegade, the speeches here affirmed my involvement in the struggle for liberation while I lived and worked in South Africa. One speaker did not even agree with the majority that suggested detachment from my previous involvement: 'Let Mr Dingake decide for himself. We do not know what motivated his commitment to the struggle in the first place, only he knows, and if he has to stop, he alone can decide when and where to stop . . .' Bobonong was a microcosmic reflection of the national opinion. The majority felt: 'You've done your bit. Relax! Others can carry on where you left off!' A minority felt: 'You're your own king. Rule yourself according to the dictates of your own conscience.'

The celebrations continued throughout the night, my primary school teachers and school mates reminisced about the olden days: 'Ah, Knowledge!' they slapped me on the back, to initiate some conversation using the translation of my Setswana name, Kitso. My father kept telling everyone: 'He is resurrected. He was dead. He is alive now!' His initial macho facade finally crumbled under the impact of the unprecedented village solidarity. He gave in to his bottled emotions and wept for joy.

In the four days we spent in the village we visited the four primary schools and the two junior secondary schools in the village. It was a far cry from our Standard IV days, when the concept of formal education was welcomed by a handful, looked on with indifference by some, and jeered by the majority. Currently, the village seemed unanimous on the value of formal education. University graduates from the village were in tens, and more children were at universities all over the world.

The village was on the move not only politically and educationally, but economically and socially as well. Small businesses, owned by the villagers, dotted the village. Housing was improving in quality, water taps were within metres of every home, unlike in the past when the women of the village travelled miles to scoop water from the river bed and carry it on their heads in approximately 25-litre containers. Means of transport and communication were far better than I had ever known them. A regular bus service operated between the village and the nearest town, Selibe Phikwe. The telephone system connecting the village with the capital Gaborone, though it left much to be desired, existed and facilitated communication occasionally. Political independence was beginning to bear fruit, and none seemed to regret the passage of colonial days. People held their destiny in their own hands. In due course, free sons and daughters of this small village would contribute not only to national development but to international development as well. Already, the Botswana ambassador to the United Nations was a son of this area, Mr J Legwaila.

It reminded me that one of the most reprehensible crimes of apartheid was the suppression of social and human talent. South Africa and the world will never know by how much humanity has been impoverished by the policy of discrimination in South Africa. The loss of qualitative human resources through denial of opportunities cannot be quantified, but it is undeniably inherent in the apartheid system. On Robben Island one came across so many young men who could have achieved outstanding success in various fields, and there they were, frustrated and bottled up in that dungeon, just because they fought for opportunities for their people to express themselves for the good of all. The spectre of the South Africa situation continued to haunt me.

There are two allied viewpoints on South Africa's apartheid policy. One states that apartheid is South Africa's domestic policy and there should be no outside pressure to end it. The other states that apartheid is an abhorrent system, but the international community should not attempt to apply strong pressure to help end it: strong pressure will only make South Africa more intransigent . . .

The first argument is of course the argument of the SA government. It also dovetails with the second part of the second opinion, namely, that pressure will only make SA more intransigent. In recent years this 'making-SA-more-instransigent argument' has been proved hollow by several concessions, albeit minor, granted under external pressure. The 'einas (ouches)!' uttered by the Bothas (the President and the Foreign Minister) under threat of disinvestment campaign in the USA are further proof of the thinness of this sort of argument.

The white South African government's Western allies have been peddling the argument of 'sensible', 'moderate', 'inexcessive', 'diplomatic' pressure against South Africa. The same block of states does not hesitate to apply boycotts, sanctions, embargoes, 'mining' of sea-coasts and even military invasions of 'unfriendly' nations or governments. The two arguments identifiable in current political parlance as 'non-interference in the affairs of another country' and 'constructive engagement' are a disastrous old hat.

These arguments and their corollary of inaction were the guiding principles of the Neville Chamberlains during the Nazi era and the holocaust. Hitler was considered the potential Moses against Russian Bolshevism and not to be upset by strong criticism. He was an ally of the West. The Jews, non-racialism and democracy could be sacrificed on the altar of anti-Bolshevism.

The obsessional hatred of the Soviet Union and its socialism continues to pervert foreign policies of the West. Their talk of democracy and humanitarianism turns into a mere shibboleth whenever their imagination scans the penumbra of socialism in the distant horizon. Any anti-Soviet satellite is an 'old ally' even at the risk of distorting written history.

The Nationalist Party, which constitutes the present apartheid regime in South Africa, was openly sympathetic to Hitlerism during World War Two, yet the most 'powerful' man in the world (Reagan of USA) says SA is an 'old ally'! Harold MacMillan, then Prime Minister of Britain, in his 'wind of change' speech, delivered in the SA parliament in 1960, alluded to the non-interference 'principle': We shall be told to mind our own business. But what if your business interferes with my business?

Apartheid *is* a matter of international concern. More so, today, after the experience with Nazi Germany, its anti-semitism, its horrors and its aggressive policies which plunged the world into a bloody conflagration. Even more so, after political independence of black Africa. Apartheid is an anachronism in the post-colonial era, more than it has ever been. Independent black Africa is right if it feels it is not free, and independent, as long as black South Africans are not free. This feeling of insecurity is amply confirmed by the current destabilisation policy of SA against its neighbours: murders of the people of Lesotho, 'Kassinga' in Angola, 'Matola' in Mozambique, parcel bombs in Lusaka, Maputo, Lubango, Gaborone, Swaziland, pot shots in Harare and above all the colonial war in Namibia.

In addition the sponsoring and support of anti-government bandits and mercenaries in a number of African countries demonstrates the inherent unfreedom of all blacks in Africa. South Africa's domestic policies of humiliation and repression of the blacks inside the country are extended and manifested in its foreign relations with the black African states. Like the blacks inside the country, the black states do not know what is good for them. Only SA, the white shiny Jewel of the West, in the zone of black 'instability' fomented by the East, can say what is good for them.

It is not only blacks in SA and black Africa that are humiliated and unfree as long as apartheid exists. Any black anywhere in the world who cherishes human dignity must feel insulted and indignant against the policy of apartheid. Many progressive whites in SA and everywhere in the world must feel ashamed and morally disfigured by an ideology which seeks to identify them with the discredited barbarism of the 1930s – Nazism.

Bishop Desmond Tutu, the 1984 Nobel Peace Prize winner, is right when he equates apartheid with Nazism. Considering that apartheid takes place in a world where certain political crimes have been declared crimes against humanity, even when committed by individuals exercising legitimate constitutional authority, it can be strongly argued that it is morally worse than Nazism. Apartheid as a matter of international concern must be fought by all men and women in the world who believe in human dignity and world peace. Unless the rampage of apartheid is halted by vigorous efforts of the international community, immediately, we may be a short step from a 'Poland trauma' that might spark off World War Three.

Black sons and daughters of South Africa are struggling gallantly against the monster in spite of the odds. They shall achieve victory in the end, for their struggle is a just struggle. They shall win even without the help of the outside world. The unknown quantity is at what cost to human life, human suffering, human relations and progress.

Since apartheid affects humanity as a whole, because of its inhuman character, it must be fought by all mankind and eradicated root and branch from all elements of society. Those who suffer most under apartheid will inevitably be in the frontline. Their major weapon will neither be the AK-47 nor the grenade, although these must form ingredients of the arsenal. The critical weapon will be maximum unity of the oppressed. In the past this has been elusive as a result of sell-outs, selfseekers and the state of political consciousness. The sell-outs' guarantee of security is no longer guaranteed, selfseekers' lack of principle is systematically being exposed, and as the level of oppression rises in its subtlety, the level of political consciousness is rising correspondingly. Maximum unity is no longer merely an idealistic concept.

The neighbouring states by their very contiguity cannot escape the immediate effects of apartheid. From the demands for political asylum to the risk of destabilisation in all its forms, the neighbouring states must share the horrors of apartheid, willy nilly. Those states who have courageously resisted tail-wagging to the apartheid master/ monster must be commended. Commended also must be all the states that have constituted themselves into the organisation of the 'Frontline States' to improve their resistance against efforts to undermine their political independence and to bantustanise them.

The weakness of the concept of the 'Frontline States' lies in its application to the governments of these states alone. The concept can be a formidable weapon if it is transferred to the masses, to insulate these states against the security agents of their big neighbour. It is the network of the National Intelligence Service (NIS) that makes it possible for South Africa to sponsor bandits, bomb refugees, apply pressure on the neighbouring states to sign the so-called non-aggression pacts, and distribute anti-government propaganda of the type that was disseminated in Botswana against President Q K J Masire in 1982. Only the mobilised masses can flush out the nests of security agents that jeopardise the security of the Frontline States. Vigilance is the watchword. The masses of the Frontline States must be involved in the noble efforts of these states to defend their sovereignty. The 1980s are not the 1910s. The eighties are an era of mass mobilisation.

In 1912 when the ANC was formed, it was enough that Kgosi Khama and other Batswana chiefs identified themselves with it. Their status not only qualified them as the representatives of their subjects but entitled them to a claim of sole representatives on foreign policy matters. Today in the era of mass participation, governments should feel more on course with the active backing of the whole nation. This implies that the masses of the Frontline States should be deliberately conscientised on the essence of apartheid and how it affects them as individuals and as nations.

Without a more vigorous participation of the international community in the struggle against apartheid, the struggle is likely to be unduly protracted. The more protracted it becomes, the more the people of the Frontline States are going to bear the brunt of the struggle. This will take place whether they support or dissociate themselves from the struggle. That being the case, their suffering, incidental or otherwise, will become more tolerable if they are conscientised in advance of the implications of the political trends emanating from South Africa's policies.

It is the task of the national leaders to educate their followers. In this context, national leaders includes leaders of opposition parties where opposition parties exist. The United Democratic Front slogan, 'UDF unites, apartheid divides' is correct inside South Africa. Externally, apartheid unites! It should therefore be easy for the government party and the opposition to unite against the menace of apartheid, the menace of destabilisation, violation of national sovereignty and military invasion. The emphasis on government and parties taking the initiative in mass education against the spectre of apartheid does not preclude private initiative.

While the liberation movements, SWAPO and the ANC, must welcome the moral and material support of the African states, they should even be more impressed by moral support organised and initiated by ordinary men of goodwill in these states. It is intriguing, even embarrassing, that in distant Europe and the United States of America, we hear of non-government, non-partisan movements operating in these countries to enlighten the public and organise protests as a mark of solidarity with the victims of apartheid, yet some blood relatives of the same victims are so indifferent and aloof. Sometimes openly hostile, to the extent of calling refugees 'Batswakwa (foreigners)'!

Before political independence we depended very much on our South African brothers when we earned a livelihood in their economy. We were never subjected to subtle discriminations as practised here against 'Batswakwa' except by the common enemy – the colour bar/apartheid state. In fact it was our black brothers who taught us how to survive, how to cheat the pass laws and how to enjoy the limited accommodation with them. We were welcome. We were welcome in the ghettos, in the factories and in the schools. The parents whose children did not find vacancies because of our admission to their limited schools did not curse 'Batswakwa'. Today we can boast of national leaders who are leading us in the righteous path of independence, who are products of the hospitality and magnanimity of our black brothers across the border.

We are free now. They still clutch on hope. But they too will be free. This process can be accelerated by some tolerance, maybe some moral support. A positive attitude will be a definite contribution. As one who for years was a fully fledged participant in the South African liberation struggle, I know the South African freedom fighters will not recruit outsiders to bear arms for them. But I also know that their fighting morale is lifted and sustained by any expression of moral support for their cause from any external quarter.

It is high time people of the Frontline States started thinking seriously of solidarity organisations to express their goodwill in more concrete terms. The fight against apartheid is a fight for universal human rights. Nobody does anybody a favour by aligning himself or herself with the struggle. In the last analysis, each, in such a role, lays a brick to the monument of social justice and peace.

Africa cannot be free until all Africans are free. It is not yet uhuru. Not yet!

PUBLISHING LIBERATION LITERATURE ON
SOUTH AFRICA AND NAMIBIA

ESCAPE FROM PRETORIA
Tim Jenkin

256pp illustrated. 1987.
Price £5.00 paperback, £10.00 hardback.

This is the amazing, true story of the break-out by three political prisoners from Pretoria Central Prison in 1979. Written by one of the escapees, the meticulous way in which the escape was planned and executed, involving the manufacture of keys which got the prisoners through 14 locked doors to freedom, makes for gripping reading.

But it is also the inspiring story of a white South African who gave up his privileged lifestyle because of a deep commitment to the liberation struggle in South Africa.

A TOUGH TALE
Mongane Wally Serote

48pp. Price £3.00

Mongane Wally Serote is internationally acclaimed as one of South Africa's foremost liberation poets. In this, his latest work, he has written an extraordinarily powerful poem depicting the protracted and bitter struggle against apartheid, and illuminating the fighting spirit of the people of South Africa.

For further details of **Kliptown Books** or for a copy of the International Defence & Aid Fund for Southern Africa catalogue, please write to IDAF, Canon Collins House, 64 Essex Road, London N1 8LR, or telephone 359 9181.